Praise for *Still Standing*

"A must-read book that proves courage and leadership are indeed alive and well in elected officials."

—**Governor Chris Christie**

"The inside story of the political 'nuclear explosion' that elected and re-elected a Republican governor in America's bluest state."

—**Chris Wallace**

"A great story about what strong, independent leadership really looks like."

—**Governor Arnold Schwarzenegger**

"Governor Hogan's story is inspiring and one we can all relate to. He showed perseverance when facing what appeared to be insurmountable odds and came out on top."

—**Cal Ripken, Jr**

"An account of how America's governors worked together to fight the unprecedented challenge of the coronavirus pandemic."

—**Governor Andrew Cuomo**

Press About Governor Larry Hogan

"If the U.S. muddles through the current crisis, it will be because America's governors stepped up to the plate—at least in part because of Hogan."

—*Time* magazine, April 2020

"I've been impressed by governors across the country, including . . . Governor Hogan and the many others who are . . . providing a model for us all to follow."

—Bill Gates on Twitter, March 2020

"Larry's at the top of a list of leaders that I admire today because what's happening here in Annapolis is the antithesis of what's happening in Washington, DC, these days. Larry embodies the strong, independent leadership America needs now."

—Governor Jeb Bush, January 2019

"Governor Larry Hogan is showing that leadership isn't restricted by politics."

—*USA Today* Editorial Board, March 2020

"One the nation's model crisis leaders."

—Mark J. Rozell for *The Hill*, April 2020

"A leader solving the problems in front of him."

—Carly Fiorina, April 2020

"[Governor Hogan] comes up in most conversations about central figures who could be well-positioned for a presidential run."

—*National Journal*, April 2020

"Larry Hogan can offer a serious and meaningful alternative to the corroded conservatism we have in Washington today."

—Brett Stephens for *The New York Times*, January 2019

"Hogan has shown an ability to win across party lines. He won re-election by double digits in Maryland, a state that last voted Republican in a presidential election in 1988."

—Chuck Todd on MSNBC, January 2019

"The Un-Trump Republican: In the shadow of the nation's storm-tossed political epicenter, Larry Hogan's governorship is seeming more and more like an intriguing test case for a radically different version of the Republican Party: What would it look like if a politician played to Trump's electoral coalition while rejecting just about every element of the president's personal style?"

—**Matthew Mosk for** *Washington Post Magazine*, **August 2017**

"The rare Republican unafraid of the president."

—**Yahoo News, April 2020**

"To his immense credit, Mr. Hogan, a Republican in a state where Democrats enjoy a 2-to-1 advantage, has largely fulfilled that pledge, rejecting what he called 'the extremes of either political party' and taking a pragmatic, centrist approach to leadership that has been a tonic in a venomous era. In polarized times, he has stuck to the political middle, from where he has fashioned agreements that will benefit millions of Marylanders. That's no easy feat."

—**Washington Post Editorial Board, October 2018**

"Now [Hogan] seems to be showing the country how to govern as a pragmatist and build bridges with Democrats."

— **Jason Russell for** *The Washington Examiner*, **September 2016**

"Maryland Gov. Larry Hogan is a pragmatic, personable Republican who governs like a working class independent in a heavily Democratic state. He makes no apologies for his conservative principles, while welcoming those who don't, giving him space to thrive in a blue state despite a president who often leaves him blue in the face."

—**Adam Goodman for** *The Tampa Bay Times*, **January 2019**

"[One] of the most lauded public officials during the coronavirus crisis."

—*Politico*, **April 2020**

"The lead GOP voice for urgent action on pandemic."

—*The Washington Post*, **April 2020**

"A leader in early action on coronavirus."

—**NBC, March 2020**

"Mr. Hogan, a Republican in a Democrat-loving state wields a hammer of common sense amid a map of political avengers."

—Deborah Simmons for *The Washington Times*, April 2020

"In Maryland, Hogan has burnished his reputation as a forceful, can-do leader."

—Robert McCartney for *The Washington Post*, March 2020

"Maryland Gov. Larry Hogan has been among the most decisive and aggressive politicians in fighting the coronavirus pandemic."

—Jennifer Rubin for *The Washington Post*, March 2020

"Larry Hogan has handled the rise of Donald Trump better than any other Republican politician. Hogan is a rare bird in American politics, a broadly popular Republican governor in a very blue state. Hogan has acquired a reputation for affable, moderate pragmatism and assembled a coalition spanning Republicans, independents, and conservative Democrats."

—Andrew Egger for *The Weekly Standard*, June 2018

"What is equally surprising—and more welcome, as a reminder to Americans that the country was not always so fractious and polarised—[Hogan] has built his career on bipartisanship and compromise."

—*The Economist*, October 2018

STILL STANDING

SURVIVING CANCER, RIOTS, A GLOBAL PANDEMIC, AND THE TOXIC POLITICS THAT DIVIDE AMERICA

GOVERNOR
LARRY HOGAN
AND ELLIS HENICAN

BenBella Books, Inc.
Dallas, TX

Live Like You Were Dying
Words and Music by Tim Nichols and Craig Wiseman
Copyright (c) 2003, 2004 BMG Bumblebee, Big Loud Shirt/ASCAP (admin. by Big Loud Bucks) and
      Warner-Tamerlane Publishing Corp.
All Rights for BMG Bumblebee Administered by BMG Rights Management (US) LLC
All Rights Reserved Used by Permission
Reprinted by Permission of Hal Leonard LLC

Photo credits:
Page 2 (bottom), page 3 (top left and right), page 6 (top), page 7, page 8 (bottom), and author photo (cover) by Steve Kwak
Page 3 (bottom) by Getty Images
Page 4 (top left) by AP Images/Patrick Semansky
Page 5 (top) and page 6 (bottom left) by Joe Andrucyk
Page 8 (top) and front cover photo by Patrick Siebert
All other photos are property of Governor Hogan's personal archive.

BENBELLA

BenBella Books, Inc.
10440 N. Central Expressway
Suite 800
Dallas, TX 75231
www.benbellabooks.com
Send feedback to feedback@benbellabooks.com

BenBella is a federally registered trademark.

Printed in the United States of America
10 9 8 7 6 5 4 3 2 1

Library of Congress Control Number: 2019059818
ISBN 9781950665044 (cloth)
ISBN 9781950665211 (ebook)

Editing by Brian Nicol   Printed by Lake Book Manufacturing
Copyediting by Elizabeth Degenhard   Text design and composition by Katie Hollister
Proofreading by Laura Cherkas and Amy Zarkos Cover design by Ty Nowicki
Indexing by WordCo Indexing Services, Inc.

Distributed to the trade by Two Rivers Distribution, an Ingram brand
www.tworiversdistribution.com

**Special discounts for bulk sales are available.
Please contact bulkorders@benbellabooks.com.**

This book is dedicated to three people I fervently wish were still here:

My mom, Nora, who taught me caring and compassion and showed me the greatest love any son could ever ask for.

My dad, Larry Sr., who was my hero and role model and taught me so much about integrity and public service.

And my amazing big sister, Terry, who I always wanted to be like when I grew up.

CONTENTS

INTRODUCTION

It was the very last morning of my very first trade mission overseas, a twelve-day barnstorm across South Korea, China, and Japan. The trip had gone really well, especially for someone who'd never been on a trade mission before. We had productive meetings with international business leaders. We were welcomed by top government officials everywhere we went. I signed memorandums of understanding that would produce jobs and business for the people of Maryland. First-year governors don't normally race off on major trade missions. Then again, *normal* wasn't what I was going for.

I was still shaking my head at the scene in South Korea. My wife, Yumi, is the first and only Korean-born first lady of any state in America. In Seoul, Yumi was a much bigger celebrity than I was. "First Lady, First Lady!" people called out in the hotel lobby and on the street. To the Koreans, I was the first lady's far less glamorous American husband. Was this how JFK felt when he took Jackie to Paris? All this stuff was new to me. I'd been the governor of Maryland for less than five months.

I had to admit I wasn't feeling so hot. My first legislative session had been successful but exhausting. The Democrats in the House of Delegates and the state senate had done everything they could to haze the new Republican governor. Our largest city, Baltimore, had erupted in riots, the worst in forty-seven years. I had to declare a state of emergency and call out the

Maryland National Guard. On the plane ride over, my back had been killing me. I told myself I must have pulled something. The thirteen-hour time difference and sixteen-hour days had also taken a toll. As we climbed the Great Wall of China, I had to stop the state troopers and say, "I gotta sit down for a minute here." That wasn't like me. I'm usually the Energizer Bunny. I just keep going and going and going.

I was up early that final morning, staring into the bathroom mirror in our Tokyo hotel room. I had shaving gel on my face and a razor in my hand. I was happy. I was tired. I was ready to fly back home.

That's when I noticed it: a lump in my throat like I had grown an Adam's apple I never had before. It seemed to have popped up overnight.

The lump wasn't painful. It was just *there*.

I called Yumi into the bathroom.

"That doesn't look right," she said to me. "Does it hurt?"

I assured her it didn't. But when she said I should go see my doctor as soon as we got back to Annapolis, the lump looked weird enough that I didn't put up a fight. I texted my scheduler, Amanda Allen, and asked her to make an appointment for me with my primary-care physician, Dr. Michael Riebman.

"I don't think it's anything to worry about," the doctor told me when I got in to see him on the day I returned. "It appears to be some kind of benign cyst. But I'm going to send you for an ultrasound."

Dr. Mark Baganz, a radiologist, was no more alarmed. "It looks like fluid in one of your lymph nodes," he said to me. "I'm going to send you to an ear-nose-and-throat guy, just to see what's going on there."

The ENT guy, Dr. Lee Kleiman, said, "I'd like to do a CAT scan of your neck."

The CAT scan took just a few minutes. Then Kleiman returned. "If you don't mind," he said, "I'd like to do a scan of your chest, as well."

"Sure."

When that was completed, Kleiman came back in, this time with Baganz, the radiologist, who said, "We're going to do some more scans of your abdomen." Baganz returned a few moments after that and said, "Let's do a final one of your groin area."

What's going on here? I wondered more intensely with each additional test. *It's only a lump in my throat. But, hey, at least they're being thorough.*

I was sitting alone in the examining room, catching up on texts and emails, letting the minutes creep by. Craig Ciccarelli, the leader of my state police executive-protection detail, was waiting for me in the hallway. Then the door swung open. Kleiman and Baganz walked back in. This time, they had a surgeon with them, Dr. Vincent Sayan.

Three doctors? I thought. *This can't be good.*

It wasn't.

"Governor," one of the doctors said to me, "I'm afraid we have some very difficult news to share with you."

The scans showed forty to fifty tumors, running from my neck all the way to my groin. Some were as large as baseballs, like the one pressing on my spinal column that was causing me all that back pain. My mind was racing so fast I didn't catch every word the doctors said. But I did hear: "Lymphoma, a cancer of the lymph nodes."

I heard the phrase "very advanced and aggressive."

And I heard "stage three, possibly stage four."

I felt like I'd been hit by the 300-mph Maglev train we had just ridden in Japan.

Sayan told me he would need to do a biopsy surgery to remove a lymph node from under my arm. "But first," he said, "we need to get you to a specialist, an oncologist, who can help you decide on the right course of treatment."

My head was still spinning. I'm sure they said some other things I can't recall. *How could the doctors say this was probably nothing to worry about, and now they're saying I have advanced cancer spread all over my body?* That just didn't seem possible.

Craig Ciccarelli walked with me back to our black Chevrolet Suburban. From the expression on his face and his quiet demeanor, I was sure he had heard most of what the doctors had told me. He'd been right outside the door. But he didn't know what to say, and neither did I.

I climbed into my usual spot in the back seat of the SUV with two troopers in the front. I pulled out my iPad and slid the earbuds in. I played a song by Tim McGraw. "Live Like You Were Dying," the song was called.

In the months to come, that song would become very important to me, my cancer-fighting anthem. But for now, all I knew was that it had an uplifting and positive message, describing someone who was trying to make the best of every day he had left. As we rode back to the governor's mansion, I felt like the song was talking directly to me. I wasn't really scared. Stunned is a better way to describe it. I just felt numb, as my mind struggled to process what I had just been told. After everything I'd been through just to get here—winning the biggest surprise upset in America, achieving "the impossible" during our first session of the Democratic Legislature, taking command of the riot response in Baltimore, *everything*—five months after becoming governor, was this really how it was all going to end?

PART I

LEARNING

CHAPTER 1

MAKING LARRY

I f the American Dream was shaped like a ladder, the Hogans were pulling themselves from the first to the second rung.

Prince George's County, where I grew up and learned a lot of what I know today, was a sprawling, blue-collar suburb of Washington, DC. Our town, Landover Knolls, just inside the Capital Beltway, was solid but a little rough around the edges. It's far rougher today, the kind of place where drugs are sold on street corners and the police much prefer to patrol in pairs. But back then, which was the late 1950s into the early 1970s, Landover Knolls was somewhere an FBI agent and his stay-at-home wife could afford a red-brick starter home with a small backyard and a stoop out front and could raise a couple of active kids. Like most of our neighbors on Osborne Road, my parents came out from inner-city Washington.

Both my folks, Lawrence Joseph Hogan Sr. and Nora Elizabeth Maguire, were the products of close-knit Irish-American families whose grandparents had left the old country with nothing more than the clothes on their backs and dreams of a better future in America. My dad's father was a union printer in Boston. When the work dried up there, he moved to Washington and got a job at the Government Printing Office. He, like all of his relatives, was a solid Democrat. My mother's people came to Washington via Baltimore. Her father worked various jobs at small hotels. Both families settled near Catholic University in a northeast DC neighborhood called Brookland. The area had so many Catholic organizations and institutions—the Franciscan Monastery, Poor Clares of Perpetual Adoration Convent, Monastery of the Holy Cross, plus assorted Knights of Columbus, Hibernian, and Sodality meeting halls—some people called the neighborhood Little Rome.

When my parents met and started dating, my mom was with the nuns at Academy of Notre Dame. My dad was under the watchful gaze of the Jesuits at Gonzaga College High School. The neighborhood sweethearts married the same year they graduated. They were both nineteen. Their first child, my sister, Mary Theresa—Terry, for short—arrived the following year. They had almost no money. But both my parents worked to put my dad through the undergraduate and law schools at Georgetown University, another Jesuit institution that had long been a launchpad for bright young Catholics. Seven years after my sister was born, I showed up at Washington's Providence Hospital on May 25, 1956, a happy, chubby baby boy bursting with energy and seemingly ready for anything. I was named Lawrence Joseph Hogan Jr.

My dad was driven, outgoing, and unapologetically ambitious. My mom was the sweet, thoughtful, caring one. Everyone said the mix was ideal, which it was until it wasn't. After ten years with the FBI, my dad started a small PR and advertising firm in Washington. He edited a trade magazine. He started writing books, mostly novels that never got published. He also taught a journalism-law class at the University of Maryland, where his students included future network anchor Connie Chung. My mom's job was the house and the family, and she was awesome at it. Preparing hearty dinners for her husband and children—meatloaf, spaghetti, tuna-noodle casseroles, and sloppy joes. Being home when my sister and I returned from school. Serving as a class mother, a scout leader, and whatever else there was to volunteer for.

My sister was the person I looked up to most. When people asked little me what I wanted to be when I grew up, I didn't say a fireman or an astronaut or a ball player. "I want to be a teenager," I said. Friends. Cars. Parties. Weekends on the boardwalk in Ocean City. Terry seemed to have it made.

I followed my sister to Saint Ambrose Catholic School, which was right across the Cheverly line. Cheverly was a middle-class town, a little nicer than Landover Knolls. The kids from Cheverly had a swim club and a tennis court. We had a rim on a telephone pole. They had grass fields. We had dirt. A few times I heard classmates say, "He lives in Landover," which I understood as a synonym for *the other side of the tracks*. They were right, I suppose. I had to earn my own spending money. My father insisted on it.

When I was in second grade—*second grade!*—I got my first paper route. Two of them, actually. I threw the *Washington Daily News* in the morning and the *Evening Star* when I got home from school. I used the earnings to buy a red Schwinn bike. I put baseball cards in the spokes. I had streamers on the handlebars. I could do perfect wheelies. And my journalism career had only begun. When I was nine, I started my own newspaper. It might have been the worst newspaper ever, but it had an avid local readership. I wrote all the stories myself and printed the paper on an 8½-by-11-inch contraption with a metal cover and purple gel inside. We featured headlines like "Bobby Cassidy's Bike Stolen" and "Angels Beat Cubs" in sandlot baseball. I guess you'd call it a niche publication, but people gobbled it up.

I had a bunch of friends in my neighborhood and at Saint Ambrose. We hung out at each other's houses and played ball in the streets until the lights came on. Guys like Dennis Miller. Dennis was the biggest kid in our class. I was one of the smaller ones. We made a distinctive pair, and Dennis was funny as hell. Our two families spent time at the beach together. I kept working after school, grabbing whatever jobs I was old enough for. I cut grass. I picked up trash with a broom and a bin. I worked at an amusement park in Ocean City called Ocean Playland. I wasn't old enough to run the rides at first, so they put me on the "Balloon and Darts," "Water Guns," "Guess Your Age or Weight," and all the other midway games.

These were carefree times. I felt loved. I felt secure. I had friends. We had a nice, suburban family life. We weren't rich, but we were happy and comfortable. I felt like nothing really bad was going to happen to me. An upbringing like that can send a kid into the world with a sense of belonging and the self-assuredness to think he can achieve anything. My universe was small, but I was pretty sure I had it mastered. Then, things got even more fun. Politics came into our lives.

In 1966, when I was ten, my father surprised all of us by announcing that he was running for Congress. He'd been around that world a little bit as a public-relations man, but he'd never expressed any interest in running for office. Our local congressman, a Democratic lawyer named Hervey Machen, was seeking re-election in a district that was 3 to 1 Democratic, and my father was going to run as a Republican. It wasn't about ideology for him. In the 1960 presidential race, he started out being partial to John Kennedy, his fellow Irish Catholic. But as a former FBI agent, my father had grown disenchanted with the party of his father and all his relatives, convinced the Democrats were insufficiently tough on crime. He somehow got himself selected as an alternate delegate to the 1964 Republican convention at the Cow Palace in Daly City, California, where Barry Goldwater was nominated.

No one gave the 1966 Hogan for Congress campaign much of a chance. Not in Maryland's fifth district. Not for a first-time candidate with no money and no major endorsements. My dad had a few signs and some enthusiastic volunteers who'd believed him when he said, "We're gonna change things." But what he really had was boundless energy, a natural gregariousness, and an unshakable faith in himself.

I campaigned with my dad many nights and nearly every weekend, passing out literature, slapping bumper stickers on cars, hammering signs in people's front yards. It was all a blast for me. It also gave me a reason to hang around with my father, and it taught me some lessons I didn't realize I was learning at the time. I was amazed by how my dad could connect with strangers almost instantly. Since he couldn't draw a crowd on his own, we campaigned wherever the crowds already were. County fairs. Shopping centers. Ball games. Carnivals. He would stand in front of supermarkets and shake all the shoppers' hands. "Hi, I'm Larry Hogan," he'd say. "I'm running for Congress. I hope you'll consider voting for me." Then he'd help the people load their groceries into their cars. He liked to burst into barbershops—and especially beauty parlors—and shake every hand. The men would say, "I don't know who that guy was, but I kinda like him." The ladies would say, "Oh, my gosh. This handsome young man came in and talked to us. He seemed so nice." He'd write down their names on three-by-five cards and follow up with everyone. It was old-school, grassroots politics, and it worked brilliantly.

"If everyone tells two friends and every one of them tells two friends," he told the campaign volunteers, "we really can win this thing." The way he said it, with such unshakable self-confidence, we almost seemed to have the election in the bag. It was all word of mouth. My dad especially loved parades. There was no parade, no matter how dinky, he wouldn't join, riding in the back of a convertible. He would shake hundreds of hands in a day. I watched him do all of that. It was a model I would follow—and keep improving on—for the rest of my life. I'd eventually skip the car and walk or run some of those same parade routes. You could shake a lot more hands that way. At every event, my dad made sure his volunteers carried "Democrats for Hogan" signs. "We'll never win if all we get are Republicans," he said. "We need the cross-overs. They're the key." It was another lesson I absorbed.

He made unexpected inroads, pulling votes from thousands of lifelong Democrats who liked his sunny personality and anti-crime message. On election night, he did far better than anyone expected him to, but he came up short against the Democratic incumbent, 46 to 54 percent. As soon as the results were in, he made an announcement that seemed almost preordained. "Tonight," he said to all his supporters, "I am declaring my candidacy in the next election. We're fighting for what we believe in. We'll win next time." And he did, toppling Hervey Machen 53 to 47 percent in 1968.

I was twelve on January 3, 1969, when Dad was sworn in as a member of Congress. My mom and my sister and I all went with him to the Capitol. Lots of members brought their families that day. Kids were running everywhere, including in the galleries and on the floor of the House of Representatives. There was real excitement in the air. Maybe the congressmen would all be fighting later, but for a few hours, at least, everyone seemed to be getting along. It felt to me like the first day of school, except that everyone wore much fancier clothes.

When Speaker John McCormack swore in all the members, I got to stand next to my father on the House floor. He leaned over and whispered to me, "Raise your right hand and repeat the oath along with me. That way, we'll get two votes for Maryland's Fifth Congressional District." As the speaker began, my dad and I were right there with him: "I do solemnly swear that I will support and defend the Constitution of the United States against all enemies, foreign and domestic . . ." Neither one of us missed a word. Even I knew our trick wouldn't work, but I still thought it was pretty cool.

My father's hands-on, constituent-focused, hardworking approach seemed to connect with the voters. He would sail to re-election in 1970 and 1972 in the overwhelmingly Democratic district. People just liked him.

After eighth grade, I went on to Saint John DeMatha, an all-boys high school where the students wore blazers and neckties and were taught by the Trinitarian Brothers. In the Washington area, DeMatha was the working-class Catholic school. High-end Catholic boys were at Georgetown Prep. The smart ones went to Gonzaga, like my dad and his brother Bill did, or to Saint John's if they could handle the JROTC military discipline. Archbishop Carroll and DeMatha were for the regular guys. DeMatha was a little cheaper and a little more down-to-earth than the rich-kid schools, and our sports teams reliably clobbered all of them. We had a chip on our shoulder, but in a good way. I loved the place from the day I arrived.

I was never the coolest kid, and I certainly wasn't the smartest. But I had a knack for getting along with all the factions, the same way I do today. I wasn't a true insider in any group, but I was okay with all the different cliques. The jocks. The brainiacs. The artsy kids. The semi–juvenile delinquents. I was outgoing and personable. I wasn't exactly the class clown, but people would say, "He's funny. He can come hang out with us." I considered it my job to entertain everyone.

I loved sports but wasn't a strong enough athlete to play on the teams at a high school like DeMatha, which was a national powerhouse. But I was fun to have around the gym or on the field. Our beloved basketball coach, Morgan Wootten, was a future Hall-of-Famer already being singled out as one of the nation's finest coaches at any level. His fan club included coaching gods like Red Auerbach of the Boston Celtics and John Wooden of UCLA. Wootten turned down coaching offers from many of the top colleges to remain at

DeMatha, where he also taught world history. His top players got major college scholarships. He sent quite a few to the NBA, including Adrian Dantley and Kenny Carr, both of whom I went to school with. Coach Wootten was a generous mentor and someone I idolized. Now that I had achieved my dream of becoming a teenager, I started telling people I wanted to be a basketball coach when I grew up. Since I had no prayer of making Wootten's squad, I decided that becoming a manager in the program would teach me how to be a great coach one day.

My pal Dennis Miller went to Archbishop Carroll, and I got to know many of his friends over there, guys like Tim Maloney, who would become a leader of Maryland's Democratic Party and a lifelong friend of mine. Guys like Michael Steele and Boyd Rutherford, who would go on to be Maryland's only two Republican lieutenant governors in history. Both African-American, both friends of mine. That they would both attend the same Catholic high school at the same time—the odds of that must be, like, a million to one.

I never stopped working on weekends and in the summers. My father insisted on it. Now that I was old enough, I ran the rides at Ocean Playland. I saved my minimum-wage paychecks and, once I got my driver's license, I put down $1,250 and bought my first car, a secondhand, dark blue 1970 Ford Pinto. It very well might have been the least cool vehicle Detroit ever produced. It was junk, but I cherished it anyway, mainly because I had worked so hard to pay for it.

Everything was going really well for me until one day, without the slightest bit of warning, my whole world changed.

CHAPTER 2

IMPEACHABLE OFFENSES

t was 1972, the summer between my sophomore and junior years of high school. I had just turned sixteen. I assumed I'd be returning to DeMatha in the fall, an upperclassman at last. But soon after school let out, I was shooting hoops beside our house when my dad came outside and said to me, "I've got something I want to talk to you about. I'm going to leave your mom. We're getting a divorce."

I had no clue. I knew my parents had been a little tense with each other lately, but I never sensed my dad was going to leave. The news shocked me, and I was unbelievably hurt by it. But I tried to be a grown-up about it. I figured, *I'll still be here. I will still have my friends in the neighborhood and at school. I'll just see my dad on weekends, that's all. Lots of kids do that.* But in the gossip-fueled world of political Washington, the story of my parents' split was everywhere, including the *Washington Post*. It seemed my father had begun a romance with a young Capitol Hill staffer named Ilona Modly. After twenty-four years of marriage, he wanted out.

My mom was devastated. She had dedicated her whole life to this man, and now he had broken her heart. I was working in Ocean City that summer with my friend Dennis. Mom came down to talk to me: "I want to go somewhere where nobody knows who I am and nobody knows who he is." Mom had a friend from our old neighborhood with a sister who lived in Daytona Beach, Florida. My mom flew down to get away and check out the area. "I love it," she said. The friend's sister promised: "We'll find you an inexpensive house and introduce you to some people in town." Under the circumstances, that was good enough for Mom.

I loved both my parents, and both of them wanted me to live with them. At the time, I was probably closer to my father. We went to Redskins games together. He took me camping. He brought me to the White House and the Capitol. I loved working on his campaigns. Whatever we did together was exciting, and I did not want to miss any of it. But my mom was in pretty bad shape, and I knew I could not leave her alone. She was the one who'd been at home with Terry and me while my father was busy with his business and being a congressman. Of the two of them, there was no question my mom needed me more. My sister was already out of the house and married by then. Was I going to stay or go? It was terrible being in this position. But I knew what I had to do.

I had to give up my chance to study under Coach Wootten and had to say goodbye to my DeMatha friends with the blazers. I packed up all my teenage possessions and pointed the Pinto toward the on-ramp for Interstate 95 and then, all alone, drove eight hundred miles south. I started a new life with my mom in Daytona Beach, enrolling at Father Lopez High School just in time for junior year. It was a major transition, that's for sure. But the terrible trauma that I expected never quite materialized.

Like DeMatha, Father Lopez was a good Catholic school. But Father Lopez had one important thing that DeMatha didn't.

Girls.

Lots of them.

Everywhere.

And this being Florida, they all seemed to have short skirts and sun-tanned legs, and they wore bikinis when they went to the beach, which was just down the street from our school. I was in the throes of puberty, and suddenly my social life was drastically improving. Although I missed my dad and my friends back in Maryland, it didn't take long before I was thinking, *You know, Florida really isn't so bad!*

I made a great new set of friends in Daytona, guys like Mike Kundid and Russell Bubb. Even though I was the new kid, everyone welcomed me. We had beach parties and sock hops and drive-in movies. A national sports power-house we were not. At our basketball games, we didn't have Coach Woot-ten or any future NBA stars. On the other hand, we did have cheerleaders! Another added bonus: Instead of twenty-one, the drinking age in Maryland, Florida's was a loosely enforced eighteen. Very loosely.

My mother had hardly any money. She was a forty-seven-year-old single parent who hadn't worked outside the home for two decades. I was a teenage boy who ate a lot. My mom answered an ad in the newspaper and took a job at the Daytona International Speedway as a secretary to Bill France, the owner of NASCAR. They loved her there, and I got to go to the Daytona 500 with my new high school friends.

Divorces are always rough, and this one certainly was. It may have been even rougher on my older sister than it was on me. My father tried hard to keep our relationship close. He came to visit me in Florida, and I spent time with him in Maryland. He knew how much I loved politics, and we talked about that a lot. He worked to keep me inside his world and to stay present in mine. That said, I felt protective of my mom and worked hard to make sure she was all right.

So, I did what millions of children before and after me have done when their parents broke up: I tried to make the best of things. Somehow, we all carried on.

Another student at Lopez, Terry O'Leary, had also just moved to town. His family had taken over the Americano Beach Lodge. "I really need to get a job to help my mom," I said to Terry, who promised to speak with his dad. The next morning, Terry told me a bellhop job was open at the hotel if I wanted to apply. As soon as he mentioned I'd get tips and a free meal with every shift, I was sold. That beat what I'd been making in Ocean City. It turned out I was a damn good bellhop. Chatting up the guests. "Where ya from? Canada, eh? Here to see the Expos play?" Telling people where to go for dinner and all the fun things to do in town. All I had to do was be friendly and fun and carry luggage.

Eventually, I graduated to a new and even better job as a lifeguard selling suntan lotion at the pool. The hotels all had contracts with suntan-lotion companies, which in turn provided the hotels with lifeguards and pool maintenance. I became their best salesman and kept getting promoted to nicer hotels, quickly working my way up to the Daytona Hilton. I earned a 50 percent commission for every five-dollar bottle I sold, and I sold a lot of them. We had "Six Steps to a Safer Tan"—Sun-Screen Gel, Sub-Tropic Lotion, Tropical Oil, Pro Oil, and Aloe Lotion for nighttime. I can't remember the sixth one, but I'm pretty sure I sold a lot of that too. Mostly, it was the female guests who bought the suntan products. I had a grass hut by the pool. My coworker in the hut was a beautiful blonde who sold scope pictures.

The tragic story of my parents breaking up and me getting yanked away from my friends ended up with me hanging out by the pool of an ocean-front resort hotel, getting paid good money to get a great tan, meet new and interesting people, and talk to girls all day. At the time I didn't think there could possibly be a better job anywhere. Without even realizing it, I was also preparing for my future careers in business and politics.

In July of 1974, I had just graduated from high school, and my dad was revving up a campaign for governor of Maryland. He had decided to give up his safe seat in Congress to challenge the Democratic incumbent, Marvin Mandel, who was becoming embroiled in a corruption scandal that would eventually send him to prison. But it wasn't my father's dream of being governor that shook the political world that summer. It was his work as a member of the House Judiciary Committee.

The Watergate scandal was heating up then, and the action was moving to the House Judiciary Committee. Should President Nixon be impeached or not for the break-in and the cover-up? My father and other members of the committee had crucial votes to cast. Dad had been a strong Nixon supporter, especially when it came to foreign policy. He admired how the president opened US relations with China. The two men were elected together in 1968. Nixon campaigned with my dad. Nixon's daughter Tricia campaigned with us too. When my father was first elected to Congress, I went with him to a prayer breakfast at the White House, where I met President Nixon. I'd also met Nixon's vice president, Spiro Agnew, who had been the governor of Maryland and resigned as vice president in 1973 over his own corruption scandal from the Maryland days.

As the impeachment vote grew closer, my father took his role on the committee with the utmost seriousness. He believed he should painstakingly review all the facts and be guided by them. Some of his fellow Republicans, he grumbled, were reflexive Nixon apologists, just as some Democrats seemed hell-bent on destroying Nixon, no matter what. My father didn't belong to either camp. He simply wanted to get to the facts of the case.

The more he learned, the more uncomfortable he seemed to get. "Dad, what do you think?" I asked him during one of our visits. "Do you think he's guilty? What are you going to do?"

My dad was like a juror sitting in judgment. He didn't want to tell me things that were too confidential, but he said, "The president wasn't well-served by the people around him. A lot of mistakes were made. I'm trying to figure out how much involvement the president had. I have an enormous responsibility and an important decision to make."

Then my father stopped for a second and said earnestly, "We'll get to the bottom of it. I'm pushing to make sure the investigation is fair."

He was a Jesuit-trained, Gonzaga–Georgetown–Georgetown Law ex-FBI agent who believed in the law and the power of evidence. Even if he'd fallen short in his personal life, Dad strongly believed in the difference between right and wrong. He was a loyal Republican and a loyal Nixon supporter. But he had seen the facts. He didn't want to believe them. He was eager to defend his president. But the evidence kept coming, and it kept getting worse. It was eating away at him. It was impossible to ignore.

Most eighteen-year-olds don't give a damn about politics, but I found the whole thing riveting. I'd been around my father's campaigns for eight years by then. I'd hung out in his congressional office. I'd played basketball with Jack Kemp in the House gym. I can't claim I was exactly reading the *Congressional Record* instead of comic books, but I was living and breathing politics a whole lot more than most teenagers ever did. And I'd definitely been following Watergate.

I didn't know what to tell my father. I just said, "Dad, I guess you have to go with your gut and do whatever you think is the right thing."

"Even if it means the end of my career?" he asked me.

"I don't want to see you ruin your career," I said, "but don't you have to do what's right for the country?"

At that point, the polls had my father with an excellent chance in the race against Governor Mandel. The Republican primary, which he had to get through first, was looking like a cake walk. The only other Republican candidate was an eccentric party committeewoman and former state senator named Louise Gore, who wasn't given any chance against the popular congressman.

On the day the House Judiciary Committee voted, July 27, 1974, my father spoke some words that would echo through the annals of American history and send a wrecking ball through his own career—and that of Richard Nixon. My dad understood the enormity of what he was doing, as he had made clear to me. And he had the guts to do it anyway. His remarks in the committee room that day were so potent, so eloquent, so bold, and so obviously heartfelt, they keep reappearing all these years later in documentary films, TV retrospectives, and American history books.

When my father addressed the committee, he started with a broad, general principle. "Party loyalty and personal affection and precedents of the past must fall before the arbiter of men's action, the law itself," he said. "No man, not even the president of the United States, is above the law. For our system of justice and our system of government to survive, we must pledge our highest allegiance to the strength of the law and not to the common frailties of men."

The room was totally silent. No other Republican on the committee had said anything remotely like that. Inside his party, my father was already out on a limb. Then, he described his own reaction to what he had learned. That's when the pace of his words got faster and a small catch crept into his voice. "The thing that's so appalling to me," my father said, "is that the president, when this whole idea was suggested to him, didn't in righteous indignation rise up and say, 'Get out of here! You're in the office of the president of the United States! How can you talk about blackmail and bribery and keeping witnesses silent? This is the presidency of the United States!' And throw them out of his office and pick up the phone and call the Department of Justice and tell them, 'There's an obstruction of justice going on. Someone is trying to buy the silence of a witness.' But my president didn't do that. He sat there, and he worked and worked to try to cover this thing up so it wouldn't come to light. He didn't have to know because he already knew, and he consistently tried to cover up the evidence and obstruct justice. As much as it pains me to say it, he should be impeached and removed from office."

It was all live on national television and appeared on the front pages of papers across the country, including the *Daytona Beach News-Journal*. All my friends heard about it. Some of them already knew that my father was a congressman and my parents had gotten divorced, but this was the first time most of them had really paid any attention to that. With his words that day, my dad sealed his place as the first Republican in Congress to call for Nixon to be impeached. When the roll was finally called, he was the only Republican to vote for all three articles of impeachment.

Most politicians would never have had the courage to do what he did. I was proud to be his son.

His brave stand made him a hero in some corners of America. History has certainly treated him well. But the reaction at the time inside the Republican party was just as my father predicted it would be: fast and furious. He received more than 15,000 pieces of hate mail, some addressing him as "Judas" Hogan and "Benedict Arnold" Hogan. People used words like *snake* and *turncoat*. As a Republican officeholder, he had no business coming out against the Republican president, they said. Packages of feces showed up at his door. The White House, his fellow Republican politicians, party leaders across America, and other Nixon stalwarts howled in outrage. Nixon's critics admired my father's courage, but his base of Republican support crumbled almost instantaneously. Nixon's resignation only eleven days later on August 8, before the full House voted on impeachment, didn't calm anyone down.

There was a very small turnout in the Republican primary for governor a month later. Slightly more than 100,000 Republicans voted in the entire state. Most people had assumed my father would sail to the nomination. But the few voters who did show up were mad as hell, and they turned out in greater numbers than the ones who weren't. Pro-Nixon Louise Gore defeated my father, 54 to 46 percent. She went on to be crushed in the general election in November by her dear friend Governor Mandel, who had encouraged her to run.

CHAPTER 3

LEARNING EXPERIENCES

I couldn't afford to attend a private college. I could hardly afford any college at all. Luckily, in Florida at that time, state residents were able to attend the state universities tuition-free. As a resident of Florida, free sounded really good to me. Florida State University had a strong government and political-science program. The campus was in Tallahassee, the state capital. They were willing to have me, and the price was right. My college choice was as simple as that.

I loved Florida State. I shared an off-campus apartment with a couple of other guys and got an internship working for Florida's House Minority Leader Tom Lewis, a Palm Beach Republican. This involved running errands, commanding a Xerox machine, and trying to learn a little of the inner workings of state government. Not the stuff I'd been reading in my poli-sci books—the way things *really* worked. Hanging out at the State House confirmed one thing I'd picked up from my dad: Much of government was built on personal relationships that had nothing to do with party or politics. The legislators in Florida, just like my dad and his friends in Congress, had different constituents, different outlooks, and, often, conflicting ambitions for higher office. But they also had a lot in common, whomever they represented and whichever party they belonged to. Dealing with each other was the only way they could get anything accomplished. I got a strong taste of that in Tallahassee, and it made perfect sense to me. And it was more fun than studying for my classes.

In 1976, before starting my junior year, I was selected to be an alternate delegate at the Republican National Convention in Kansas City, where former California governor Ronald Reagan was challenging President Gerald Ford. My dad was chairing the Maryland effort for Ford. The two of them had served in Congress together. And, of course, my father had played a role in making Ford the president.

I stood on the floor of the Kemper Arena with my Maryland alternate delegate badge around my neck, mesmerized by Reagan's speech. I loved the way he reached out to "all those millions of Democrats and independents who I know are looking for a cause around which to rally." He tried to heal his own party's divisions, not to exacerbate them: "We must go forth from here united and determined. What a great general said a few years ago is true: There is no substitute for victory, Mr. President." Reagan really was the Great Communicator, I decided that night.

I marched across the convention floor in a demonstration, wearing my Reagan hat and holding my Reagan sign. Dad wasn't too happy about that. Ford narrowly won the nomination and then, unfortunately, was defeated by Jimmy Carter in November. But I had no doubt even then: Reagan was the kind of optimistic leader the Republican Party and America needed in the years to come.

There was one rattling development in my senior year: Serial killer Ted Bundy, facing murder charges in Colorado, pulled off two daring escapes and turned up on the Florida State campus. He began brutally attacking young women again. On January 15, around 2:35 AM, he slipped into the Chi Omega sorority house, where he sexually assaulted and brutally murdered

Margaret Bowman and Lisa Levy, then bludgeoned two of their sorority sisters before breaking into a ground-floor apartment eight blocks away and attacking yet another Florida State student.

Until Bundy was arrested a month later in Pensacola, the female students of Florida State were in an understandable panic. To be truthful, it wasn't just the girls on campus. Everyone in Tallahassee was on edge. This was before the internet and social media, but rumors were flying everywhere. In every rumor, Bundy had supposedly been sighted in some of the places we all knew well. Detectives combed the campus for clues. I didn't know how to be helpful until I learned of an opportunity that made perfect sense: I volunteered with other upperclassmen to escort female students at night. This was no joke. Walking across the dark campus, we all knew: This killer could be lurking anywhere. Everyone breathed a huge sigh of relief when Bundy was caught.

All through college, I headed back to Daytona on weekends and in the summer and picked up lifeguarding shifts at the hotels along the beach. I drove up to Maryland from time to time to see my dad and my high school buddies. They always wanted to know, "When are you moving back?" I knew I'd probably return to Maryland eventually—but, hey, why rush? When all was said and done, I got a good education in Florida. I graduated in 1978 without a nickel of student debt. I learned tons about government and politics, and I became a lifelong Seminoles football fan. I made some close friends, and I had a blast. After finding a lot to love about finishing high school in Florida, I also felt like I'd put the pieces together for a first-class college experience.

My bachelor's degree in government freshly in hand, I headed north to help my father resurrect his political career. Some people were pushing him to run for his old seat in Congress or to go for governor again. His controversial stand against Nixon had been somewhat vindicated, and the fallout from Watergate was starting to subside. But my dad decided to stick closer to home and challenge Win Kelly, the Prince George's County executive. The county in those days was in the iron grip of the O'Malley Democratic machine, painstakingly assembled by Peter O'Malley, brilliant land use attorney and president of the Washington Capitals hockey team. O'Malley's field lieutenants included future governor Parris Glendening, future state senate president Mike Miller, and future US House majority leader Steny Hoyer.

I got a day job on Capitol Hill working for California congressman John Rousselot to pay the rent. "In this family, everybody works, and you can't be a lifeguard selling suntan lotion forever," my dad kept reminding me. As far as I was concerned, being a lifeguard selling suntan lotion had its pluses. But I had to admit Dad was probably right.

I didn't love being a low-level congressional aide, but I got an up-close view of the sharp-elbowed staffers and faceless bureaucrats who run so much of Washington. And I got to know John McCain, whose first wife, Carol, worked in the same office with me. She was really nice.

Nights and weekends, I did the job I was passionate about, the unpaid one, busting my butt on my father's campaign. Despite Kelly's incumbency and the entrenched O'Malley Democratic machine, a property-tax revolt was brewing in Prince George's that year, and my father rode it to victory, easily dispatching the stunned incumbent Kelly with 60 percent of the vote. That same day, county voters approved a property-tax cap called TRIM, while California voters shocked the nation by passing their anti-tax referendum Proposition 13.

When my dad won, I said to him: "I have to be a part of this."

"I can't hire you," he told me. "I'll get accused of nepotism."

"I'll work for free," I offered.

"You can't do that," he said.

Some key players from the campaign leaned on my dad and made it clear that he needed me around. He relented under one condition—that I would be the lowest-paid person in all of county government. My starting salary was about $14,000, half what my administrative assistant earned. As the county's intergovernmental liaison, I dealt with all the municipal governments, handled the political appointments, negotiated with the county council, filled in for my dad at Kiwanis luncheons and firefighter banquets, and sometimes dealt with the media when he couldn't. I was just out of college, doing several jobs at the same time and already thinking maybe I'd like to run for something myself someday.

I stayed involved, locally and nationally, getting elected to the Republican

Central Committee and becoming more active in the state party. I was elected president of the Young Republicans and was named chairman of Youth for Reagan. I kept saying *yes* to things. I was also elected as a delegate to the 1980 Republican convention in Detroit, where Reagan sealed his place as our party's nominee. As Young Republicans president, I brought a bunch of other hyped-up twenty-somethings with me to Detroit.

Reagan was even more inspiring than he'd been four years earlier. I liked everything he was talking about. Facing down the Soviets. Standing by our allies. Peace through strength. Turning the economy around. Cutting taxes and job-killing regulations. Shrinking the bloated federal bureaucracy. Never negotiating with terrorists. Reagan's approach sounded a whole lot better to me than President Carter's recession, malaise, higher taxes, unemployment, and long gas lines. I was especially enthralled by Reagan's optimism, eloquence, and talk of a "big-tent" party, being inclusive and drawing new people to the cause. He was winning converts every day, including the millions of "Reagan Democrats" who would help him send Jimmy Carter back to Georgia and would define what soon became known as the Reagan Revolution. I was proud to be a foot soldier in that fight.

The way Reagan spoke, his positive world view, how he seemed to care about people, his willingness to reach across the aisle—I had found my kind of Republican. Those ideas really connected with me. They would form the foundation of my future political beliefs.

As his four-year term was winding down, my father decided not to seek an easy re-election as county executive. Against my advice, he chose to challenge US senator Paul Sarbanes. The two of them had been on the House Judiciary Committee together in the Watergate days. My dad lost the race badly. "You were right; I should have listened to you about that one," he would concede to me years later, a rare admission on his part.

Dad went off to teach, practice law, and write books that actually got published, including novels, poetry collections, a pre-9/11 anti-terrorism handbook about Osama bin Laden, and a fascinating investigation into the early-1920s Osage Indian murders. He also worked on a dense textbook called *Legal Aspects of the Fire Service*, which became required reading at fire academies across the country. "I can't believe that's the one that became a bestseller," my father would say, shaking his head in disbelief. "The most boring thing I ever wrote!"

With my father out of elective office for good, I went into real estate. I wanted to do something out of my dad's shadow, something that would help me grow beyond the "junior" that always seemed to be tacked onto my name. After three years learning the real-estate business at a large commercial brokerage called Kenneth H. Michael, I opened my own firm, Larry Hogan & Associates. It was 1985. I'd just turned twenty-nine. We were a full-service land company, which meant we helped farmers and other landowners enhance the value of their property by connecting them with developers and guiding them on what to do next. We put large parcels together and won zoning and environmental approvals. We were the firm in the middle that understood how to get everything done. Thankfully, I knew my way around government. I could talk to suspicious farm owners, sharp-eyed developers, busy home builders, municipal bureaucrats, and the lawyers and bankers who made these deals happen. Sometimes, I was the only one talking to all of them.

I started in the basement of my townhouse with one part-time associate, Barbara Richman, who'd become a friend when we worked together in my dad's Senate campaign. The business grew from there. Finding deals. Getting referrals. Adding people as we went. My first big project was resurrecting a dormant 6,000-unit residential development in southern Prince George's County called Marlton. By the late 1980s, we had grown into the largest land and commercial firm in the county, then the largest land-brokerage firm in the state. Over time, we began investing in some of these projects, and we connected developers with others who wanted to invest. We grew to a team of nearly fifty people in the company.

The money was nice, but what I really enjoyed was bringing people together. Unless the deal got done, we didn't get paid. It wasn't so different from my idea of politics, helping people on opposite sides reach agreements that everyone considered a win-win. I liked doing that. I was good at it. I had written off politics as anything more than a sideline interest, which pleased my father. "Do something else as a career," he told me. I felt like I'd found my niche in real estate, and that's what I devoted myself to for a solid decade, though I never got politics entirely out of my blood.

Like a lot of people, businesspeople especially, I grumbled about the high taxes in Maryland and all the rules and regulations from Annapolis and Washington that made things more complicated than they needed to be. This was becoming more of an issue by the early 1990s as housing starts fell and a national recession was kicking in.

My local congressman, Steny Hoyer, was a denizen of the Prince George's County Democratic machine. He'd first been elected to political office in 1966, becoming the youngest state senate president in Maryland history. For the decade leading up to the 1992 election season, Congressman Hoyer had been busy clawing his way into the leadership of the US House of Representatives. He'd been deputy majority whip and then co-chair of the Democratic Steering Committee, two insider posts that actually carried some weight. By early 1992, the aggressively ambitious Hoyer had risen to chairman of the Democratic Caucus, making him the number four Democrat in the entire House of Representatives. Already a candidate for re-election, Hoyer was loudly bragging about the extensive power he'd amassed in Congress and touting the big loads of federal bacon he'd been bringing home to the fifth district of Maryland.

None of that scared me at all.

With all the self-confidence of a thirty-six-year-old who'd never been elected to anything, I announced that winter that I was running against one of the most powerful men in Washington.

CHAPTER 4

NEAR KNOCKOUT

Steny Hoyer wasn't just my local congressman, holding the seat my father once held. To me, he also represented everything that was wrong with Washington. And that's exactly how I intended to run against him. Thankfully, I had plenty of material to work with.

Ralph Nader's group Public Citizen had named Hoyer the number one abuser of junkets, saying no one in Congress wasted more public money on lavish overseas travel than he did. He'd been on sixty-four of these taxpayer-funded trips out of the country. During this time the public also learned of the major scandal of the shockingly mismanaged House bank, in which congressmen from both parties had been repeatedly overdrawing their accounts with what amounted to millions of dollars in secret, interest-free personal loans.

I knew my campaign wouldn't have much money—not compared to

what Hoyer could collect from lobbyists and interest groups. I'd need to run a clever, provocative, disciplined campaign on a shoestring. And since the district was still more than three-to-one Democratic, I couldn't win with just Republican votes. I'd also have to attract a large swath of Democrats, just like my father once did.

I hired a young Democratic campaign manager, Ron Gunzburger, who'd worked for Missouri congressman Dick Gephardt and others. Ron was great on messaging and loved creating funny, low-cost stunts that were designed to grab attention, what campaigns call "earned media." Along with our normal palm cards, we started handing out "rubber checks" mocking the banking scandal: "House Bank . . . Pay to the Order of Myself . . . $10.8 million . . . 20,000 interest-free loans . . . (signed) Your Congressman Steny Hoyer and 354 others." The gag checks, stamped "Insufficient Funds," doubled as jar openers. We ran a catchy "Lifestyles of the Rich and Famous" radio commercial with a voice actor who sounded just like Robin Leach. "What's next for the jet-setting congressman? The casinos at Monte Carlo? Or maybe schussing down the slopes at Saint Moritz? Champagne dreams really can come true when you're Congressman Steny Hoyer." Even the disclaimer at the end had a little twist: "Paid for by the Larry Hogan for Congress campaign. Travel and promotional considerations for the incumbent paid for by taxpayers." We bought as much radio time as possible, but we didn't have enough money to run even a single TV ad.

Hoyer tried to ignore me at first. But when he refused to appear with me at public forums, I showed up with life-sized cutouts of "the two Stenys" and explained, "Candidate Hoyer says the middle class is being squeezed, but Congressman Hoyer is the one who's been doing all the squeezing. He's voted for every single tax increase since he's been in Congress. Candidate Hoyer says the government spends too much, but Congressman Hoyer is the biggest spender in Congress."

We knew our anti-incumbent message was getting traction when the Hoyer campaign scrubbed the words "re-elect" and "Congressman" from their messaging. The revised slogan was a pared-down "Hoyer for Congress," and he started peppering his presentations with, "*If* I'm elected in November . . ."

"If you are happy with the job that Congress is doing," I kept telling

people, "then you should re-elect my opponent and keep him as a leader."
That was a low-risk proposition. Nobody liked Congress the way it was being
led. "But if you are fed up with Washington, then you should join our fight
to sweep out Congress."

Things got kinda crazy in our big televised debate. Hoyer set so many
ridiculous pre-conditions before he would even agree to show up, Ron told
me to just say yes to everything up front—then do whatever I wanted once
the cameras started to roll. I knew this was my best shot at getting our message out. I didn't hold back. I even interrupted Hoyer's opening statement to
correct something he said.

"I didn't interrupt your opening, Larry," Hoyer admonished me in his
usual pompous and dismissive tone.

"Yeah," I answered, "but I told the truth in mine. If you had, I wouldn't
have interrupted you."

I'm not sure the poor Maryland Public Television moderator got in more
than one or two questions the whole thirty minutes, as Hoyer and I went toe
to toe on our insider-versus-outsider punch-and-counter-punch routine. We
had a great debate, and I felt like I got my message out.

The Thursday before the election, Hoyer and I met at Anne Arundel
Community College for our final debate. There were nearly a thousand people in the auditorium, and our face-off was broadcast on local cable TV. I
hammered Hoyer all night on crime, taxes, and the free-spending culture of
Washington. Then, a question came from the audience. "Congressman, is it
true that you've taken more of these taxpayer-funded junkets than anyone
else in Congress?"

"I'm glad you asked that question," Hoyer said, before explaining that
as the chairman of the Helsinki Commission on Security and Cooperation
in Europe, he'd often been "carrying the torch of freedom behind the Iron
Curtain."

"Steny," I responded, "the last time I checked, Paris, London, Switzerland, Barbados, the Bahamas, Bermuda"—I listed some of the places he'd
recently junketed to—"they're not behind the Iron Curtain. While most of
us struggle to save a few dollars to take our families to Ocean City for the
weekend, you took sixty-four vacations paid for by the taxpayers. We added

up all the frequent-flyer miles. You traveled more than the distance from here to the moon and back again at our expense."

I could see him getting red in the face, as if to say, *How dare you talk to me like that!* He'd clearly gotten used to the kowtowing from his lobbyist pals in Washington.

After a few more questions were asked and answered, we got to the knockout punch.

"Congressman," a woman said, "we've heard a lot about this House bank scandal. Can you please explain your role?"

"Thank you for asking that question," he said. "If you listen to my opponent, you'd think that I was a teller in the House bank, and that somehow I was responsible for my colleagues bouncing twenty-two thousand bad checks for millions and millions of dollars. I'm angry and frustrated about it, but I'm not a teller in the bank."

"Congressman," I said, "with all due respect, we all know what an important guy you are. I would never try to give anyone the impression that you were a lowly teller in a bank. But as the chairman of the Democratic Caucus, you're responsible for hiring Jack Russ, the sergeant at arms. Every single person that worked in the House bank was hired through your office as a patronage employee." I went on for quite a while, citing the congressman's role on the House Oversight Committee, which set rules for the House bank and had responsibility for the oversight. Then, I said, "Congressman, you weren't a teller in the bank. You were more like the chairman of the board, and nobody in America bears more direct responsibility for the entire scandal than you do."

By then, the veins were practically popping out of Hoyer's head as he leaned over and hissed at me, "You're such a fuckin' liar, Hogan."

It was four days before the election. Hoyer's campaign had outspent ours six to one. He should have been winning in a walk. Yet there were fresh polls saying we were nearly tied. He could see his whole career passing in front of his eyes.

I put my hand on his shoulder. "Steny," I said with a smile, "you've got to relax. It's just an election."

At that point, he started to rise out of his chair, and I really thought he might take a swing at me. To tell you the truth, I was hoping he would.

Once he bolted off the stage, he ran into Ron and sputtered, "I have never been treated with less respect than the way I have been tonight."

"Steny, it's a campaign," Ron said with a chuckle and a shrug.

We spent election night at the Greenbelt Marriott. The vote totals were quickly coming in from four of the district's five counties—Charles, Calvert, St. Mary's, and Anne Arundel, all four of which we won big. We were up all night long by solid double digits overall. In Prince George's County, the stronghold of the Democratic machine, the results were maddeningly slow.

"You think they're trying to figure out how many extra votes they need?" Ron joked darkly to me as the evening wore on.

"With these guys, anything is possible," I said.

Hoyer had never faced a tough challenger before. The media weren't expecting much. They seemed to think the race was a foregone conclusion. They'd hardly paid attention at all. But by 11 PM, I was up nearly 20 points.

The TV-news updates began expressing alarm. Hoyer was shown with his family, looking stricken and glum. He complained about "the negative campaign" that his opponent had run, saying we'd "misled the voters." Turnout was heavy. Nineteen ninety-two was a presidential year. Bill Clinton beat George Bush that night, badly in this congressional district. But we were running far ahead of the Republican president. Our numbers experts, State Senator Marty Madden and Delegate John Morgan, both good friends, were still up in one of the suites, poring over the figures with Ron. Our victory party was going wild in the ballroom downstairs. We knew that Prince George's County would narrow the margin, but this was a huge gap. Hoyer wasn't publicly conceding, and we hadn't declared victory yet.

Hoyer came downstairs at his headquarters and told his people not to give up hope yet. "It's going to be a long night," he said. I went downstairs at our place and said, "Thank you for all your wonderful work. It looks like an actual possibility that we could pull off the biggest upset of the year. But we probably won't have the final numbers tonight."

The headline in the *Washington Post* the next morning had the race too close to call.

The turnout in Prince George's, the majority-minority county adjacent to Washington, was the largest in history. Throngs of base Democrats turned out in huge numbers to vote for Bill Clinton against George H. W. Bush. The final tally from the county was so massive, it swung the district-wide result against us. Instead of a double-digit victory over one of the most powerful men in Congress, our ragtag campaign came up just shy of victory. In the final count, Hoyer won with 53 percent.

What can I say? It was the thrill of victory and the agony of defeat all within twelve hours. We'd done far better than anyone ever believed was possible. We ran a brilliant campaign without the benefit of any real money. If it weren't such a hotly contested presidential election year in such a heavily Democratic district, we surely would have won. We gave one of the most powerful people in Washington the fight of his life and the closest election of his entire career.

Thankfully, I had a day job to return to, though the economic pressures on the real-estate industry were growing more challenging by the day.

CHAPTER 5

ROCK BOTTOM

Steny Hoyer's House bank wasn't the nation's only troubled financial institution. There was a national problem at the time with the savings-and-loan industry. Some S&Ls were making overly risky loans. But Congress's response, something called FIRREA, the Financial Institutions Reform, Recovery and Enforcement Act, was so rigid, it was starting to paralyze much of the lending in the homebuilding and real-estate-development industries. As a result, more than a thousand S&Ls eventually collapsed across the country.

When many of our clients found their own credit abruptly withdrawn, their companies began collapsing right along with their lenders. And that meant they couldn't pay the fees and commissions they owed us. But we were still managing.

Our company did a lot of business with First American Bank. We had perfect credit. We'd never missed a payment to anyone. Our cash flow was always strong. But when First American began spiraling downward, we quickly found ourselves in a horrible squeeze as well. New owners took over the bank. Then the federal regulators came in. They withdrew our line of credit and all our business loans. Like many of our clients, we were suddenly forced to come up with millions of dollars in cash we didn't have.

I could have washed my hands of it all, the way Donald Trump and many other real-estate developers did at the time. We could have left our lenders holding the bag. But I made the decision not to do that. I said, "We need to find a way to pay these loans back, keep our people employed, and save our company."

We flew into frantic motion. We liquidated whatever assets we could. But the real-estate market was contracting, and values were sinking fast. Some of my clients thought I was crazy for not filing for bankruptcy at the first sign of trouble. "If you don't file for bankruptcy in the nineties, that just means you were nobody in the eighties," one of them said to me. Under that popular theory, skipping out on your debts was just another shrewd business move, and I was a sucker for trying to live up to my commitments.

After struggling for more than a year to pay everyone back, I agreed to sign personal guarantees on all the business indebtedness. That bought me some time. I put up my house. I put up my other personal assets. I pleaded with the creditors: "Just don't close down the business. Give us some time to generate cash."

In the end, the new regulations and the new people taking over the failing lending institutions made it impossible for anyone to make logical business decisions. As a result, I lost everything. I lost my beautiful house with a swimming pool. No more nice vacations or fine dining out or any of the other trappings of business success. I had to sell my furniture. I got to keep my clothes and a few personal items, but that was about it. Sadly, I had to tell longtime employees who were like family, "I'm so sorry. They won't let us continue. I can no longer keep paying everyone." I filed for bankruptcy.

My net worth had sunk from millions of dollars to zero. It was a depressing, gut-wrenching, humiliating experience—and a defining moment for me. Everything I had worked so hard for was now gone. I'd been proud of our accomplishments and my good reputation. I was well known in the business world. I had excellent relationships with my clients, my lenders, others in the industry, even my competitors. I had just nearly beaten one of the leaders of Congress.

And now I was at rock bottom. And I had no idea what might be next.

Would I ever be able to pull myself back again? Everyone now knew: Hogan was out of business and broke.

I tried to tell myself that it wasn't my fault. It was a government-caused collapse that wiped out thousands of businesspeople across the United States, me along with them. That was true, but it didn't make me feel any better or offer any kind of lifeline.

It was the toughest challenge I had yet confronted in my life. It literally made me sick to my stomach. People I thought were good friends disappeared. I'd never experienced this kind of stress before. My self-worth was in tatters. More than once, I found myself in tears in a ball on the floor. I learned what failure felt like. It didn't feel good.

When everything that defines you is stripped away, what are you then? It took some soul-searching for me to figure that out. Though my immediate future looked as dark as my recent past, I asked myself, *Where do I go from here?* I knew I didn't want to stay where I was. I was determined not to let my biggest failure define the rest of my life. *I'm going to climb out of this and start over*, I resolved, *even if it's ten times harder the second time.*

It was.

I rented a house in Bowie and hung my license at a residential real-estate company, which was starting again from scratch in every way. Seeking clients. Searching for deals. Figuring out what services I could provide that others could not. I was still the same person I'd always been. I had the same brain and the same drive and the same personality, even if my self-confidence had been badly slapped around.

After a while, I was able to scrape together a few dollars, and I went back into business on my own, opening the Hogan Group, a second-generation version of what we'd had before.

I knew the business well, but after the bankruptcy I couldn't get credit. We had to close a new deal before we could bring on another employee. Everything had to be covered cash on the barrel as we went. We had to climb back from below zero. But climb back we did.

I moved out of Prince George's County and bought a townhouse in Annapolis, a foreclosure, and fixed it up myself. We moved our office to Annapolis and grew the business to twenty-five employees.

Almost everyone forgot about the tsunami we'd been through. But I never have, and I never will. Going through all of that had a profound impact on me. It humbled me, I think, and helped me to see which things are important in life and which things are not. I learned who my true friends were and who was around just for the pleasures of the ride. That whole experience made me more empathetic to the struggles of others.

Hearing about something is different from actually going through it. After the collapse of my business and the bankruptcy that followed, I had a whole new level of understanding for someone who'd lost a job or for a family whose home had been taken in a foreclosure. I didn't just feel bad for them. I *was* them.

I knew what it was like to struggle to climb to the top of the mountain, and I also knew what it was like to go tumbling off the edge of the cliff. I've had incredible highs, and I've had incredible lows. And there is no question that I learned more from the challenges and the incredibly difficult times.

I hated going through it, but I know that I am a stronger and a better person as a result.

CHAPTER 6

INSTANT FAMILY

I was a thoroughly confirmed bachelor.

There were a couple of times in my twenties and thirties when I came close to getting married. Each time I was the one who backed off. Maybe part of it had to do with my parents' divorce. I certainly didn't want to put another woman through what my mom had experienced. Part of it was that I was so focused on my career and building my business. But the truth is, mostly, I just really enjoyed being single. I thrive on relationships and interactions with people. Whatever the combination of reasons, let's just say I didn't rush to the altar, that's for sure.

I worked hard. I had tons of friends. I dated a lot. I had a series of really wonderful and interesting relationships. My life felt full to me, and I didn't have a burning desire to turn it upside down.

And time seemed to race along.

At some point, I thought, *Hey, you're in your thirties.*

I had an easy answer for that: *So, what?*

Then, it was, *You're forty.*

My answer: *Who cares? I'm a really young forty!*

My mother wasn't pestering me about settling down like a lot of moms do. Surprisingly, my father was the one who kept bugging me. He was constantly saying to me, "You can't keep this lifestyle up forever. When are you going to find a nice girl, settle down, and give me some grandkids?"

I did have a snappy comeback for him!

By that point, my dad had four much younger sons with his second wife, Ilona. Matt, Mike, Pat, and Tim were twenty to twenty-five years younger than me, young enough to be my children. In fact, plenty of people thought they were my kids when they saw us together! "Give me a break, Dad," I told him. "You don't need me to give you grandchildren. You went ahead and had your own."

In 2000, as I was turning forty-four, I began thinking that there must be more to life than working, dating, and having fun with my friends. For the first time, I was at least open to the possibility of becoming more serious and eventually settling down with someone. If I found the *right* someone.

Maybe it was just the right person at the right place at the right time. But a wonderful woman came along just by chance, and I fell in love with her. If it had happened earlier, maybe I wouldn't have been ready, I don't know. But here's what happened: I was dragged to an art show at Howard County Community College, which was not an event I would normally attend. The art was nice, but it wasn't the art that grabbed my attention. It was the artist. She was an attractive young South Korean woman named Yumi Kim, and she had made some of the paintings in the show.

At the time, I didn't know it would lead anywhere. But I gave her my card along with the best line I could think of on the spot. "I'm in the real-estate business," I told her. "We have buildings. We sometimes have art in some of the lobbies. You and I should talk."

Okay, maybe it wasn't so romantic, but I really did want to talk to her again. And in my defense, all that was true. I was certainly no art expert, but we did have buildings, and her abstract landscape paintings were beautiful. "I'd love to follow up," I said.

I called her a couple of times. She was busy.

I called again. She was still standoffish. Maybe her playing hard to get is what made me follow through. I like a challenge. Finally, I convinced her to have lunch with me.

We met at a casual dockside restaurant in Annapolis called Pusser's Caribbean Grille. We got a table outside where we could see the sailboats passing by. It's a very romantic spot.

At first, we had a little trouble communicating. Her English wasn't that strong but was certainly much better than my Korean, which was nonexistent. I was trying hard, and she was trying hard, and I was really enjoying the conversation. She told me she came from a traditional Korean family and had raised three daughters as a single mom. She taught art and singing lessons in her basement, she was active in the Korean community, and she was the lead singer in the choir in her Presbyterian church. She said she had never been to Annapolis before, even though she lived nearby in Howard County. "I am very busy," she said. "I don't get out too much. I don't have time for dating."

I was surprised when she told me she was forty-one. I figured she was in her early thirties, mid-thirties at most. She ordered a salad. I had crab cakes.

"Would you care for some wine?" I asked.

"No, thank you," she said.

"Maybe a frozen drink, a cocktail or something?"

"No," she repeated.

"Are you sure?" I asked her. "I'm going to have something."

She hesitated and then said, "Okay, maybe I can have a shot of tequila."

What?! At lunch?

This nice, soft-spoken, churchgoing Korean mom who didn't have time to go out and had just said "no, thank you" to a glass of wine was now asking for a shot of tequila? Then, she explained. "I don't really drink, but we recently went on a church mission to Mexico. They showed us about the tequila with the salt and lime."

"I'm not sure we should start with that," I said. "Why not try something else and see if you like it."

We agreed to meet again and started very slowly.

Yumi was different from anyone I'd ever dated before. I was an outgoing guy. I knew everybody. Cocktail parties and happy hours. Boating and ball games. The social scene back and forth between Baltimore, Washington, and

Annapolis. She was a quiet, reserved, humble person who had been focused on her children, her art, and her church. You know how they say that opposites attract? To me, there was just something completely different and compelling about her. For our first nighttime date, we went to an Italian restaurant called Maria's and talked all night.

Yumi had a dignity about her that was magnetic to me and a life story that was truly inspiring. The youngest of seven children, she grew up on a chicken farm in the rural southwestern corner of the Korean Peninsula, gathering vegetables, drawing with ancient sumi ink, and dreaming of one day becoming an art teacher. I was especially intrigued by the story of how she came to America. At eighteen, she married a Korean-American man and moved to Texas with him. They started a family quickly, but it wasn't a happy marriage. They divorced, and Yumi was soon raising three girls alone in a strange country with an unfamiliar culture and a language she had only begun to learn. Money was tight. She knew hardly anyone. She and the girls moved from Fort Hood, Texas, to Diamond Bar, California, and then to Columbia, Maryland. She became a US citizen in 1994. Along the way, she owned a pizza parlor, hosted a Korean-language show on the radio, and earned an associate's degree at the Maryland College of Art and Design in Silver Spring. At graduation, she won a full scholarship to the world-renowned Maryland Institute College of Art in Baltimore. She dreamed of getting a MICA degree, then maybe teaching art one day in college.

Everyone agreed that her art was exceptional. Unfortunately, Yumi was unable to pass the college admission department's English-proficiency exam and couldn't enroll. "But I never gave up on myself," she said, "and that's how I raised my girls."

We didn't rush anything. I got to know her daughters, three incredible young women who were building successful lives for themselves. The oldest, Kim, was working in a Washington law firm and was in the US Army Reserves. She'd met her future husband, Louis Velez, when they were deployed together in Afghanistan. Middle daughter Jaymi was attending the University of Michigan, thinking about law school and a future career as a prosecutor. Julie, the youngest, was still in high school, into dance, and hoping to follow Jaymi to Michigan. Julie looked at me with some suspicion at first, as if to wonder, *What's his agenda?* The other two girls were instantly welcoming, and Julie came around eventually. I introduced them all to Lexi, my rambunctious little Shih Tzu. She was a point in my favor, I believe. They'd never really had a dad on the scene as long as they could remember. I started to like the feeling of having the family I had missed out on. They seemed happy that their mom had met someone and that she was finally taking some time for herself. The girls liked having me around. And I loved them all.

Yumi bonded easily with my dad, doting on him and listening to all of his stories. He treated her like an answered prayer. I told my mom that I'd met a woman named Yumi who was Korean-American and had three daughters and was very special to me. Mom was living outside Charlotte, North Carolina, near my sister, Terry, and her family. I flew down for my mother's seventy-fourth birthday in April. Yumi sent a little present, a set of Korean teacups and chopsticks. She was looking forward to coming down with me next time. It wasn't to be.

On June 13, 2002, my mom had a heart attack in her sleep and died. She hadn't been sick. She had no history of cardiac problems. My sister's husband, Bob Lazarus, found my mom in bed in her condo. Her beloved Yorkie, Peanut, was resting quietly on her chest. Her last day had been a happy one. She'd spent time with her grandkids, gone to lunch with a friend, worked in her garden, taken Peanut for a walk, and gone to bed.

I was relieved she went so gently, but her death was the hardest thing that had ever happened in our family—definitely worse than my parents' divorce, which was the second hardest. She was the most loving and supportive mother I ever could have hoped for, and I wasn't only a son to her. In many ways, I was also her protector, from the time I moved to Florida at sixteen because I couldn't stand the thought of her being alone. She was just as close to my sister and her family. She'd been a daily presence in the lives of my niece, Becky, and two nephews, Keith and Kevin. They all adored their Nana. Yumi came down with me for her memorial service at Saint Thomas Aquinas Catholic Church in Charlotte. It was one of the saddest things I've ever experienced: a very simple service—just prayers and reminiscences. Mostly what we did was cry and hug each other. I was so sorry that Mom never got to meet Yumi and the girls. I know they would have loved her. And without any doubt, my mom would have loved them. One of the greatest tributes of all would come years later when Jaymi and her husband, Ben, would name their own daughter Nora, even though they and Mom had never even met. But they'd heard enough stories to know how special she was.

Before I left North Carolina, I agreed to adopt Peanut and took him back on the plane with me to Maryland. Let's just say my own dog, Lexi, was not entirely supportive of that decision. But for Mom, we learned to make it work.

It was soon after I met Yumi and just after the 2002 elections that I agreed to take a job I didn't really think I wanted. It involved stepping away from my business to join the cabinet of Bob Ehrlich, who had just been elected governor of Maryland. We'd known each other since he was a young lawyer right out of school. I got him involved in my father's Senate campaign. We'd attended Republican conventions together. He'd volunteered in my 1992 congressional race against Steny Hoyer.

We were about the same age and both from blue-collar backgrounds. While I focused on business, he served eight years in the Maryland House of Delegates. Two years after my near-victory against Hoyer, Republican congresswoman Helen Bentley vacated her second-district seat in Baltimore County. So, in 1994, while I was battling creditors and fighting for my financial life, my friend Ehrlich decided to run for the open seat and was elected to Congress, where he served eight years. In 2002, he ran for governor. His designated lieutenant governor, Michael Steele, another old friend, had taken my spot on the Republican Central Committee and later became the state party chairman. With Steele at his side, Ehrlich pulled off a stunning upset against Democratic lieutenant governor Kathleen Kennedy Townsend, 52 to 48 percent, making him the first Republican to be elected governor of Maryland since Spiro Agnew in 1966.

"I really want you to join us in the administration," Ehrlich said to me the week he won. "You can have any position you want."

"What, like secretary of state?" I answered.

"No," he said. "That's a bullshit job. I need you to do a real job. I'd like you to be secretary of appointments."

My first reaction: "Seriously?"

"This is going to be the most important position," he said. "I need you to help put together the cabinet and get everybody confirmed. You'll have all the appointment power of the governor." It was, in fact, a very big job. The appointments secretary helped choose thousands of department heads, judges, and members of state authorities, commissions, and committees. Since our party hadn't had a governor elected in thirty-six years, there wasn't much of a Republican bench to recruit from.

Many of the key appointments required state senate confirmation. So, a key part of my job was maintaining a good relationship with Democratic senate president Mike Miller—and not just to smooth appointment confirmations. Mike and I got along well. I'd known him since I was a kid. He came from Prince George's County and had known my dad for years. He liked to tell people that one time, he had even been my babysitter, driving around with little me in the car in some long-forgotten campaign. Now, he was a savvy, scotch-drinking pol with allies everywhere and a knack for pulling the levers of power in the State House. He and the new governor were not natural soulmates. Whenever Ehrlich had an important bill to push in the Legislature, he'd say to me, "Time to go get drunk with Mike Miller." Ehrlich didn't drink at all, which was probably a liability in his job. "I never trust a son of a bitch that doesn't drink," the senate president grumbled to me about the new governor.

My position, which few people understood, was a source of extraordinary influence. I served as both a cabinet secretary and a key advisor on the governor's executive staff, helping to choose, vet, and shepherd 7,800 state appointments. I gave him frank advice, even when he didn't want to hear it. I learned about every nook and cranny in Annapolis, knowledge that would serve me very well later in life. Serving as Governor Ehrlich's appointments secretary, I knew almost everything about state government, especially where all the landmines were buried.

Finally, I thought I might be ready to take a big leap in my personal life. In early 2004, I surprised Yumi on a trip to Key West, Florida, by asking her to marry me. I actually bought the ring at a jewelry store in Key West. We went out to a romantic dinner, then had a moonlit walk on the beach, where I got down on one knee under a palm tree. She wasn't that familiar with the custom. She left me hanging there for a few seconds, not knowing what to do. But after that brief pause for dramatic effect, she said yes.

Everyone was thrilled when we broke the news during a family reunion in the Outer Banks of North Carolina—no one more than my dad. My brothers made fun of how Yumi spoiled him. In the Korean culture, it's very important to respect the elders. Older people are revered. We tend to forget that sometimes in America. Yumi doted on my father constantly. She brought him his slippers. She asked if he wanted a glass of wine. "Can I get you anything, Dad? Would you like another dessert?" He loved it!

We had a beautiful wedding at the historic William Paca House and Garden in Annapolis, an eighteenth-century Georgian mansion built by one of the signers of the Declaration of Independence. The wedding was a thoroughly bicultural affair. Yumi invited her friends from church, the art world, and the Korean-American community. I had lots of relatives and people I knew from school, business, government, and politics. All three of the girls were in the wedding as their mother's bridesmaids. My best friend and business partner, David Weiss, was the best man. My youngest brother, Tim, and my old friend Steve McAdams were groomsmen. We had an American ceremony with the typical prayers and vows. Then Yumi changed out of her lacy bridal dress, and I took off my tux, exchanging those for traditional Korean wedding attire. She wore a *chima*, a full-length, high-waisted wrap-around skirt; a *jeogori,* a short jacket with long sleeves and two long ribbons tied together; a pair of boat-shaped silk shoes; and an elaborate headpiece. I went *gwanbok*-style—a jacket with loose sleeves, trousers tied with straps at the ankles, and a special black *moja* hat with a humpy thing in the back. Of course, I didn't know about any of this, but I wanted to embrace Yumi's culture.

When Bob Ehrlich saw me dressed like that, he couldn't restrain himself from making fun of my hat, which he seemed to think resembled a certain Disney character. "M-I-C," the governor of Maryland began to sing, "K-E-Y—" By the time he got to the second M, he was laughing so hard at his own performance, he couldn't go on.

Following the rituals of Yumi's homeland, we bowed to our parents, present and not, and promised to honor them always. Since the governor and first lady were there, we also did a ceremonial bow to them. Ehrlich quipped that he thought that would be a great way to begin future cabinet meetings.

After both ceremonies were over and the cake was cut and champagne was poured, several of the guests delivered affectionate toasts. Then, I raised my own flute to thank and welcome everyone. "I know that a lot of you thought this day was never going to come. I admit that I didn't settle down with the first girl who came along, or the second . . . or the third." That provoked some intended and well-deserved laughs. "I waited until I found my soulmate, the woman I wanted to spend the rest of my life with. I am so amazingly lucky. Yumi is just as beautiful on the inside as she is on the outside. And not only did I find this one incredible woman to be my wife, but I've got these three wonderful, beautiful, incredible young women to be my daughters. I love them all very much."

We really did become a family that day in every sense of the word.

Early on, I made a promise to Yumi: "I want to help you get your dream back." I wanted to find a way for her to receive the art education she had missed out on earlier in her life. With my encouragement, Yumi enrolled in English-as-a-second-language classes at the community college, and I hired a tutor for her. She got to work right away, just as diligently as I expected. She really did a wonderful job improving her English skills.

Eventually, she applied again at MICA, the prestigious art college where she had once won the scholarship. The scholarship with the tuition waiver was long gone, but she was accepted into the highly competitive program. Impressively, Yumi graduated cum laude and then went on to receive a master of fine arts degree at American University in Washington. Ultimately, she would earn an appointment as an adjunct professor on the MICA faculty, teaching a popular class in the sumi ink techniques she had first learned as a little girl in Korea.

What could I possibly accomplish in life that could be any better than that?

PART II

RUNNING

CHAPTER 7

FED UP

When I first told people I was thinking of running for governor in 2014, they thought I must be joking.

"Really? Of what state?" one of my closest friends joked.

"No, I'm serious," I said. "Maryland."

I understood the skeptical eye rolls. This was bold talk for any Republican, much less one who'd never been elected to anything before. With so many federal workers in the DC suburbs and such a high percentage of African Americans statewide—the highest of any state outside the South—Maryland was among the very bluest of blue states, right up there with California, Massachusetts, Vermont, and New York. Despite Bob Ehrlich's surprise victory in the 2002 governor's race, he'd gotten clobbered when he ran for re-election four years later against Democratic Baltimore mayor Martin O'Malley and lost even worse to O'Malley when he ran again in 2010. Before Ehrlich, you had to go all the way back to Spiro Agnew in 1966 to find a Republican governor. Republicans hadn't won a presidential race in Maryland since 1988, when

George H. W. Bush squeaked past Michael Dukakis. In 2014, Maryland had the highest percentage of registered Democrats of any state in America.

The you've-gotta-be-kidding response to my political musings soon gave way to what I would describe as a sort of friendly tolerance. "I mean, I agree with everything you're saying," another friend told me. "I'm as mad as you are. But come on—*really?* A Republican can't get elected governor in Maryland!"

Even I had to agree it was a real long shot.

It wasn't that people didn't think our state needed fresh leadership. We'd lost 8,000 businesses and 100,000 jobs since Martin O'Malley was elected governor in 2006. Our unemployment rate had nearly doubled. Sadly, our overall economic performance ranked forty-ninth out of the fifty states. Taxes, fees, and tolls had gone up $10 billion. Not surprisingly, we had a huge exodus of residents fleeing the state. People were finally saying in disgust, "I don't want to live here anymore," or, more often, "I just can't afford to live here anymore." Lifelong Marylanders were packing up their belongings and fleeing in droves. Retired people were saying, "I don't want to leave my kids and grandkids, but I can't afford to stay here on a fixed income." Business owners were saying, "They're taxing me to death. I'm moving my company to Delaware. Or to Virginia. Or to South Carolina. I'm shutting my doors and laying my people off. It breaks my heart, but what choice do I have?"

And it wasn't just Republicans and business owners talking this way. My Democratic and independent friends were all expressing the same frustrations. Back in July of 2011, I'd joined the board of directors of a group called the Maryland Public Policy Institute, a business-oriented think tank that was just as boring and earnest as the name makes it sound. We produced important research on improving competitiveness and revamping the tax structure and that sort of thing.

But normal people don't read policy papers. Candidly, most politicians don't either. Everyone seemed to agree, but no one could answer the obvious follow-up: *So, what are we supposed to do about it other than toss our hands in the air in frustration and just give up?*

"I'm not sure," I said. "But we need to talk to people directly. Explain exactly what the state is doing wrong. Say it in a way that will make sense to everyday people. Then, come up with some practical solutions about how we can change Maryland for the better."

Change Maryland. Straightforward. Direct. An idea that a lot of people could rally around. To me, that sounded like the perfect name for a nonpartisan, grassroots organization that would take all these ideas and try to get some traction for them.

I started it on a shoestring. A few friends. No money. Working out of my house and then out of my real-estate office in Annapolis. The original team was a political consultant named Steve Crim; a young woman named Marina Hardy, who had interned for me in the appointments office; and Justin Ready, who had directed the state Republican Party until they ran out of money and couldn't afford his salary anymore. Later, we added a data specialist named Matt Proud and Hannah Marr, who volunteered to help us with social media. As Change Maryland chairman, I was the message guy. I would do most of the writing and most of the posting on Facebook, which was pretty much where Change Maryland lived at first.

Instead of long position papers, we took quick shots at the latest mistake that Governor O'Malley or the state Legislature had made. *Another job-killing regulation! Another painful tax increase! How many is it now?*

Early on, we had just a few hundred Facebook followers. But our hard-hitting commentary seemed to strike a nerve. At least someone was speaking up now. Pretty soon, we had a few thousand followers, and I was being invited to talk to business and political groups and getting calls from reporters at the State House. "Another Maryland company just moved to Virginia. Do you have any comment?"

Who else were the reporters going to call? The Maryland Republican Party barely had phone service anymore. They'd lost the last governor's race—O'Malley versus Ehrlich, the rematch—by fifteen points. They were broke. The Democrats ran everything—the executive branch, the House of Delegates, the state senate. And that was just begging for trouble, one side controlling everything. For all practical purposes, Maryland was an arrogant monopoly. Our shoestring organization was no match for the all-powerful machine. It was like David versus Goliath. But we plowed straight ahead.

We focused strictly on economic issues. Jobs. Taxes. Infrastructure.

Economic development. Transportation. Quality of life. "Let's not argue about all the social issues," I said. No divisive debates over guns or abortion. No bashing immigrants or playing to people's darkest fears. "We want to unite people, not separate them the way both political parties and most politicians try to. Let's push the things that people can agree on and bring Republicans, Democrats, and independents together." Almost everyone wanted the economy to improve, even if the folks currently in power seemed hell-bent on crashing it.

Then O'Malley and his enablers in the Legislature found something else they could tax. They decided to tax the rain.

On May 2, 2012, the governor signed into law what was officially known as HB 987, the Watershed Protection and Restoration Program. The idea was to reduce runoff into the Chesapeake Bay, a perfectly worthy goal. But the chosen method rubbed just about everybody wrong: forcing nine counties and the city of Baltimore to impose an annual fee on "impervious surfaces"—roofs, driveways, sidewalks, patios, garages, and anything else that wouldn't absorb water when it rained. The calculations were complicated and differed from place to place. Homeowners were supposed to determine the Equivalent Residential Unit and the Impervious Unit, whatever those meant, then multiply that by some other figure—the whole thing was going to be a nightmare. It was so confusing that nobody really understood what any of it meant. But I understood this much: The new tax, on top of all the other taxes, would cost Marylanders another $3 million a year. And no one in any other state had to pay it.

But remembering our experiences from the think-tank days, I didn't want to get into a wonkish debate over impervious surfaces, Equivalent Residential Units, and other bureaucratese. I thought we'd call this money grab exactly what it was: the Rain Tax.

"And now they're even taxing the rain!" we started thundering on the Change Maryland Facebook page. "What's next? A blue sky and sunshine tax?!"

By our Change Maryland count, the rain tax was the forty-third consecutive O'Malley tax hike.

People howled in outrage. This one really struck a nerve. O'Malley and his supporters in the Legislature tried to explain why the Watershed Protection and Restoration Program was perfectly fair, reasonable, and necessary. The *Baltimore Sun* editorial page kept insisting that it wasn't really a tax on the rain. The governor's allies accused me and Change Maryland of wanting more pollution in the bay. None of those attacks convinced anybody. People could see immediately what an absurdity the rain tax was.

"Everyone wants a clean and healthy Chesapeake Bay," I told a reporter from the local-news website *patch.com.* "This is more about increasing people's taxes than protecting our bay. It's time for us to start electing real leaders who will fund important projects like cleaning up the bay without breaking the backs of taxpayers."

I wasn't sure at first how much we were really going to be able to change things. But there was no denying that our message was breaking through and we were getting heard. A consultant named Jim Pettit joined our team and helped us do an economic-competitiveness comparison between Virginia and Maryland, showing how the tax increases were making us less competitive with our neighbors in the region. We talked about all the things Virginia was doing to attract new jobs and everything Maryland was doing to drive those jobs away. I was invited on the Fox Business Network to talk about the comparison. I'm not sure how many people saw the segment when it ran live. But when we posted the video on the Change Maryland Facebook page, O'Malley definitely saw it—and he went nuts!

Governor O'Malley wasn't accustomed to criticism. The Legislature was more like a cheering squad, going along with almost any crazy thing he wanted to do. We seemed to be getting under his skin now, and we were not letting up. He lashed out at me as a "failed congressional candidate and failed would-be candidate for governor." He accused Change Maryland of twisting the facts. The swipes from O'Malley gave us even more attention. Every time he trashed me, our Facebook page lit up with thousands of new followers. People started saying maybe we really should run somebody for governor. You can't really change Maryland without changing governors. There weren't too many obvious candidates. The truth was that there wasn't anyone with a chance to win. That's when the idea first occurred to me: *Maybe I'll have to think about running myself.*

CHAPTER 8

CHANGE MARYLAND

Things kept getting worse for the state I loved, and people kept noticing. Higher taxes, declining services, politicians who seemed to be completely disconnected from the people in the real world. Change Maryland kept focusing attention on the facts, on the issues, and on the governor. O'Malley and his administration didn't have much of a response. The governor's popularity was falling too. Soon enough, he dropped to fiftieth place, the least popular governor in America.

Then a Gallup poll was released: A whopping 47 percent of all Maryland residents said they would move out of the state if they could. As a lifelong Marylander who loved my state, that broke my heart. It also made me say, "Enough is enough." I could certainly understand all the skepticism about my own potential as a candidate for governor. After all, I was just a small-business guy who had started a bipartisan grassroots organization. But I was talking about solutions to the problems everyone was concerned about. I was good at simple messaging and social media posts. Perhaps most importantly, I had a knack for getting under the governor's skin. But I had never held elective office before. I had no money, no early endorsements, and no broad-based support. To a person, my friends were all warning me against running. "You're a Republican—*in Maryland!*" they kept reminding me.

The party I was a member of was beset by debt and internal division—and, oh, by the way, had only 26 percent of the registered voters in the state. O'Malley was term-limited and couldn't run again. But another strong Democrat, most likely Lieutenant Governor Anthony Brown, would be on the ballot. He had spent the last eight years as a statewide elected official, traveling all over Maryland. Most people had never even heard of me.

What could possibly go *right* here?

I'm not going to run, I told myself, *unless I believe there's at least a chance of winning.* Then I kept looking at Governor O'Malley's falling approval ratings and the two-thirds of Marylanders who said the state was going in the wrong direction, and I started convincing myself that winning might actually be possible. I also fell back on something long-shot candidates always tell themselves: *Somebody has to get out there and at least talk about these issues and make the arguments. Who better than me?* Before I went much further, I needed to discuss all this with Yumi, the girls, and my dad.

Yumi was a bit shocked when we had the conversation. She knew I dabbled in politics. She knew how focused I'd been on building Change Maryland. She loved my dad and had listened to all the stories about his political career, even when he repeated them three or four times. I would describe her first reaction as skeptical. "You're a businessman," she said. "I don't know if you want to try to run for governor." It wasn't like I'd been telling her ever since we met, "I plan to run for governor one day." But Yumi is a very centered person. She asked all the right questions. "Is this the best thing to do? Do you really want to do it? What will it be like for the family?" Then quickly she came around to: "I believe in you. We should pray about it. If it's in God's plan, then you should do it. If you believe in it, I will be there with you."

What more could I ask for?

The girls needed no convincing. "Sounds like fun . . . Let's do it . . . We're all in."

My dad needed even less. "Great!" he said. "It's about time!"

I knew that if I jumped in, my family would be one of my biggest assets. They'd campaign with me. They'd give me plenty of advice. They'd talk me off the ledge when I needed it.

Before I made a final decision, I needed to sit down with my key people in the business: my youngest brother, Tim, who had started with us as a University of Maryland intern and was now my partner in the firm, as well as Hogan Companies' chief operating officer Victor White and vice president Jake Ermer. "Guys," I said, "here's what I'm thinking about doing. What do you think?"

I just laid it out for them.

"There's good news and bad news," I said. "The good news is we're going to actually try to do something to fix the state, which could help the business environment and help everyone. The bad news is that, for the next year at least, I'm going to be gone a lot, and you guys are going to have to step up. Chances are, I'm not going to win so I'll be back to work in November. Then again, I could be the next governor of Maryland and be gone for quite a while."

They all basically told me, "We hate what's going on in Annapolis. We don't think you can win. But if you want to try, go for it."

Now I had the support I needed—at work and at home. In the end, my decision was part political analysis and part leap of faith. The next step: Build a campaign.

When I started to recruit a campaign team in the middle of 2013, the political pros were no more enthusiastic than my friends had been. I'd known a lot of these guys for years. But they weren't exactly jumping at the chance to join a Hogan-for-governor campaign. My Change Maryland cohort Steve Crim agreed to be the campaign manager. We brought in a professional consultant, Mike Leavitt, who was willing to work at a reduced fee. My old friend Russ Schriefer, a nationally known media consultant, said he would make my TV commercials, if we could afford to run any. Russ seemed especially skeptical. After winning with Ehrlich in 2002, he had done the work on the last two losing Republican races in Maryland. "Come on, Larry," he said. "Are you sure you really want to do this?" Since Russ would be working with half a dozen other campaigns that political season, he luckily wouldn't be counting on revenues from our campaign to feed his family.

By the fall, six other candidates were already in the race, three Democrats and three Republicans. As predicted, Anthony Brown, the Democratic lieutenant governor, was running. So were Democratic attorney general Doug Gansler and progressive state delegate Heather Mizeur. Whichever one of them survived the June 24 Democratic primary would almost certainly be the next governor of Maryland, according to all the political experts.

Harford County Executive David Craig, State Delegate Ron George, and former congressional candidate Charles Lollar were the three Republican candidates. They had been running for almost a year. They were all trying to out-conservative each other to win the Republican primary in June, which would surely be the kiss of death for the general election on November 4. My strategy was to ignore them as much as possible and to stay laser-focused on the Democrats in power. But before I could get my crack at the winning Democrat in the general election, I'd have to survive the Republican primary.

Steve Crim and I decided that a short race was better for me than a long one. I didn't want to actually launch a campaign until January, giving us less than six months to become the nominee and then another four months for the general election. Some of my advisors were warning me that January was too late. The other candidates were already out campaigning. They were already raising money and lining up support. If I was going to make the race at all, now was the time to jump in.

"So, let's do a hybrid," I said. We wouldn't officially launch until January 21, exactly one year before the new governor would be inaugurated. But we'd host a huge pre-launch event at the Republican state convention in November, one year before election day. "Without actually announcing," I said, "we'll make sure everyone knows I would be the strongest Republican in the race."

"At the GOP state convention?" Mike Leavitt asked skeptically. "Nobody even goes to that. It's pathetic. It's a hundred and fifty party insiders who don't give a damn about us."

That was true, I conceded. "But we're going to go to their convention and show them what a winning campaign could look like," I said. "We'll rent out the biggest ballroom at their hotel in Annapolis. We'll show them there's more to our organization than they can possibly imagine."

We rented out the Mainsail Ballroom at the Doubletree Hotel. We ordered a full buffet, an open bar, and hired a terrific party band. We printed up tickets that said $250 and hand-stamped every one of them *Complimentary.* "We'll call it the Change Maryland Harvest Party," I said. "It'll be just like a fundraiser, but we won't charge anyone." We invited old friends, political people, Change Maryland supporters, business associates, and everyone who'd already be attending the state party convention.

The other three Republican candidates for governor had sad little hospitality suites in the hotel with a few people trickling in and out. Our Change Maryland bash was the state Republican equivalent of Woodstock. The ballroom could hold seven hundred people. Fourteen hundred showed up, eating, drinking, dancing, and having an excellent time. The guests spilled into the hallways, the lobby, and the parking lot. There were traffic jams trying to get in. The Annapolis fire marshal was not pleased.

The delegates couldn't help but notice they were joined by another 1,300 people they'd never seen before, all trying to cram into the ballroom for the convention's biggest event ever. And the Republican regulars couldn't help but notice who else was there: several risers filled with reporters and cameras from the *Washington Post*, the *Baltimore Sun*, the Washington and Baltimore TV stations, and other media from around the state.

At the last minute, I asked Boyd Rutherford, a lawyer from Howard County and a friend who'd served with me in Governor Ehrlich's cabinet, if he would introduce me to the crowd. Later, people would read that choice as an early sign of who might run as my lieutenant governor. Truly, it was just a coincidence. We hadn't even gotten close to choosing a running mate.

Everyone thought I was going to make a dramatic announcement that night. But I threw a head fake and didn't announce anything. I delivered my speech, hammering at the many faults of the monopoly in power, and I promised an update on my own plans after the holidays, when I would speak with my family and close out my business year.

"Everyone who knows me knows that I love this state," I said in the packed ballroom at our not-quite-a-launch event. "I hate to let people down, and I've never walked away from a tough fight. I happen to believe very strongly that the people of Maryland simply cannot afford another four years of O'Malley-Brown-Gansler tax-and-spend policies . . . It's about time we got the government off our backs and out of our pockets so we can grow the private sector, put people back to work, and turn Maryland's economy around. This isn't a fight between right and left. It's a fight between right and wrong."

"I've never seen anything like the turnout Hogan had tonight," former Baltimore County Republican delegate Don Murphy told the *Baltimore Sun*. WBAL radio called our Harvest Party "the largest political event of the year," marveling at the "sold-out crowd of over one thousand people at the event."

Point made, I'd say.

CHAPTER 9

THE MOLEHILL

I t snowed on January 21—a massive, road-closing blizzard. The official campaign launch we'd planned that night at Mike's Crab House outside Annapolis had to be postponed, so I sent out my official announcement by email.

Not exactly the seamless lift-off of my dreams.

"No amount of snow is going to stop our grassroots army of 75,000 fed-up Republicans, Democrats, and independents from bringing real change to Maryland," I wrote, all but ignoring my Republican primary opponents. "The establishment in Annapolis has just been expecting another coronation in November. But today, regardless of the weather, we're putting them on notice that we're going to give them the toughest fight of their lives."

We finally held our kick-off rally at Mike's on January 29, beneath a giant banner that declared, "The Change Starts Now." We passed out rain-tax umbrellas.

"One thing is clear," I said. "We can't change Maryland without changing governors . . . This isn't just another fight between Democrats and

Republicans. It's more important than that. This is a fight for Maryland's future, and it's a fight worth fighting."

But the big news for our nascent campaign was the man I had asked to be my running mate, the same man who'd called me to the stage at the jam-packed Change Maryland party at the state GOP convention: Boyd Rutherford. Besides serving with me in the Ehrlich administration as secretary of general services, the fifty-six-year-old attorney had deep management and government experience. He'd been President George W. Bush's assistant secretary of agriculture and the associate administrator of the General Services Administration, the federal government's landlord. Boyd was smart, honest, and level-headed, and he knew his way around state government. He was also African-American, bringing some racial balance to the ticket in a state where 29 percent of voters identified as black or African-American.

"I needed to recruit the most capable and most experienced lieutenant governor I could possibly find," I said. "Tonight, I want you to know I have found that partner."

Raising money was really hard. People like a winner—or at least a perceived potential winner. "I have no doubt you'd be a great governor," one of my business friends told me. "But I just wrote a four-thousand-dollar check to the Anthony Brown campaign because I think he's going to win." That was typical, though a few of my friends started kicking in a few bucks. We knew we could never raise the kind of money we would need to run a well-funded campaign, not compared to the mega-dollars Maryland Democrats would be raking in.

So we did something major Republican candidates almost never do: We decided to join the state's public-financing system, which drastically limited the amount of money we could spend. But if we raised enough in small donations—$250 or less—we would qualify for public matching funds, enough to at least give us a voice. We knew that no one in Maryland had ever won a statewide race that way. But we were not likely to raise big dollars, anyway—so why not accept the match? One positive: It meant we could spend a whole lot less time chasing money and a lot more time messaging and meeting voters.

My three Republican primary opponents all ran hard.

David Craig and Ron George were both current officeholders, each with his own base of support. Charles Lollar, a former Marine Corps officer who'd run for Congress against Steny Hoyer, was an energetic campaigner, and the conservative base was fired up about him. I was the politically moderate businessman who said we needed to attract Democrats and independents to win. That was not the perfect message for a Republican primary, especially not halfway through Barack Obama's second term, when the party was drifting further right.

The hard-core Republican activists didn't seem to realize that you couldn't win in Maryland without the support of Democrats and independents. I didn't attack my Republican opponents or get pulled into hot-button social issue debates. Believe me, they tried to draw me into some of those, but I just kept talking about taxes, jobs, and the economy and how we needed to unite Republicans, Democrats, and independents to change Maryland for the better. I was laser-focused on the pocketbook issues that mattered most to people in their everyday lives.

My opponents kept calling me a moderate, which they intended as an insult. But I stayed focused on the larger target I hoped to face in November. I didn't reinvent myself for the benefit of the audiences who showed up at Republican debates and candidate nights. I just stayed *me*.

My strategy worked. On primary day, I handily defeated the other three Republicans, winning 43 percent of the party vote and finishing 14 points ahead of my nearest opponent. I think the Republican voters liked the idea that I might actually attract some Democrats and independents and wouldn't be intimidated by O'Malley's hand-picked candidate, Lieutenant Governor Anthony Brown, who vanquished his nearest opponent in the Democratic primary by 27 points.

The pundits thought the Brown–Hogan race looked awfully lopsided in this overwhelmingly Democratic state. It would pit a two-term Democratic lieutenant governor who had unlimited amounts of money and all the entrenched machine support against a Republican businessman who many people hadn't even heard of and nobody thought could possibly win. In

Brown's eyes, beating me looked like a foregone conclusion. Now that he had ascended the mountain of the Democratic primary, he declared condescendingly, "We've got a little bit of a molehill to take in November."

A *molehill?*

I'd been called a lot of things over the years. *A molehill* definitely wasn't one of them. I responded with a taunt of my own. "We're gonna turn this molehill into the biggest mountain he's ever seen," I promised. "He expects a coronation. We're gonna give him the toughest fight of his life."

I still don't think many people believed in me yet. They thought I was all talk. Brown certainly had a high-flying résumé, even before his two terms as O'Malley's number two. He graduated from Harvard College and Harvard Law School, where he'd been a friend and classmate of Barack Obama. He was a colonel in the US Army Reserves. While serving in the Maryland House of Delegates, he was deployed to Baghdad, Fallujah, Kirkuk, and Basra as part of Operation Iraqi Freedom. On a personal level, he wasn't the most charismatic candidate to come along, but he seemed like a serious, solid, decent guy. As an African American, he also had a political advantage with one of the state's most important voting blocs. And he was stomping me in all the early polls. A *Washington Post* survey taken in early June put him 18 points ahead.

Just to let our Democratic opponents know we were alive, Steve Crim came up with an idea, and Russ Schriefer threw together a quick web video. It wasn't a TV ad. It never appeared anywhere except on our own campaign's Facebook page. The short video mimicked the memorable "Most Interesting Man in the World" commercials for Dos Equis beer. Except in our version, Brown was the "most incompetent man in the world" for botching the Maryland launch of Obamacare, among other political flubs.

"It'll be a head fake," Steve confided. "Brown will think we're going to be running negative TV ads against him. Let's see if we can bait them into overreacting."

That's exactly what happened. The Brown campaign quickly answered our "ad," which no TV viewer ever saw, with an expensive barrage of negative TV ads, real ones, hitting me relentlessly. Voters quickly began to view Brown as running a mean, negative campaign. And it helped improve my name ID.

Our actual TV commercials, when we finally started running them, stayed positive throughout the entire campaign.

Brown took a leisurely two-week vacation right after the primary, then spent most of the summer on the phone raising money, a total of $18.3 million by the time he was done. And that didn't include the millions more that the Maryland Democratic Party and the Democratic Governors Association kicked in. Like I said, raising money is easy when everyone thinks you're going to win.

Our campaign, by contrast, had agreed to abide by public-financing fundraising limits, and we had to cap our total spending at the $2.6 million we received in public financing, which was not much in a state of six million people with several TV media markets. Unlike the Democratic Governors Association, which was lavishing financial support on the Brown campaign, the Republican Governors Association wasn't swooping in to help us at all, despite our constant pleas. They had states they thought were worth investing in. Maryland was at the very bottom of their no-way-in-hell list.

My opponent had a fortune in the bank and all the staff, consultants, and TV ads an eight-figure war chest could buy. We had an energetic corps of volunteers and a full-sized Thor Windsport RV—part transportation, part mobile campaign office, and part rolling Hogan-Rutherford billboard. "The bus," as we called it. That would be my home away from home. "Change is Coming," the destination sign on the front said. We drove that thing everywhere. To every county fair. To every crab feast and oyster roast. To every local parade. It was one-on-one campaigning wherever people were, just like my dad had done at the supermarkets and beauty parlors all those years ago. "I'm Larry Hogan. I'm running for governor. I hope you'll consider voting for me." Even the words were his. We talked to a lot of people. But could we really reach millions in a five-month campaign?

Sure, we could—one at a time.

We got occasional flashes of encouragement, random hints that we might actually be onto something here. We were on the Eastern Shore, pulling the campaign bus into a Holiday Inn parking lot on Route 50 in Easton, when I noticed a large beer truck leaving the parking lot of the restaurant next door. The driver was waving at us and blasting his horn.

"Hogan!" the driver called out. "Larry Hogan!"

As we pulled to a stop, I jumped out to say hello and shake his hand.

He clearly had something on his mind.

"Mr. Hogan," he said to me, "I'm a black man, I'm a lifelong Democrat, and I've never voted for a Republican in my life."

I nodded.

"But I'm definitely voting for *you.*" He really punched that word, *you.* "Everybody in my whole family is voting for you. And I'm telling everybody I know to vote for you."

"Well, thank you," I said. "That really means a lot to me."

Then, he made clear why.

"They're taxing the rain?!" he asked incredulously. "They're taxing the fuckin' rain?!"

I laughed, took a selfie with him, and thanked him again for his support. Then he asked, "Can I get some of those Democrats for Hogan bumper stickers and a couple yard signs?"

In the months to come, Brown's ads would saturate the Baltimore and Washington TV markets. We could barely afford any TV time. Brown had dollars pouring in from national donors and state contractors, eager to grease their relationship with Maryland's next governor. I had my dwindling public-financing dollars. So how could we possibly make inroads here?

We did some limited polling with the little money we had. Even though I'd won the Republican primary, we discovered, many voters still hadn't heard of me. But when our internal pollsters asked if the state was on the right track or the wrong track, two-thirds of them answered, "Wrong track."

That made me think. If two-thirds of the people are convinced the state is headed in the wrong direction, why would they want to keep the same people in charge? Martin O'Malley, the man largely responsible for two-thirds saying the state was on the wrong track, wasn't on the ballot this year, and Anthony Brown didn't have the current governor's high negatives. People had a generally favorable opinion of Brown. "I've heard of him," people said, which was more than they were saying about me at the beginning. "He's the lieutenant governor . . . He's a military guy . . . Maybe we should have our first black governor in Maryland . . . He seems pretty good." But when the pollsters asked about O'Malley, the reaction was much stronger and far more negative. The forty-three tax increases. The rain tax. Driving businesses and retirees away. The sagging economy. People were mad about all of it. People basically said they hated O'Malley. They were okay with Brown. And they'd never heard of me.

I'd been around politics long enough to know exactly what to do with information like that: Tie O'Malley and Brown together and make sure everybody knows that I'm not them. Keep reminding voters about the "O'Malley-Brown Administration . . . the O'Malley-Brown tax increases." The two men had served side by side for the past eight years. Did voters really want more of the same?

I could really have a chance here. I was convinced of it. I just had to avoid getting dragged into the divisive social issues. So, when people asked, "What do you think of abortion?" I said, "I'm focused on turning the economy around." When people asked, "What do you think of gay marriage?" I said, "That's already been decided. I want to turn the economy around." Whatever it was, I wanted to put people back to work and get the economy going again after eight years of "O'Malley-Brown." I kept telling people, "Enough is enough. We can't afford a third term of the O'Malley-Brown administration."

I knew I was getting somewhere when people started responding, "Hell, no. We don't want that at all."

Slowly, ever so slowly, I could feel it. We were chipping away and gaining support.

"I don't know who that dude is, but he's working his ass off," people were saying. "What's his name? He's talking about things I care about. He's everywhere."

We were the little engine that could, still pressing on. Though no one in the media or the national Republican Party was giving us much of a chance yet, my confidence was growing. That's more important than it might sound. If you don't believe you can win, your campaign staff and volunteers won't believe it either. And voters are far more likely to support you if they think you have a chance. I started out telling myself, *Maybe there's a 10 or 20 percent chance we can pull it off in November.* Then, I thought, *Maybe there's a 30 percent chance.* Then 35 or 40. Slowly but surely, we were gaining momentum, and we weren't the only ones who were noticing.

Something special happened at the Dundalk Fourth of July Parade.

Dundalk, Maryland, is an amazing community. A beer-and-a-shot kind of town on the east side of Baltimore County. A patriotic place of strong Catholic parishes, beehive hairdos, and a proud, proud past. Bethlehem Steel's Sparrows Point plant was once the largest steel mill on Earth, stretching four miles from end to end and employing 30,000 workers. Sparrows Point steel is in the girders of the Golden Gate Bridge, in the cables of the George Washington Bridge, and in dozens of battleships from World War I and World War II. Since the big mill shut down, the people of Dundalk have had plenty to fret about, including shaky retirements and a lack of other well-paying jobs. Solidly Democratic, Dundalk hadn't elected a local Republican in seventy-three years.

I knew we could win western Maryland and the Eastern Shore. I knew we would lose liberal Montgomery County and the Democratic machine powerhouses of Prince George's County and the city of Baltimore. Baltimore County was a real battleground, especially on the east side, where on this Independence Day thousands of people were already in lawn chairs and on porches by 7 AM, sipping their first Bud Lights and Natty Bohs of the morning, waiting for the Dundalk Fourth of July Parade to step off at 8.

We had the campaign bus in position. We had a big pile of Hogan-Rutherford t-shirts and a good-sized crew of sign-carrying volunteers. I ran the whole parade in front of the bus, zigzagging from one side of the street to the other, shaking as many hands as a human being could. I ran into the yards and up on the porches in my shorts and Change Maryland polo and ball cap. I'm sure I logged ten miles on the three-mile route and must have sweated off at least five pounds.

I was paid back for every ounce of effort I made.

"I'm a lifelong Democrat, but I'm voting for you," one Dundalk resident called out to me.

"I'm sick of all those taxes. O'Malley's gotta go."

"I never voted for a Republican in my life, but I'm voting for you."

Those words were sweet music to my ears. If I was getting this kind of reaction in Dundalk, I could smell victory ahead.

As I rounded corners, whole crowds of people stood and cheered like they were doing the wave at a ballgame.

It was a solid Democratic area, but Brown didn't bother to show up for the big parade. Instead, his running mate, Howard County executive Ken Ulman, filled in for him. And the crowd was booing Ulman and cheering for me.

At the end of the parade, I guzzled a large bottle of water and collapsed into my seat on the bus. A dozen people from the campaign were in there with me. "We are going to win the election," I said to them. Not "I think we can win." Not "Wow, maybe we can actually pull this off." But "We *are* going to win this election." I just knew it, even if nobody else believed me quite yet.

From January to July, we'd gone from "never heard of him" to "he doesn't have a chance" to "he seems like a nice guy" to "he's everywhere" to thousands of enthusiastic Democrats in the streets of Dundalk saying "go get 'em" and "I've never voted for a Republican before, but you've got my vote this time." They had somehow heard our message, and it was starting to resonate with them—big time!

Now, all I had to do was convince the pollsters, the political pundits, the media, and even the leaders of my own party, who were all still adamantly insisting I had no chance whatsoever to win, not in a solid-blue Democratic state like Maryland.

Really, how hard could that be?

CHAPTER 10

JAYMI'S ANSWER

There was one big problem with Anthony Brown's summer-long strategy of ignoring us: It wasn't working for him.

We didn't need the Democrats' attention to keep us going. We were finding our own oxygen. Our message was right on target. Regardless of party, a lot of people felt like I did. People hated the tax increases. They hated the toll hikes. They hated the sagging economy. They hated the job losses. They hated that living in Maryland was getting harder and more expensive every year. And who else could they blame but the one-party monopoly controlling all of state government, with O'Malley and Brown sitting at the top?

Our internal campaign polls—and theirs too, I suspected—showed we were getting uncomfortably close. The media didn't pick up on any of this. How could they? To save money, they'd quit polling this foregone race, and they viewed internal campaign polls as unreliable—*too self-serving*.

But the Brown campaign was clearly becoming alarmed. In September, they unleashed the dragons—a brutal, vicious series of negative attack ads portraying me as a radical and dangerous right-winger, panicked spots that no confident front-runner would ever air. Brown's ads were running constantly on the Baltimore and Washington TV stations. One ad showed assault weapons in a shopping cart and next to a schoolyard swing set. Another claimed I planned to take away a woman's right to birth control and to outlaw abortion, even if the life of the mother was at risk. But when those attack ads against me started airing, I knew we couldn't afford to ignore them. We had to respond somehow. The ads were outrageously negative and slanderously false, but they could still do terrible damage, I knew.

My daughter Jaymi called, really upset, the first morning the ads started running. "How can they say these lies about you?" she wanted to know.

I called an emergency meeting of my top campaign advisors. I asked Steve Crim, Russ Schriefer, and Mike Leavitt to meet me in the campaign headquarters first thing that morning. "I want to find a way to immediately respond to these attack ads, especially the one saying I am anti-woman."

"We have very limited resources," Steve reminded me. "We really can't spend that money until the end of the campaign."

"It would be a mistake to play into their hands," Mike said. "We want the debate to be about *our* issues, not *theirs*. We don't want to wage this campaign on guns and abortion. We want to keep talking about taxes and the economy."

Russ agreed with both of them. "Besides," he added, "even if we wanted to, we don't have enough cash to make a big enough buy. We can't put enough points on television to make any difference. As uncomfortable as it is, we just have to take the incoming."

"Everything you've all said is true," I answered. "But if we don't respond, this election is over. We might as well forget whatever our message is. It'll never be heard. If we allow these false attacks to define me, our campaign is dead."

I don't think I persuaded anyone. They kept arguing the logic of not responding. But I was absolutely convinced that this was the defining moment, and it was for all the marbles. "I have heard everyone, but I am vetoing all that advice," I said. "Russ, we need to produce an immediate response as quickly as possible—like today. Then, I want to take every single penny we can scrape together and buy every available spot we can get our hands on." Russ had a brilliant team, including his partner, Ashley O'Connor, and Shannon Chatlos, talented women who were assigned to work on scripts and a concept for a woman-focused ad. The first idea was for me to look directly into the camera and tell the truth about my positions. "But I also want to try something else," Russ said. "Maybe we get Yumi to cut an ad."

English wasn't my wife's first language, and I told Russ I didn't think she would be comfortable doing an into-the-camera spoken ad.

"Then, what about your daughter?" Russ asked. "The prosecutor."

"Jaymi?" I said. "I think she would be great."

A couple hours later, Jaymi and I were sitting in my living room with Russ, Ashley, and their whole video crew, along with Kara Bowman, Amanda Allen, and some other key folks from the campaign. I recorded my version of the spot, answering the attacks directly. Everyone felt good about my read. Then, it was Jaymi's turn. One of the crew applied professional full makeup, a rare event for Jaymi. On her first read, she was a second or two over. She did it flawlessly the second time, and that was it. Russ called me a couple of hours later: "I'm sending you two rough cuts."

I opened the email attachments immediately. I looked at the two ads and called Russ back: "Take the one with me and throw it in the trash. Take the Jaymi ad and buy every single spot you can find. Get it on the air as fast as possible. Drain our accounts."

The ad hit Baltimore TV the next morning. We couldn't afford the more expensive DC media market.

"Let me tell you about my dad, Larry Hogan," Jaymi said, speaking straight to camera. "He married my mom and became the father of three independent, strong young women. These ads attacking him as anti-women are just wrong. He's the only candidate who favors over-the-counter birth control covered by insurance. And he's committed to not changing current Maryland law on choice. Dad encouraged my sisters and me every step of the way. He loves the state almost as much as he loves us. He'll make a great governor."

The spot was so powerful, I think we recaptured the momentum right there. Jaymi's message was so positive and so direct and so obviously heart-felt, it couldn't help but move people. This confident, young Asian-American woman, talking about the father she so obviously loved—Jaymi spoke with moral authority. I was so grateful to her. The ad was designed to reach women. But men were coming up to me saying, "That spot with your daughter is incredible. It made me think of my own daughters." It completely neutralized Brown's heavy-handed smears.

We were still being pummeled with attack ads around the clock. His hits on me were coming at a ten-to-one ratio, and Brown still had all the money in the world compared to us. But despite the huge financial advantage, Brown's campaign had suddenly lost its punch. We stayed positive. The other side looked reckless and mean. People were saying, "I hate that Anthony Brown guy. Why is he saying those terrible things about that good guy Hogan with the nice family?" Our one thirty-second commercial with my daughter Jaymi turned a major threat into a major triumph.

Don't get me wrong. At this point I was still seen as a prohibitive underdog. But people were starting to recognize that I wasn't going to quit, and the comparison between the two sides couldn't have been starker. I was now being viewed by voters as a positive, down-to-earth guy next door who was fed up with politics as usual. Brown was more and more being viewed as arrogant, entitled, negative, and dismissive. He was ready to get on with the coronation just as soon as he could get rid of this pesky token opponent the Republicans had put up. At some point it dawned on him that I could withstand a lot of punches. I wasn't going down as easily as he thought I would. The molehill was a little taller than he had imagined. I was campaigning my heart out.

Campaigning hard was one thing. Having the right message and answering the attacks—those were important too. But if I was going to be the next governor of Maryland, I would also have to show that I could go toe to toe with my opponent in a debate and find a way to rattle him.

Brown was plenty smart. He had a glowing résumé. But he also had a stiff personality. He wasn't a real open, friendly guy. When he was campaigning, he was highly scripted and carefully coached. This stiffness really worked to my advantage during the televised debates. We had three of them. The first debate, on October 7, was a predictable affair. I slammed Brown on the state's sagging economy and tied him to O'Malley's tax increases. "Taxpayers in Maryland are suffering," I said. "They just can't take it anymore."

Brown tried to distance himself from his two-time running mate. "There will be no new taxes," he promised before accusing me of being a right-wing extremist. *Ho-hum.* A *Washington Post*–University of Maryland poll released the day of the first debate said Brown was now ahead of me by 9 percentage points among likely voters, 47 to 38 percent. Eleven percent were undecided. We had cut the lead in half from 18. We were gaining ground—but we still had a long way to go.

It was at the second debate, on October 13, where things got fun. Instead of standing at podiums, we sat side by side at the WJLA NewsChannel 8 anchor desk. As soon as I took my seat, I noticed that Brown had a stack of 11-by-17-inch sheets in front of him with boxes and diagrams like flow charts. It was a detailed road map reminding him, *If he says this, you say that . . . If he says this other thing, you should respond with this answer.* All I had in front of me was a mug of water.

The cameras were on us. The debate was about to begin. I could tell Brown was nervous, which seemed strange to me. He had been the sitting lieutenant governor for almost eight years. He was an Ivy League lawyer. He had nearly $20 million to spend. I was the underdog challenger, the small businessman who'd never been elected to anything. I had my public-finance pittance and my ragtag volunteers. I thought to myself: *I don't know why this guy is so nervous, but I've got to rattle his cage.*

There was a big digital time clock on the camera straight ahead of me, counting down to the start of the live debate. Ten seconds, nine, eight, seven, six, five . . . I leaned over and whispered to the lieutenant governor, "You know, Anthony, I can see all your notes and read all your answers." And then, we were *live!*

NewsChannel 8 anchor Bruce DePuyt did his best to help Brown. I'd never seen a debate moderator quite so partisan. For his opening question to me, DePuyt ticked off four hot-button referendum topics—gay marriage, the Dream Act helping young immigrants, abortion rights, and gun control—and then asserted: "If you are a mainstream Republican, you likely voted no on each of those. Are you this year asking voters to elect someone who doesn't share the state's basic values?"

What a jackass! I thought to myself. *Where did that come from?* But I refused to take the bait. I just thought, *This is going to be fun.* And I said the same thing I'd been saying on the campaign trail. "You know," I answered, "all of those decisions are settled law at this point. The voters of Maryland have made their decision. As governor of Maryland, when I take the oath of office, I take an oath to uphold the laws of Maryland. We're not going to be taking actions to roll back or change any of those measures."

And we were off.

I hammered Brown hard on excessive state spending: "Our economy is a mess. Everybody in Maryland seems to know it but you." I hit him on the problems with Maryland's Obamacare website, which crashed almost as soon as it went live. Maryland lost $261 million as a result. "It's been a complete disaster," I said.

Brown admitted that he shared responsibility for the botched website launch but said that many more Marylanders were now getting health insurance. "The cost of inaction would have been greater," he said. Brown said he was the candidate who would make tough choices to protect the environment, to which I countered: "We're the only state in the nation that taxes the rain."

After the debate was over, all the rest of the media waited for us outside. I went out and answered everyone's questions. Brown snuck out the back door and drove away with his entourage and the state troopers. I don't think he ever recovered from my telling him I could see all his answers in advance.

The final debate, on October 18 at the Maryland Public Television studios in Owings Mills, was the most contentious of all. We were supposed to focus on issues of special concern to the rural parts of Maryland. We discussed natural-gas drilling and fertilizer regulation. But we also exchanged plenty of punches.

Brown insisted he was no O'Malley puppet. He proceeded to mention a few times he said the two of them had quietly disagreed behind the scenes. "I've disagreed with him on the mortgage interest deduction that he proposed several sessions ago," he said. "I did not speak out publicly on that. I disagreed with the governor when he signed the bill that passed the tech tax in Maryland several years ago," a tax that was ultimately repealed.

The truth was there was no separating the two of them.

It went on like that for much of the hour. When I brought up the economic devastation caused by the forty-three O'Malley-Brown tax hikes and the collapse of the health care website, Brown accused me of "rooting for failure," another soundbite line that sounded carefully rehearsed.

"I'm rooting for failure?" I shot back incredulously. "If I was rooting for failure, I would just let you be governor!"

I could hear the gasps. Brown looked dazed. He twitched and blinked and licked his lips. He couldn't talk for a couple of seconds.

The video of that exchange was widely circulated on blogs and social media and started to put our underdog campaign on the edges of the national radar. One headline read, "Watch the GOP nominee eviscerate the Maryland lieutenant governor."

CHAPTER 11

RED ZONE

We'd gotten to the five-yard line all on our own in the toughest state in America. We did it with a great message, a nonpartisan grassroots organization, a nimble staff, and an army of energetic volunteers. Very little money but a lot of sweat equity.

So where was the big fullback who would power us into the end zone?

For months, we'd been pleading with the Republican Governors Association to pay attention to our race. The RGA exists to elect Republican governors across America. What about Maryland? The group's chairman, New Jersey governor Chris Christie, had raised $130 million for this election cycle, an all-time record, and had been pouring money into a couple of dozen states. When we inquired, we kept being told the same thing: *Maryland isn't on the list of winnable races. The RGA doesn't invest in impossible causes.* With a little pushing, they did agree to review our internal polling. They also noticed the attack ads the Democratic Governors Association was running against us. That had to mean something, right? The Democrats must be feeling threatened, at least a little.

On September 17, Christie came to Bethesda to do a fundraising lunch for me. He and I instantly clicked. We got along like old friends. He was a moderate Republican with a regular-guy appeal who'd been elected governor of a Democratic state—not quite as blue as Maryland, but still. "You're talking to a guy from New Jersey, who won twice in the same kind of atmosphere," Christie told the reporters camped outside the Redwood restaurant. "These races can be won."

Nice, but Christie still wasn't ready to open the RGA checkbook.

Russ Schriefer had been leaning on him. Besides advising the presidential campaigns of Bush 41, Bush 43, and Mitt Romney, Russ had also worked on the New Jersey governor's 2009 and 2013 campaigns. Now, the two men were flying around the country, helping elect other Republicans. "What about Maryland?" Russ said to Christie on their next trip together. "Larry Hogan."

"Give me a break," the governor said. "I know Hogan's a client of yours. But come on, it's Maryland!"

"I know it doesn't make any sense," Russ allowed. "But I'm telling you—something's going on there."

"Russ, please," Christie snapped. "I have all these states to worry about, and Maryland ain't one of them."

In the coming weeks, Russ brought it up a second time and a third time.

"Russ," Christie said, sounding a bit exasperated. "The Maryland thing again?"

"We have a poll that shows us within five points," Russ told him.

"No fuckin' way," Christie said.

Russ showed him the poll. "Is this real?" Christie asked.

"Yeah, it's real," Russ assured him.

"How? It's Maryland."

"Governor," Russ said, "I've been trying to tell you this for months. We've been inching up since April."

"He doesn't even have any money. What did he do? It's a two-to-one Democratic state."

Russ laid it all out—the message discipline, the frustration with O'Malley, the uninspiring Brown, the movement we'd been seeing among Democrats and independents. "I don't know, Russ," Christie said. "It doesn't make sense. We would have to do our own poll."

At the same time Russ was leaning on Christie, our other consultant Mike Leavitt was pressing his friend Phil Cox, the RGA's executive director. But Phil was telling Christie there was no money in the group's account to do anything in Maryland. "Just to shut Russ up," Christie insisted, "let's scrounge up the money to do a poll."

They couldn't share all the results with me because the Governors Association has to maintain independence from the individual campaigns. But from what I heard later, the RGA poll said our race was a tie. Their poll was *better* than our poll!

Cox called Christie. "Governor," he said, "I've got good news and bad news. The good news is Hogan is doing better than he thinks he's doing. He's actually tied in Maryland."

"What's the bad news?" Christie asked.

"The bad news is we don't have any money."

"We've got to help this guy," Christie said, finally coming around. "He got this far all by himself in the most hostile territory imaginable. I want to win one more race."

"We can't do anything," Cox said. "There are only a couple of weeks left, and we don't have any money."

"What about that line of credit we have?" Christie asked.

"We can't use that for a race," Cox warned. "That's for our operating expenses after the election."

"Who says we can't use it?" Christie asked.

"We've never used it before," Cox said.

"What do I have to do to use it? Do I need to go to the executive committee?"

"I think you just need one other person on the committee to go along with it."

Christie called Indiana governor Mike Pence. "Mike," he said, "I want to talk to you about borrowing money to try to add one more race into the mix."

"Okay," Pence said.

"I want to talk about getting involved in—Maryland," Christie said.

There was a long, perceptible pause before Pence responded, "Chris, have you been drinking?"

They borrowed the entire $1.3 million available on the line and plowed all of it into a hard-hitting message on Maryland taxes that sounded a lot like what we had been saying for the past year. It was our first real penetration into the expensive Washington media market. Our campaign spent our last remaining dollars on Baltimore TV, which is about half the cost.

Would it be enough?

I will tell you how worried the Democrats were at the end.

They recruited all four of the party's marquee endorsers to come into Maryland and campaign for Anthony Brown. Barack Obama, Michelle Obama, Bill Clinton, and Hillary Clinton.

Bill Clinton got there first, drawing a big crowd of supporters to a Brown fundraiser on October 12. Barack Obama arrived a week later, packing the gym of the Dr. Henry A. Wise Jr. High School in Prince George's County with 8,000 people just as early voting was set to begin. Backed by a high school marching band, Hillary Clinton pleaded on October 30 with students at the University of Maryland to get out and vote for Brown, though some of her remarks at the Ritchie Coliseum were drowned out by pro-immigration hecklers. The Brown campaign held their biggest gun of all until election eve, when First Lady Michelle Obama addressed an overflow crowd in Baltimore's War Memorial Building. "If we stay home tomorrow," she said, "we're just letting other folks decide the outcome for us."

That was the Democratic dream team right there, two Obamas and two Clintons. Democratic endorsements don't get any more forceful than that.

Our campaign didn't have any current or former presidents or first ladies. But I liked the closer we had. No one can rev up a crowd like Chris Christie can. He came down the Sunday before the election and stood in front of a thousand people at a Baltimore bingo hall.

On our way in, with the TV cameras all pointing at us, Christie and I shook hands with excited supporters along a rope line. A large man reached his hand out and said, "Remember me?"

He looked familiar. "I'm the truck driver from Easton," he said, "the guy who told you, 'They're taxing the fuckin' rain.'"

I gave him a big hug. "I can't believe you came out here," I said. "But thank you for your support."

"You're gonna win this thing," he shouted over the rising cheers.

There was no keeping Christie off the stage. "I read something very interesting today on my way in from the airport," the New Jersey governor told the crowd. Christie said he'd seen a story in the *Washington Post* reporting that Governor Martin O'Malley was "a little nervous" about his hand-picked replacement, Lieutenant Governor Anthony Brown. "I want to look directly at the camera and talk to my friend Marty," Christie said in that taunting way of his. "Hey, Marty! Don't waste your time being nervous. Just get ready to clear out your office and turn it over to Larry Hogan."

The crowd erupted in cheers.

"I mean, don't you just love it," Christie went on, continuing to tie Brown to the unpopular governor. "Big, bad Marty O'Malley. Big-taxing Marty O'Malley. Big-spending Marty O'Malley. And in two days, big loser Marty O'Malley."

Christie had a promise for the crowd about my running mate Boyd Rutherford and me. "If we spend our time in the next forty-eight hours working for them," he declared, "they are going to spend their time for the next four years working for you."

It was pure Christie. And so was this.

After he introduced me and I went up to the podium to make my closing speech, the New Jersey governor walked over and stood next to my eighty-three-year-old father, who was sitting in a chair onstage. I only heard about this after. But while I was talking, my dad tugged on Christie's jacket.

Christie looked down at my dad.

"Governor," my dad said, ignoring my eloquent words, whatever they were. "Do you really think my son can win?"

Christie was still staring at my dad. "Sir," he said, "your son is going to be the next governor of Maryland."

Tears welled up in my dad's eyes.

And still the media and the so-called experts didn't have a clue.

The day before the vote, famed election prognosticator Nate Silver gave Anthony Brown a 94-percent chance of beating me in the Maryland governor's race. The most likely outcome, Silver concluded, was that Brown would win by 9.7 percentage points. This wasn't just some guy's gut feeling. Silver's FiveThirtyEight blog, which claims to use "hard numbers and statistical analysis to tell compelling stories about elections" and other subjects, was famous for accurately predicting the outcome of the 2012 presidential race in all fifty states. Now, Silver was leaving me like Beltway roadkill on the way to another big Democratic win.

The *Baltimore Sun* and the *Washington Post* were so confident in their predictions of a Brown victory, they hadn't bothered to poll in weeks, convinced that Brown would win in a walk. Their final surveys, taken between October 2 and 8, had me losing by an average of 8 percentage points. By contrast, our final survey, taken a week out by the polling firm WPA Intelligence, gave us a 5-point lead. (According to WPA, we'd been 5 points behind in September and 1 point behind in mid-October.) That confirmed what I was feeling on the ground and what the RGA pollsters had picked up: The trend was moving our way.

But who believes internal polls? Not the media, the experts, or the election prognosticators.

We didn't have to win everywhere. But we had to do a whole lot better than Republicans normally do in deep-blue Maryland. Hopefully, those July 4 parade fans in Dundalk hadn't forgotten about us. As I read the race, we needed to rack up 80 percent of the vote in the western and Eastern Shore counties where Republicans normally get 60-something percent. At the same time, in the three strongest Democratic areas—Montgomery County, Prince George's County, and Baltimore City—we had to shave their totals from 90 percent down to 60-something percent. We had to win all the swing areas. We needed to win all the Republicans, almost all the independents, and a huge chunk of Democrats. That meant we had to run the tables and everything had to fall just right.

With our own final dollars—and the independent infusion from the Republican Governors Association—we hammered hard until the end.

We kept banging our economic message.

We kept reaching out to people who had never voted for a Republican before.

We kept saying, "O'Malley-Brown."

And as the voters headed to the polls in what the experts were all still convinced would be another Democratic blowout in Maryland, in my mind at least, a once far-fetched possibility was genuinely hanging in the air, the enticing prospect that this time the huge underdog might actually win.

CHAPTER 12

NUCLEAR EXPLOSION

'll tell you how I first learned we'd won the biggest surprise upset in America.

It wasn't an announcement by any of the networks: "We have a winner in Maryland." That didn't come until nearly midnight.

It wasn't a concession call from Anthony Brown. That came even later.

It wasn't the carefully crunched numbers from the data jockeys and polling experts on our campaign team.

It was a knock on the door of our hotel suite.

Yumi was with me and our daughters and my dad. So was Boyd Rutherford, my running mate, and his wife, Monica, and key members from the campaign team: Steve Crim, Russ Schriefer, Mike Leavitt, Kara Bowman, and a handful of others. We were all at the Annapolis Westin. Our supporters were downstairs in the Capital Ballroom, nervously eyeing the giant TV screens and fortifying themselves at the bar.

Everything was taking forever. Nobody was calling, declaring, conceding, or announcing anything.

Our campaign team had been collecting raw totals from across the state since the polls closed at 8 PM. These guys were pros. Within an hour, they were confident we had the numbers and were on our way to the biggest political upset in America. We'd turned out our people in the traditional Republican areas. We'd made surprising inroads with the Democrats in Baltimore County. *Thank you, Dundalk!* We'd avoided a Democratic blowout in Baltimore City and Montgomery County. We were losing Prince George's County but not nearly as badly as Republicans usually do. We'd even gotten a respectable number of black and Hispanic votes—against an African-American opponent who was strongly backed by the Obamas and the Clintons!

But the Maryland Board of Elections was late in releasing the totals. Much later than usual. Why were they taking so long? The media hadn't bothered to do exit polls because they didn't think our race was going to be competitive. Now, without the board's confirmation, they didn't want to call the race. And Brown was refusing to call us and refusing to show up at his election night party to concede.

As this dragged on and on, I was stressing out in the suite.

"I'm not waiting any longer," I finally told Steve. "I'm going downstairs. These people have been waiting all night. I'm going down there to make the victory speech."

Several of my cooler-headed team members were literally holding me by my jacket. "We have to wait," Russ said. "Either Brown has to concede or the AP or one of the networks has to call the race. You can't just go down there and say, 'I'm the winner.'"

"Why not?" I said. "We won."

I was pacing back and forth. The campaign staffers were trying to distract me. I was getting more and more agitated. Russ was especially insistent. He said he'd been in situations like this one before. "I know you want to," he said, as if he were talking to a six-year-old, "but we have to wait."

Everybody was trying to dissuade me, even Kara and some of the other younger staffers. Suddenly, they too were experts in election-night protocol.

My dad sounded angrier than I did. "Goddamn it," he fumed. "How come that son of a bitch hasn't conceded yet?"

Maybe Chris Christie was tying up the phone line? It seemed like the New Jersey governor was calling me every half hour. "How's it looking? What do you know?"

Christie was as excited as I was. Some of it was personal because he and I had become friends. Some of it was business because he was chairman of the RGA. It was a huge night for him. He was winning gubernatorial races all over the country—but this one he wasn't supposed to win. He'd personally stepped up for me. He figured he deserved some credit too. "If we pull this off," he said, "it's going to be the greatest thing ever."

"It's looking good," I kept telling him.

"Are you sure?"

"Yeah, I'm sure."

If we waited much longer, I was concerned that our supporters would start going home. I didn't want to miss my own victory party or talk to an empty room.

The staffers told me not to worry. The crowd was excited, and nobody was going anywhere.

At the same time, we were getting reports from the alumni center at the University of Maryland, the site of the Brown campaign "victory party."

"They're suicidal over there," someone said. "Everyone's leaving. His people are trying to drag him onstage and make him concede. He just won't do it. He keeps saying, 'Not yet.'"

We waited and waited some more.

Finally, there was a knock on the door of our suite.

The governor of Maryland, like the governors of all the other states, is protected by a special, plainclothes security detail, the executive-protection team of the state police. Four Maryland state troopers were standing outside the door.

"Governor," one of them said, "we're here to protect you, sir."

I'd never been called *governor* before.

I'm not sure if that knock can be counted as an official notice, but that's how I chose to take it—the unofficial official confirmation that I had been elected as the sixty-second governor of Maryland.

"We did it," I called out to Yumi, who came over and gave me a big hug. The three girls were right behind her with my two sons-in-law, Louis and Ben, followed by all four of my brothers. Everyone was ecstatic. I turned to Boyd and Monica and hugged them. It wasn't very eloquent, but this is what I said: "The shit just got real."

I walked over to my dad, whose hearing had declined. He was sitting in front of the TV and telling people, "Be quiet, be quiet. I'm trying to listen."

He was so focused on the TV he didn't notice me at first.

"Dad," I said once I got his attention, "it may have taken us forty years, but we're finally going to have a Larry Hogan in the governor's mansion."

He didn't say a word. But in a matter of seconds, the tears of joy were streaming down his face and would not stop.

I had spent all those years measuring myself against my father, defining my accomplishments in terms of his, which was a challenge to say the least. I had been proud of him most of my life. When we both understood that I had been elected governor and I looked into my father's eyes, it was the first time I truly felt just how deeply proud he was of *me*.

With those two moments—the troopers at the door and the tears on my father's face—there was no denying this was real. I hugged my dad. Then he went around the room, hugging everybody, and so did I.

Finally, with 87 percent of the precincts reporting, the Associated Press called the race. The AP declared me the winner, the news flashing across televisions nationwide, saying Larry Hogan at 52 percent of the vote was going to defeat Anthony Brown, who had 46 percent.

It must have been the hardest phone call Anthony Brown ever had to make. But when he called, he couldn't have been more gracious. "Mr. Hogan," he said, "I just want to congratulate you and wish you the best of luck."

I thanked him and said, "Anthony, I really appreciate the call. I have a great deal of respect for you. Thank you for your service to the state and your service in the military. I hope we can get together in the coming days and talk."

He said he would like that.

More and more of the campaign people were coming upstairs by then. Some of our biggest supporters, contributors, volunteers, and people who'd been with us from the start, including Jim Brady, Gary Mangum, Tom Kelso, and Ed Dunn. The suite was really starting to swell. Christie called again. Now, he was almost yelling into the phone.

"Hey," he said. "I want to be there! I'm gonna get on a helicopter and fly down there to be with you! Can you wait? Don't make your victory speech until I get there."

"Gov," I told him, "I really appreciate that. I would love to have you with us, but these people can't wait any longer. They're literally about to tear this hotel down."

He kept pushing, but I interrupted. "You've done enough," I said. "I can't thank you enough for believing in me. We would not have won without the cavalry from New Jersey! But I have to go."

When I finally reached the ballroom, there was complete pandemonium. I know my confidence had bolstered my supporters, but most of them still seemed absolutely shocked that we had actually won. I could see a large bank of TV cameras as I made my way to the podium.

I started with a long list of thank-yous. I had a lot of people to thank. Yumi and our family. My dad, who was still crying, interrupted my thank-yous to kiss me on the cheek. Boyd and his family. Our lean campaign staff and our Change Maryland volunteers. I told the crowd how badly Chris Christie was itching to be there. And I publicly thanked Martin O'Malley and Anthony Brown for their eight years of service to Maryland.

Election night is always exhilarating when you've won the race, especially if you're a challenger and nobody thought you had a chance. I'd been to "victory parties" over the years for losing candidates, including myself. Believe me, they weren't nearly this fun. These people had poured their blood, sweat, and tears into this campaign for a year. They had earned the right to celebrate. Many of them had also been drinking for four hours by the time I came downstairs. So to say they were exuberant would be an understatement.

"Wow," I said, "what a historic night in Maryland! They said it couldn't be done here in Maryland. But together, we did it." Now, I knew, people everywhere would pay attention.

"Ladies and gentlemen," I said, "we have sent a loud and clear message to Annapolis that they have heard all across the country. Thanks to the help of everyone in this room, this is the largest mandate for change in Maryland in sixty-three years," a reference I am certain almost no one in the room recognized. (It was in 1951 that Theodore Roosevelt McKeldin, the past and future reform mayor of Baltimore, was elected the fifty-third governor of Maryland. He was the first and, so far, only Republican governor to win re-election in the state's history, which instantly gave me something further to shoot for.)

But this wasn't a night for gloating. It was a fresh opportunity to bring people together in a deep-blue state that had just shockingly elected a Republican as its governor. As America was getting more and more bitterly tribal and divided, Maryland was going the other way. "From the beginning," I said, "this race was never a fight between Republicans and Democrats. It was more important than that. This was a fight for Maryland's future, and it was a fight worth fighting. Tonight, the voters of Maryland rejected the politics of deception and division . . . Tonight, countless Democrats crossed over and affirmed the wisdom of John F. Kennedy, who said, 'Sometimes party loyalty demands too much.'"

Just because we had won the election, I emphasized, that didn't mean we should forget about the people who had supported the other guy. "It doesn't matter what party you are," I said. "It doesn't matter if you voted for us or not. Starting tomorrow, let's all work together to turn our great state around. These serious problems we face, they aren't Republican problems or Democrat problems. And the only way we're going to solve them is to sit down together, reach across the aisle, and come up with real, bipartisan, common-sense solutions."

People cheered at that. I'm not sure if they thought we'd really do it, but it was a message they'd spent the past year believing in. Now it was actually coming true. We'd been through a very difficult campaign together, but I swear there was no hate between the Republicans and Democrats in that diverse crowd of ours. There was only hope.

"Tomorrow," I said, "let's turn the page together."

Now it was time to get off the stage and celebrate. When I wrapped up my speech, the room was going wild. I noticed that we now had at least a dozen state troopers, and they were forming a perimeter around me, peering intently into the frenzied crowd. I leaned over to the sergeant and said, "I'm going down into that crowd."

"I wouldn't advise that, sir," he responded.

"Well, I appreciate that," I said, "but I'm doing it anyway. So you guys might want to get ready." I could see the troopers tossing glances at each other as if to say, *Uh-oh, he's really going down there.*

I don't think Governor O'Malley spent a lot of time marching into large crowds. The soon-to-be-ex-governor and I had very different personalities, even apart from our politics. He wasn't much of a people person or a warm and engaging guy. He would slip into events backstage from the kitchen and slip out the same way.

But, troopers in tow, I pushed right into the cheering crowd, spending the rest of the night shaking hands, hugging people, posing for selfies, thanking everyone, and just celebrating with the people whose hard work helped make this night come true.

Eventually I got a call from Governor O'Malley. He wasn't quite as friendly as Anthony Brown had been. "Hey, Governor, how are you doing?" I asked him.

"Not nearly as well as you are," he said.

He congratulated me and offered to help in the transition. We'd have to see exactly what he meant by that.

I stayed up most of the night, wishing the celebration would never end. I wanted to take it all in and remember every last second of this amazing night.

Our victory sent shock waves across the media and political worlds.

"A stunning upset," said the main lede in the *Baltimore Sun.*

The *Washington Post* used exactly the same phrase: "Republican businessman Larry Hogan pulled off a stunning upset in heavily Democratic Maryland."

"Hogan shocks Brown in Maryland," *Politico* declared.

"How could a Republican win the governorship of Maryland?" the *New Yorker* wanted to know. "That is a question many Democrats posed on Tuesday night, as it became clear that Larry Hogan had defeated Anthony Brown, the current lieutenant governor, in an upset that the *National Review* called 'stunning.'"

Stunning was a very popular word that week.

On Fox News, syndicated columnist Charles Krauthammer had an even more vivid term. He called the win a "nuclear explosion." Marveled Krauthammer, "Anthony Brown was considered such a shoo-in, no one spoke about the Maryland race. No one. You didn't hear a word. The Republican, Larry Hogan, came out of nowhere."

Actually, I came out of Landover Knolls and Annapolis. But you get the point.

The movie references were flying.

"The *Rudy* of politics," one television reporter called me, a tip of the helmet to the walk-on player who'd overcome every obstacle to take the field for Notre Dame, then sacked the Georgia Tech quarterback and was carried off the field on his teammates' shoulders while the whole stadium erupted in cheers. It's never a bad thing to have the luck of the Irish.

"The *Seabiscuit* of politics," someone else insisted, referring to the come-from-behind thoroughbred who beat the Triple Crown winner at Pimlico and was voted American Horse of the Year. That one even had a Maryland angle.

I loved that talk, of course. But as long as we were picking role models from Hollywood, I had my own nominee: I was thinking I was more like Rocky to Anthony Brown's Apollo Creed. The blue-collar guy getting up at six in the morning and drinking raw eggs and punching meat for a shot at the championship. That's how I felt the whole way, like I was arriving in my dirty sweatpants while my opponent's handlers were suiting him up in a beautiful silk robe.

David Zurawik, the *Baltimore Sun's* sharp-eyed media columnist, poked some much-deserved fun at FiveThirtyEight's 94 percent certainty that I'd be clobbered. "I can't wait to hear all the political insiders who worship at the altar of Nate Silver explain how he could have been so wrong about Maryland's gubernatorial race," Zurawik taunted.

Silver sent out one of his senior political analysts to do damage control under the headline "Flying Blind Toward Hogan's Upset Win in Maryland."

"Of all the upsets Tuesday night, one stands above the rest: Maryland governor," Harry Enten wrote. "FiveThirtyEight's gubernatorial model projected that Democrat Anthony Brown would defeat Republican Larry Hogan by 9.7 percentage points—Brown was a 94 percent favorite. In fact, Hogan beat Brown by 5 percentage points. Our forecast wasn't even close."

Well, give Silver's guy points for facing the facts. Then, take a couple of points away for the weaselly defense.

"What happened? First, 94 percent favorites are supposed to lose sometimes (6 percent of the time, to be exact). Hogan's chance of winning was roughly equivalent to the chance No. 14 seed Mercer had of beating No. 3 seed Duke in the NCAA men's basketball tournament this past March. Underdogs can win."

Enten went on to add that the FiveThirtyEight prediction model relied on public polls and that there'd been no recent public polls in the Maryland race, since everyone thought it was going to be a blowout, and FiveThirtyEight doesn't like to rely on internal polls.

Whatever. It wasn't a great night for any of the so-called experts.

When all the votes were counted, including the early ballots, the write-ins, and the absentees, the Hogan-Rutherford ticket received 884,400 votes or 51 percent. The Brown-Ulman team had 818,890 or 47 percent, with the remainder split among a Libertarian Party candidate and various write-ins.

Not bad in a state we had no chance whatsoever of winning.

I had a meeting the next morning at 7 AM after just a couple of hours of sleep. Charlie Ardolini, the commander of my new executive-protection detail, wanted to meet before I left the Westin, where Yumi and I had spent the night. He said he needed to explain to me exactly how my life and the life of my family were going to change.

"We'll take your vehicle," he said matter-of-factly. I had a black Chevrolet Tahoe SUV. Let me rephrase that: I *used to have* a black Tahoe. "You won't be driving anymore," Charlie said. "We'll be with you twenty-four hours a day from now until the end of your term."

This wasn't my first time meeting Charlie. I had known him from my time in the Ehrlich cabinet. He was very professional, then and now. But this was going to be different. I would be his team's round-the-clock focus for the next four-plus years.

He laid out some of the mechanics of our new relationship. He didn't ask me, really. He just laid them out. How the security staffing worked. How the members of his team would interact with my family and my staff. How the troopers would try not to be any more intrusive than they needed to be, but they had a job to do, and they intended to do it.

All this was going to take some getting used to.

Yumi and I wouldn't move into the governor's mansion until I officially took office in January, but the troopers would be stationed outside our waterfront home in Edgewater starting immediately that day.

By the time I got done with Charlie, the media were waiting for me.

Not just the usual campaign correspondents and State House political beat reporters. I was the surprise governor-elect of Maryland, the candidate who had come out of nowhere, and everybody—local, national, print, TV, digital—wanted to have a look at me. I didn't have to travel far. The media seemed perfectly happy showing up at my hotel, in what was the most crowded press conference I had ever attended. After the exhausting campaign, the celebratory drinks I'd downed at the victory party, and a quick nap, I wasn't close to looking my best. But good news can cover a rash of imperfections, I have learned.

"The campaign is over," I said. "Now, the governing begins. My wife and I looked at each other this morning, and I said, 'Good morning, First Lady,' and she said, 'Good morning, Governor.' It was an interesting feeling."

The reporters asked about the election. They asked about the transition. They asked who'd be joining the new administration as cabinet members and senior staff. I didn't have many specifics to share with the reporters, but I knew what a massive job lay ahead.

"We will get things done in a bipartisan fashion," I said.

I announced that I would meet soon with the leaders of the state Legislature, all Democrats. I would also name a transition team, and it would include people from both parties. That group, I said, would be co-chaired by Boyd Rutherford, the incoming lieutenant governor, and our campaign chairman, Jim Brady, who'd headed up the transition for two recent former governors, Parris Glendening and Bob Ehrlich, a Democrat and a Republican. Bipartisan from the start.

CHAPTER 13

NEW GOV

The grueling campaign finally over, I knew exactly what I felt like doing next: putting my feet up, pouring a stiff Maker's Mark, and taking a long weekend with Yumi to relax and reflect on our unexpected triumph.

Not a chance.

Instead, I needed to assemble an entire state government, and I had just two and a half months to do it. Ready or not, Boyd and I would be inaugurated on January 21. Between now and then, we had to wrap up our campaign, build a transition team, hire a staff for the governor's office, and recruit hundreds of cabinet secretaries, agency heads, and other top officials. At the same time, we had to lay out our major priorities, assemble a legislative package, draft a state budget, and move our new administration into the State House and all the state agencies, ready to take over on day one. Oh yeah, and we needed to plan an inauguration and an inaugural ball, write an agenda-setting inaugural address and a state of the state speech, pack up and move out of the house in Edgewater and into the historic governor's mansion in Annapolis, and do lots of other things I wasn't even thinking of yet.

The year-long campaign was hard, but this was going to be no walk in the park either.

Though I'd never held elected office before, in some ways I may have been more prepared for the job than many previous governors. Unlike most of my predecessors, I'd been a business owner. I'd actually hired people and run something. Although I was an outsider, I'd been around politics my whole life. And my four years as a cabinet secretary were a big help. Those four years gave me a head start when it came time to build a state government of my own. Starting with, who might be willing to help?

I'm not the smartest person in the world, but I was smart enough to know that I should surround myself with the best team I possibly could. It didn't matter to me if they had government experience or not. In fact, I was specifically looking for people from the private sector, folks who knew how to lead and knew how government impacted people in the real world. It didn't matter to me if they were Republicans or Democrats. For our transition team and for the administration, I was simply looking for the best. I wanted honest men and women I could trust.

I named Craig Williams to be my chief of staff and also to run the day-to-day operations of the transition team. Craig was one of the smartest and most capable people I knew. He had served as deputy chief of staff for Governor Ehrlich and was now a senior executive with an international bio-pharma company. It took some persuading to convince him to leave a lucrative career in the private sector after all these years to come back into public service. But I'm pretty persuasive.

When Ehrlich was elected governor in 2002 and when he turned over the reins to O'Malley in 2006, hundreds of thousands of dollars in state funding was provided to pay for staff, office space, and other transition costs. But now that O'Malley was leaving office, he wasn't nearly as generous with us. He budgeted just $50,000. We had to raise all our own money to pay for the transfer of power. We continued to work out of our campaign headquarters and continued paying our own staff. But most of the transition team's important work was done with scores of volunteers.

Sam Malhotra was a highly successful businessman who owned a defense-contracting firm and had hosted our very first fundraiser at his home. Wanting to give back in a public role, Sam told me he was ready to take on the toughest job we had, whatever that might be. I appointed him secretary of the Department of Human Resources. His mission was to transform the behemoth that provided critical services to people who desperately needed them. Mike Gill was a principal in a venture-capital and investment firm. He had never served a day in government, but he was a natural-born salesman. In his new job as economic development secretary, he would need to convince skeptical businesspeople that Maryland was a state worth investing in. Businesswoman and Democratic state senator Rona Kramer took on the Department of Aging. Republican state senator David Brinkley, who owned an insurance and investment business, became budget secretary.

I kept one O'Malley cabinet member, Secretary of Juvenile Services Sam Abed, who'd been doing an impressive job in a tough position. I named James Fielder, who'd been with me in the Ehrlich cabinet, as my new appointments secretary, the job I'd held with Ehrlich. "Widely regarded as a stepping stone to higher office," I deadpanned at the press conference announcing his appointment.

We hired Republican state delegate Kelly Schulz, who also had a great private-sector background, to be labor secretary. The longest-serving House majority whip, Democrat George Owings, a Marine who'd served in Vietnam, signed on as our new veterans secretary.

For the secretaries of the Department of the Environment and Department of Transportation, we did national searches to find the most experienced leaders in the country, hiring Ben Grumbles from the US Environmental Protection Agency and Pete Rahn, who'd run transportation in both Missouri and New Mexico.

The list went on and on. Building a team wasn't easy, but we were putting together a strong one. This was the most bipartisan, most diverse, and most inclusive cabinet ever assembled in Maryland. In my opinion, it was easily the most talented and most capable too.

As Inauguration Day grew near and our budget proposal was already being printed, the State House reporters were pressing me for details on our agenda. I wasn't ready to say much beyond the general principles I'd been articulating for months. But I did make the point that my strong commitment to bipartisanship didn't mean I'd be the only one who had to compromise. I'd expect the Democrats in the Legislature to do some bending too.

"Every bill or action that crosses my desk will be put to a very simple test," I said at an economic development conference in Annapolis. "Will this action make it easier for families and businesses to stay and prosper in Maryland? And will it make more families and more businesses want to come to Maryland and help us grow our economy? If it doesn't meet that test, I will veto it. It's that simple."

The governor of Maryland lives in Government House, a 26,900-square-foot, 54-room, 150-year-old Colonial mansion that sits on State Circle in Annapolis, meaning I would have a two-minute commute, give or take a few seconds, to the governor's office on the second floor of the Maryland State House. With seven formal public rooms, many historic portraits, and a dining table that could seat the starting offense and defense of the Baltimore Ravens, I knew it would be both an honor and a responsibility to live in a house like that. Yumi and I were all set to move in the night before the inaugural.

We thought so, anyway.

But when we showed up at the house for our first big night there, we were shocked to find that almost all the furniture in the living quarters, a large portion of the house, had disappeared.

When the O'Malleys moved in eight years earlier, the state had purchased all new furniture. It had all been there, looking great, a few weeks earlier when the outgoing governor's wife, Baltimore district judge Catherine Curran O'Malley, showed us through the house. But the O'Malleys had decided they wanted to take the state-owned furniture with them to their new home. They made a list of what they liked and then declared it "surplus," skipping the proper procedures for disposing of excess state property. No open bidding. No public notice. No eBay listings. Instead they declared fifty-four pieces of furniture—beds, chairs, tables, armoires, mirrors, lamps—as "junk." If it was junk, I'm not sure why they so badly wanted to take fifty-four pieces of junk with them. But they got away with a pretty good deal, paying just $9,638 for furniture that state taxpayers bought for $62,000 just a few years earlier. It would later become the subject of an ethics investigation and a grand-jury presentation by Anne Arundel County State's Attorney Wes Adams. No indictments were ever returned.

But for now, Yumi and I needed something to sleep on. My dad was also spending that first night at the mansion, something he'd been waiting forty years to do. In one room, there was an old bed the O'Malleys had left behind. We put my dad in that. But since the armoires were missing and the historic mansion had almost no closets at all, my dad came into our bedroom and asked, "Hey, Lar, where do I hang my suit?"

"I don't know, Dad," I told him. "Just hang it on the door or lay it on the floor. We don't even have a bed in here."

Chris Christie had agreed to introduce me at the next day's inaugural ceremony on the State House lawn. "I might come down early so we can throw Marty O'Malley's shit out the window," he'd joked to me over the weekend. Actually, it was good Christie's arrival got delayed. O'Malley didn't really leave anything to discard.

I gave my credit card to one of my campaign staffers and asked, "Can you call Mattress Warehouse and see if you can get a mattress delivered to the mansion for tonight?" And that's where Yumi and I slept that first big, exciting night at the governor's mansion, on a mattress on the floor. The next morning, with a huge crowd of people on the way to the inauguration, I was in my best suit, sitting at the edge of that new mattress, struggling to tie my shoes. I didn't even have a chair. Later, we had all the old furniture delivered from our house in Edgewater. I didn't want my first official act as governor to be having the taxpayers buy a houseful of new furniture as they had done for my predecessor. But I could hardly wait to hear the governor's mansion tour guides: "This piece is from the Federal period. This is the Victorian Room. This piece is from the 1730s. And these pieces over here? They're from the early-1990s Edgewater basement period."

We started the day's inaugural events with an interfaith prayer service at Saint Mary's Church, followed by a small brunch at the governor's mansion and then a larger gathering in the Governor's Reception Room of the State House. Then several hundred dignitaries filled the House chamber for the first of two swearing-in ceremonies. Boyd was sworn in first. Then, Yumi held the Bible for me. I raised my right hand as Mary Ellen Barbera, chief judge of the Maryland Court of Appeals, led me through the oath of office. I swore to "support the Constitution of the United States and . . . be faithful and bear true allegiance to the State of Maryland." I signed the court's official register, at which point I officially became the sixty-second governor of the state of Maryland.

It was a blustery and cold January day but more than a thousand people were waiting outside the State House steps for the official public inauguration ceremonies.

There is a lot of pomp and ritual when a new governor takes office: an invocation, "The Star-Spangled Banner," another swearing-in, several speeches, a nineteen-gun salute (presidents get twenty-one; governors get nineteen), a synchronized fly-over from the Maryland Air National Guard, and plenty of good wishes and applause. When Chris Christie began his introduction of me, the snow began to fall. The State House grounds suddenly looked like one of those beautiful winter-scene *Welcome to Maryland* postcards.

Christie called me "someone who isn't afraid to be known as bipartisan . . . He doesn't claim to have all the answers, but I know that he knows how to bring people together because he's been doing it his whole life."

He went on at some length, prophetically, I hoped. "I have every confidence," he said, "that Maryland is in good hands, and I look forward to coming back here four years from today to watch Governor Hogan get sworn into his second term."

When I stepped up to the podium, the snow started coming down much harder—large, fluffy snowflakes gently falling on the shoulders of my overcoat. It couldn't have been better timed for dramatic effect. This sent me right off script even before I started my prepared remarks: "They said it was going to be a cold day in hell before they elected a Republican governor!" The crowd roared with laughter. My nervous staff seemed relieved.

"I am a lifelong Marylander who loves this state," I said. "Every great experience, every great memory, every great moment I have ever had in my life has happened right here, in Maryland. It is such an incredible honor to be standing before you today as the sixty-second governor of the great state of Maryland. I am truly humbled and deeply grateful for the opportunity to serve my fellow Marylanders, and I vow to work tirelessly every single day to prove worthy of this great honor that you have granted me."

Our state has always faced challenges, I said, going all the way back to "those brave Marylanders who first came to this land seeking freedom and opportunity when they landed in Saint Mary's City in 1634. While the challenges facing us today are different, I know that the courage and the spirit of Marylanders is the same. We seek the freedom to compete without the undue burden of high taxes and bureaucratic regulations, which make us less competitive. We seek opportunities to build better communities, better businesses, and better lives for ourselves, our children, and our children's children. And most of all, we cherish both the freedom and opportunity to decide our future."

A lot of people heard me in Annapolis that day. But it sure doesn't seem like anyone in Washington did.

I did face one small glitch during my inaugural address.

About two-thirds of the way through, the teleprompter suddenly blacked out. I'm not sure if the snow got the wires wet or if the cold was to blame. Maybe it was the shocked ghosts of past Democratic governors seeing me standing at the podium. I'd never used a teleprompter before. During the practice run, I'd asked about what would happen if the teleprompter broke. My aides all assured me that these wonderful machines never malfunction. Well, mine did—while I was delivering the most important speech of my life.

I was able to wing it for a few moments. I had been through the speech so many times, I remembered what the next few lines were. Then, there was a flicker and thank God the screen on the right popped back on. The one on the left never did. I finished the speech that way. I don't think anyone even noticed. But for me, it was like landing a plane with one wing. And it was the first time I had ever flown a plane.

Maybe I set the expectations bar too high. But that was the idea, as I built toward the stirring close. "One hundred years from now, I want Marylanders to say, 'This was when Maryland's renaissance began.'"

Following the ceremony, Yumi, Boyd, Monica, and I all stood for hours in a receiving line on the first floor of the State House, shaking the hand of every citizen who came to celebrate with us. I also went up to the governor's office on the second floor of the State House to sign a series of official documents and executive orders, beginning the changes that would come with our new administration. I hadn't been in the governor's office since the Ehrlich days. The O'Malley staff had vacated during the inaugural ceremony. There was nothing on the walls but holes where their pictures had been. There was hardly so much as a pen or paperclip in the drawers of the historic, handcrafted Wye oak desk. We would literally be starting from scratch.

The snow kept falling all day, but it wasn't nearly enough to keep anyone from the inaugural gala that night at the Baltimore Convention Center. More than 3,000 excited people were ready to party, celebrating their hard work on the campaign and their fervent hope that we really could change Maryland for the better.

Yumi looked stunning in a red dress. She and our granddaughter, Daniella, who'd turned two just a week earlier, got far more attention than the short speeches that Boyd and I gave. My job, as I saw it, was to shake every hand in the room and thank everyone. I did that for four solid hours before I finally went to a private holding room, sank into a chair, and guzzled a bottle of water. I was exhausted. Yumi was exhausted. The state troopers from the executive-protection detail were definitely exhausted.

"Are you ready for bed?" Yumi asked.

"I don't think I can sleep," I told her. "And I don't think I shook every hand yet."

She thought I was joking. "I'm serious," I said. "I want to go back out there again for an encore." And back out to the floor of the convention center we went. It was after 4 AM before I finally got back to hit my new mattress on the floor of the governor's mansion.

CHAPTER 14

FAST START

I t's a crazy system, expecting a new governor to propose a state budget on his first full day on the job, after the Legislature has already been in session for two weeks. But that's how the political calendar works in Maryland, and we were right on time with our first budget the morning after the inaugural ball. The budget was fully detailed in a stack of black books five inches thick. Bobby Neall, David Brinkley, Craig Williams, and their volunteer budget crew had pulled some all-nighters during the transition to make that a reality. This was a historic event. Our $42 billion spending plan would be the state's first balanced budget in a decade. We had to make some difficult choices to reach that goal, including reducing state-agency spending by 2 percent and slightly lowering the reimbursement rate paid to Medicaid doctors. But the news wasn't all gloomy. Our balanced budget had no tax hikes, no layoffs, and no furloughs. It preserved all important state services and provided record funding for K–12 education. And most importantly, we eliminated the $5.1 billion "structural deficit" that we inherited from the free-spending O'Malley-Brown administration.

Delegate Maggie McIntosh, the powerful Democratic chairwoman of the House Appropriations Committee, asked if we really had to move so quickly toward a balanced budget. "We could do it a bit slower now and still get to the goal line, you know?" she proposed. Doug Mayer, our deputy communications director, who had worked for Chris Christie and Nikki Haley, grabbed the chairwoman's football analogy and ran with it: "With two minutes left in the fourth quarter, the people of our state needed a touchdown, and that's exactly what Governor Hogan and our budget team threw. Punting on the tough fiscal issues isn't an option anymore."

Our budget was a bold and important document that protected the things that were important to the people of Maryland—education, public safety, transportation, the environment—and gave new flexibility to agency heads to choose the cuts that needed to be made. "We want them to have discretion as to where they can make some of the adjustments without impacting services to the citizens," said our new budget secretary, David Brinkley.

I wouldn't say the legislative leaders, all Democrats, were overly cooperative with our efforts to bring a pro-jobs, pro-business, pro–fiscal sanity agenda to Maryland. Quite the opposite, in fact. They spent the early part of the ninety-day session rolling grenades at us. When they got tired of that, they started launching missiles. To them, we were a bunch of outsiders who had somehow snuck into their sandbox and were refusing to leave.

You want bipartisan? they seemed to be saying. *Fine, we'll give you bipartisan . . . if you do everything exactly our way.*

Bipartisanship and compromise, I had to keep reminding them, were two-way streets. And now that we were here, they wouldn't be alone in their sandbox anymore. The Democrats had the votes in the Legislature to do almost anything they wanted. I recognized that. When I'd been elected in November, I'd brought a few extra Republicans along for the ride—two more in the senate and seven more in the House—but the Democrats still had overwhelming, veto-proof majorities in both chambers. That would remain a reality during my entire time as governor.

On the other hand, I did have some power. My appointees ran all the state agencies. I named state judges and the people who sat on state authorities. I could issue executive orders on all kinds of things. I could cut tolls without the Legislature. I could cut fees without the Legislature. I could cut regulations without the Legislature. We could run the government more efficiently without the Legislature. We could improve customer service without the Legislature.

A lot of this simply involved setting a new tone, having government officials begin the conversation with "How can we help you?" instead of "No, that's not the way it's done." Attitude flows from the top.

So, as we began to negotiate with Democratic senate president Mike Miller and Democratic House speaker Michael Busch, they had the votes—but I had a secret weapon: the people of Maryland. They'd just elected me, hadn't they?

Right away, I got busy fulfilling my number-one campaign promise, repealing the wildly unpopular rain tax. This would test my ability to move the Maryland Legislature somewhere the members and their leaders definitely did not want to go. But on this issue, I knew I had the public firmly on my side.

When the rain tax was signed into law by Martin O'Malley in 2012, the tax had the votes of 70 percent of the Legislature. Could I really get all those Democratic senators and delegates to change their minds? Politicians almost never like admitting they are wrong, even when they secretly know they are. This time, the *Baltimore Sun* was constantly railing against me for even suggesting the rain tax should be repealed. "Hogan doesn't care about the environment," the Democrats kept saying, even though they knew repealing the rain tax wouldn't do any environmental damage. I was elected on an anti-tax mandate. Now that I was openly trying to get the hated rain tax repealed, calls and emails were pouring into the offices of Maryland legislators, demanding the tax be repealed.

We introduced the repeal measure on February 10. Various alternate proposals were floated, and we negotiated back and forth. When the final vote was taken April 14—lightning speed for the Legislature—every single Democrat in both chambers voted to repeal the mandatory tax. With such a massive public outcry, they wouldn't dare vote to retain it. Killing the rain-tax mandate was a stunning reversal, achieved before we'd even been in office for three months.

As for the claim that I didn't care about the environment? We would end up investing twice as many state dollars in protecting and restoring the Chesapeake Bay in my first four years alone as the O'Malley Administration had in eight years. The Bay would become the cleanest it had been in recorded history.

We couldn't stop there, of course. The rain-tax victory just whetted my appetite for more positive change. I pulled my team together and asked, "What can we do without the Legislature to put more money in people's pockets? I want to find every fee charged by every state agency that we can cut or eliminate on our own." After all, a government fee is just a tax by another name.

The next things I had in my sights were the state's road and bridge tolls. O'Malley had raised them by 150 percent. Cutting them, we confirmed, wouldn't require any cooperation from the Legislature. We quickly set in motion the process of getting that done, rolling back the tolls on the Chesapeake Bay Bridge, the Harbor Crossings, the Intercounty Connector, the new I-95 express toll lanes, and every single toll facility in the state. That right there would put $270 million back into the pockets of hardworking Maryland families, retirees, and small businesses.

"We are proud to announce what by far is our largest tax relief package to date and marks the first time tolls have been lowered in Maryland in nearly fifty years," I said in my official announcement.

I stressed to our team: "With or without the Legislature, we are going to keep doing exactly what we said we were going to do. It's what the people of Maryland voted for, and it's what they deserve."

PART III

LEADING

CHAPTER 15

BALTIMORE'S BURNING

It was the van ride that nearly destroyed Baltimore.

When Freddie Gray arrived at the hospital on April 12, 2015, some facts were known already, with one key fact remaining a topic of hot dispute. The known facts included these: Gray, a twenty-five-year-old black man from the Sandtown-Winchester section of West Baltimore, was arrested after a police chase near the Gilmor Homes housing project and charged with possessing an illegal weapon. He was handcuffed and placed in the back of a police wagon. There, he fell into a coma from which he would never return. An autopsy would conclude that Gray died from injuries that included a severed spinal cord.

The key fact in dispute was how exactly Freddie Gray came to be harmed. Were his injuries the result of a tragic, unforeseeable accident as the police drove him to the Central Booking and Intake Center on East Eager Street?

Or was he a victim of police misconduct, banged around during a purposely rough ride in the van? What responsibility, if any, did six city officers bear for the severe injuries suffered by their handcuffed suspect?

There is no point in confusing Freddie Gray with a singer in the church choir, the way some in the media did. He was a Crips gang–connected, street-level drug dealer with a long criminal rap sheet, well known to the Baltimore City police. Officers would say later that they kept the handcuffs on because Gray had been so unruly while they were attempting to place him in the van, the cuffs couldn't be safely removed. None of that, to be clear, would justify any mistreatment on the way to jail.

The case hit the news at a time of rising uproar across America over police behavior in urban neighborhoods, coming eight months after Ferguson, Missouri, erupted in riots in response to a police officer shooting a young black man. This was just as the Black Lives Matter movement was really taking off. But nowhere would this loaded national debate play out with any more drama than in the streets of Maryland's largest city. The city and the state would be severely tested, and so would I.

The anger bubbled up gradually, but I could feel it early on. By then, I'd been governor for not quite three months.

On Saturday, April 18, six days after Gray's arrest, a couple of hundred protesters gathered outside the Western District police station on North Mount Street. The demonstration was spirited but peaceful. Gray died the next morning around seven o'clock. On Tuesday, the Baltimore Police Department released the names of the six officers involved in Gray's arrest. That evening, protesters were back at the Western District police station, having marched eight blocks from the site of Gray's arrest on Presbury Street. Tensions flared. The mood was a bit angrier this time but still resulted in only two arrests.

Saturday, April 25, was the day the violence really began to escalate.

Hundreds of people marched from Baltimore City Hall to the Inner Harbor, where the city's downtown revival had begun in the early 1980s. Some were simply concerned citizens demanding answers and seeking justice. But mixed in the crowd were gang members and radical out-of-town agitators. Some of the marchers stopped to stage a "die-in," halting traffic briefly along the route. Near the end of the march, small groups of violent protesters smashed a few car windows and storefronts.

Around 6 PM, one group of protesters broke off and headed to Camden Yards, where 36,757 baseball fans, including many of my young staffers, were watching a game between the Baltimore Orioles and the Boston Red Sox. Some of those demonstrators tussled with fans outside the stadium. Scattered but ugly, as the assaults were described in news reports. Then, some violent protesters flipped over a police car.

A couple of dozen arrests followed, but mostly the police stood back. When the game ended after the tenth inning with a 5–4 Orioles win, an unsettling announcement flashed onto the giant electronic scoreboard in right center field: "Due to an ongoing public safety issue, the Mayor of Baltimore City and the BCPD have asked all fans to remain inside the ballpark until further notice. Thank you."

The gates were closed. No one was allowed to leave.

Instead of confronting the law-breakers on the streets, Mayor Stephanie Rawlings-Blake and police commissioner Anthony Batts chose to lock the law-abiding fans inside the stadium—though not for long. Less than half an hour later, the gates were reopened and the people were sent on their way with a warning: Avoid Howard Street going north, one of the city's main commercial thoroughfares, and Harborplace.

I was getting a sense of the mayor's approach to the gathering threat: Back off. Stand down. And try to wait it out.

To most people, this appeared to be a small uprising of angry kids who were letting some of their frustrations out. But I could see how volatile the situation really was, and my gut was telling me it could get a whole lot worse. The death of Freddie Gray was not sitting well with a lot of people.

All that pent-up anger was growing. It was sure to boil over. I had an urgent message for my senior leadership team, my cabinet, and homeland-security folks: "We need to get prepared. Now!"

I didn't run the Baltimore Police Department. I wasn't the Baltimore City prosecutor. I wasn't the mayor's "boss," despite what some people thought, and I didn't want to step on her toes. But as the governor of Maryland, I had a lot to be concerned about. I was concerned about the safety of Maryland citizens. Concerned about fraying race relations. Concerned about the community's distrust of the city police department. Concerned about the cops' ability to do their job. Concerned about a lot of things. The potential here was too explosive for me to simply sit back and see what might happen—which proved to be the correct assessment, as events would quickly demonstrate. Baltimore would soon be overwhelmed.

I immediately called in Keiffer Mitchell. "I want you to attach yourself to the mayor," I said. "I need an open line of communication with her, twenty-four–seven. I'm going to need up-to-date information—what the city's needs are, how City Hall is responding, what we're hearing on the street, everything we can possibly find out."

Keiffer was one of my senior advisors, a Democrat who had served on the Baltimore City Council and in the Maryland House of Delegates. His family, going back generations, were leaders in the civil rights movement in Baltimore. He lived in the city's historic Bolton Hill neighborhood. He knew all the players. He'd known the mayor since middle school.

With Keiffer on his way, I summoned more than a dozen other key people into the governor's conference room, the ones I would count on most in a major state emergency. The group included my chief of staff, Craig Williams; my counsel, Bob Scholz; my communications director, Matt Clark; and other members of my senior staff as well as the members of our security cabinet: Colonel Bill Pallozzi, the superintendent of the Maryland State Police; and Major General Linda Singh, the adjutant general of the Maryland Army National Guard. If all hell was about to break loose, these were the people I would need at my side.

I had an urgent message for everyone at the table: "No one can say for certain how bad this is going to get. We need to be prepared for the worst."

I think everyone grasped the intensity in my voice.

"Cancel leave for all state troopers," I said. "Put the National Guard on standby," meaning the state's part-time soldiers should alert their employers, have their bags packed, and be ready to report to the armory immediately.

Then I turned to Bob Scholz, my counsel. "I want you to draft up whatever paperwork we need to declare a state of emergency," I said. "What I have to do, how we go about that, and what all the ramifications are." Bob was on it.

While we were preparing for the worst, Mayor Rawlings-Blake and her staff continued to downplay everything. "We don't think anything else is going to happen," the mayor told me on the phone.

The city police were saying the same thing to the state police: "We don't have any issues." The unmistakable message, delivered to me directly and through the media, was that the city had everything under control.

In a press conference, the mayor called for peace. But when a reporter asked her to comment on how Baltimore police had responded to Saturday's violence, she said she had instructed officers to allow protestors to express themselves, adding, "We also gave those who wished to destroy space to do that as well."

What did she just say? "Space" for "those who wished to destroy"? I could hardly believe my ears.

"It's a very delicate balancing act," was how the mayor put it. "Because while we try to make sure that they were protected from the cars and other things that were going on, we also gave those who wished to destroy space to do that as well. And we worked very hard to keep that balance and to put ourselves in the best position to de-escalate."

In other words, unless the gang members and the out-of-town agitators injured or killed someone, the mayor was going to let them destroy property and cause other kinds of mayhem. It was as close to a hands-off response to urban violence as I had ever heard from a political leader. It was dangerous and reckless, and it threatened innocent lives and property. Paralyzed with fear and indecision, the mayor was truly making some very poor decisions: ordering the police to stand down and missing in action when her city was desperate and needed her most.

I'm sorry, but giving rioters "space" to destroy their city wasn't what most Baltimore residents were craving at that dicey moment. They wanted a mayor who believed in justice but was equally committed to public safety and to keeping the city from burning down.

The mayor's staff struggled on Sunday to clean up the furor her words had caused, insisting that she merely wanted to give "peaceful demonstrators room to conduct their peaceful protests." Unfortunately, she also said, "those seeking to incite violence also had the space to operate." For her part, the mayor tried to blame it all on the media, scolding the reporters: "It is very unfortunate that members of your industry decided to mischaracterize my words and try to use it as a way to say that we were inciting violence."

Actually, no. The TV stations merely played the video—a lot—and let her words fully sink in.

Her priorities were obvious. Her message was loud and clear. The stage was now set for real disaster.

On Monday morning, April 27, nearly a thousand people packed the New Shiloh Baptist Church for Freddie Gray's funeral, a service that was equal parts personal and political. As the mourners arrived, video screens flashed the messages "BLACK LIVES MATTER" and "ALL LIVES MATTER." In a soft voice, the young man's stepfather, Richard Shipley, read a poem he said the family wrote for Freddie: "You're still here in my heart and mind. I feel you, and this gives me strength and courage."

But it was the fiery eulogies that got most of the attention, especially in the wall-to-wall media coverage.

"With everything that we've been through, ain't no way you can sit here and be silent in the face of injustice," Reverend Jamal Bryant thundered from the pulpit to a congregation that included Mayor Rawlings-Blake, former mayor Sheila Dixon, Reverend Jesse Jackson, civil-rights activist and comedian Dick Gregory, and Congressman Elijah Cummings.

"The eyes of the country are all on us," Gray family attorney Billy Murphy warned. "They want to see if we have the stuff to get this right."

So how would people respond?

After the funeral, Freddie's mother, Gloria Darden, tried to send a calming message. "I want you all to get justice for my son," she said. "But don't do it like this here. Don't tear up the whole city just for him. It's wrong."

Unfortunately, the streets grew only hotter. The fuse had already been lit.

We were monitoring the situation very closely that afternoon as I headed to a long-planned meeting with the Korean ambassador in Washington. Yumi was going to meet me there. But just as we neared the ambassador's residence in the Cathedral Heights neighborhood, my assistant Alex Clark handed his iPad to me. On the live TV feed, a Baltimore police car was on fire. What looked like hundreds of people were breaking windows. The growing mob was throwing rocks, bricks, and garbage cans at police officers and attacking cars at West Baltimore's Mondawmin Mall.

I quickly called Keiffer and had him get the mayor on the line right away. When Mayor Rawlings-Blake said, "Hello, Governor," I got right to the point. "I just want you to know we are prepared to provide whatever assistance and support the city could possibly need," I said. "Everyone is at the ready. The Maryland State Police. The National Guard. The Emergency Management Agency. We have the full resources of the state ready to back you up."

The mayor's answer was just as direct as my offer. "We don't need your assistance," she said. "We have everything under control."

I took a breath, but just a short one. "With all due respect, Madam Mayor," I said, "it doesn't look like anything is under control. It looks like hundreds of people rioting in the streets and police cars on fire."

The mayor didn't budge. "We don't need any help," she repeated. "The police commissioner says it's manageable."

"Well," I said, "our senior security leadership team has been meeting all day at the State House. I'm on my way there now. I want to stay in constant communication with you. We're going to have to work closely together to ensure that the city and its citizens are safe."

I jumped out of the SUV in the driveway. I apologized to the ambassador, Ahn Ho-young, and his wife, Sen-hwa Lee, who were there to greet us. "I've got to return to Annapolis immediately," I said. "There's an emergency."

They completely understood. Like the rest of the world, the ambassador and his wife had been watching the live TV coverage of the mayhem in Baltimore. Yumi agreed to stay behind and smooth over my abrupt departure.

We sped off, lights flashing and sirens wailing for the full thirty miles back to the State House. The whole way to Annapolis, we kept trying to get the mayor back on the phone.

"She took off," a frustrated Keiffer said when I called. "They're trying to find her."

He asked the police commissioner, who said he didn't know where the mayor was. He asked her other aides. They didn't know either.

By now, the city was literally on fire. Stores were being looted and torched. The violence had spread from Mondawmin Mall to other parts of the city, including the historic Lexington Market. People were rioting now in many different neighborhoods.

Roaming bands of young men clashed with police officers. Bricks and bottles flew everywhere. Doors were smashed open at local businesses. People ran off with cash and whatever merchandise they could grab: Groceries. Cell phones. Sneakers. Televisions. Someone loaded a pickup truck with men's and women's clothing. Someone grabbed all the cigars from a neighborhood tobacco shop. A wig store was looted and totally trashed. ATMs were busted open for the cash.

The big CVS pharmacy at the corner of North and Pennsylvania Avenues was set on fire. As firefighters rushed to the scene, people hurled cinder blocks at them. Fire hoses were slashed.

The city's pharmacies were especially ripe targets, sparking some rare cooperation among the city's violent street gangs. A pattern began to repeat itself all over town. A group of young kids would throw bricks through the drugstore's front windows, and a big mob of young looters would rush in, clearing the aisles of candy, makeup, toiletries, and other grab-and-go merchandise. Meanwhile, organized gangs were backing up trucks to a rear door, cleaning out the pharmacy of all manner of drugs. This happened over and over again. Rival gangs had some kind of joint-venture agreement, dividing up the yet-to-be-looted drugstores among themselves.

We got calls from top executives at CVS, Rite Aid, and Walgreens, all pleading for help. It was the worst outburst of violence in Maryland's largest city in forty-seven years. Baltimore had seen nothing like it since the riots that followed the 1968 assassination of the Reverend Martin Luther King Jr.

Homeowners and small-business people stood outside their properties, helpless and scared. Their stories were painful to hear, even in short snatches on TV news reports. The police were mostly playing defense—ill-directed, under-equipped, and ordered to stand down and not respond.

When I got back to the State House, my homeland security team was waiting for me at the long wooden table in the governor's conference room. What an impressive group they were! Linda Singh, adjutant general of the Maryland National Guard, was the first woman and the first African American ever to hold that job. The state police superintendent, Colonel Bill Pallozzi, was a retired US Army Reserves captain who'd spent twenty-five years as a state trooper working his way up through the ranks. These people were tops in their field, and so were the others who filled the long table, including my chief of staff Craig Williams, homeland security director Tim Hutchins (a Marine Corps veteran and former superintendent of the state police), crime control director Chris Shank (a former state senator), governor's counsel Bob Scholz, public affairs director Steve Crim, communications director Matt Clark, and deputy communications director Doug Mayer. They'd all been in constant communication for days. They were monitoring everything. They were more than ready to take on the mission.

A formal state of emergency would give us the authority to provide important assistance. Normally, the state police did not patrol city streets. Once an emergency was declared, they could. The declaration would enable us to stand up and activate the National Guard. The Emergency Management Agency could cut through the usual bureaucracies and fast-track state aid. Whatever Mayor Rawlings-Blake cared to believe, the violence on the street wasn't subsiding. It was getting worse.

I kept calling Keiffer, insisting he put the mayor on the phone.

"Gov," he said to me. "We're trying everything. We still can't find her. The police commissioner doesn't even know where she is."

"Listen to me," I said. "Tell the police commissioner he needs to get the mayor on the phone immediately before I send in the National Guard. Tell him to find her!'"

Ten minutes later, the mayor called.

"Madam Mayor," I said sharply, "I have two executive orders sitting in front of me. One of them says that, at the request of the mayor of Baltimore, I'm declaring a state of emergency and sending in the National Guard. The other one says that, as governor of the state of Maryland, I'm declaring an emergency and sending in the National Guard. We would prefer to execute the first one. But either way, we're coming in to help handle this crisis in the city."

The mayor didn't say a word. So I continued.

"I believe that it would be better for you and better for us if we do the emergency declaration at your request."

"I need more time," she said.

The city was on fire. As far as I could tell, the mayor had not done much more than wring her hands and make the situation worse. And now she needed more time? Not after we'd spent two hours trying to find her and get her on the phone! "With all due respect . . . ," I started. I found myself using that gritted-teeth expression quite often with Mayor Rawlings-Blake.

"With all due respect, Mayor, there is no more time. The city police are overwhelmed. The violence is escalating. The situation is out of control. There is no more time."

"Can you get me fifteen minutes?" she asked.

"What do you need fifteen minutes for?" I pressed.

"I need to consult with the police commissioner."

"Okay," I answered reluctantly, "we'll give you another fifteen minutes."

I hung up the phone. The people at the conference table, who'd overheard my end of the conversation, were all staring in disbelief. Many were shaking their heads.

Fourteen minutes later, the mayor called back.

"Governor," she said, "since you have a gun at my head and are going to do it anyway, I guess I'll ask you to come in."

That's all I needed to hear. "Thank you," I said before hanging up and reaching for my pen.

It was 6:46 PM when I signed Maryland Executive Order 01.01.2015.14 declaring a state of emergency in Baltimore, the version with the mayor asking for our help. The state police superintendent, the adjutant general of the National Guard, and the rest of the people in the conference room immediately got on their phones, their iPads, and their laptops and gave the official call to action.

"Go!"

CHAPTER 16

TAKING COMMAND

We poured out of the State House and into a caravan of SUVs, police cars, and other state vehicles, racing to Camp Fretterd in Reisterstown in northwestern Baltimore County, which was home base for not only the Maryland National Guard but also the Maryland Emergency Management Agency (MEMA) and the Joint Operations Center. A dozen vehicles all roared down I-97 and I-695, lights and sirens all the way, carrying the entire leadership of the state government. Cabinet secretaries. Generals. Police chiefs. All flying down the highway in this rolling caravan, everyone working the phones on multiple conference calls. This isn't the way state government normally operates. But I can tell you there wasn't a bureaucratic hand-wringer in the bunch.

As we screeched up to the Joint Operations Center, we were met by Emergency Management Director Clay Stamp and some heavy military and police presence. Over the years, Clay had been involved in pretty much every aspect of emergency response—fire, rescue, emergency-medical treatment, natural-disaster response, arson investigation, hazardous materials mitigation, you name it. This time, he would be dealing with almost all those areas at once. The emergency operations center looks like a place you could launch the space shuttle from. There were more than a hundred people already manning the command center when we got there, all totally focused, all on high alert, communicating with people across the state and the nation.

A huge crowd of media was camped in a large, open room—all the major TV networks, news crews from Baltimore, Washington, and New York—jockeying to catch glimpses of the action through windows where the curtains hadn't been pulled closed.

My team had everything we needed in this high-tech beehive: TV screens with live shots from around the city. Computer monitors and constant data streams. Updates pinpointing the latest violent eruptions. And wall-to-wall media links to the outside world.

The people in this building had a daunting job ahead of them. They had to coordinate the massive response that would eventually include 4,000 members of the Maryland National Guard and 1,000 additional state, county, and local police officers from across Maryland and neighboring states, all of whom needed to be mobilized, coordinated, directed, equipped, communicated with, housed, fed, and led. It was organized chaos. And standing on top of all of it was me.

If I was going to get everyone pointed in the same direction, I knew I had to lay down some clear, basic principles right from the start. "This will require a show of overwhelming force on the streets of the city," I said as soon as I'd had a quick update. "But I also want an equal measure of restraint." Both were vital. So was a clear tactical approach. After consulting with our senior police and military leaders, I had a strategy in mind. "The city police officers will be on the front lines," I explained to the people at MEMA. 'We will back them up with the best guys we have from the Maryland State Police and the Maryland National Guard and all our other police agencies."

Our state troopers were Maryland's finest, but they were not used to patrolling city streets or battling rioters. The guard is well trained and professionally supported, but they are citizen-soldiers. A few had military police training, but none had urban-riot experience. They'd just left their civilian day jobs to be here. And with all the other support we had from the counties and from out of state, we had sufficient manpower to respond. If we provided the leadership and personnel to the city police's efforts, I had no doubt we would get the job done.

"This will be a coordinated, multilayer deployment, assertive and restrained," I emphasized. "The city police, our Maryland State Police, our Maryland National Guard, the people from other jurisdictions. We are not there to occupy the city. We are there to protect it and to help restore law and order and peace."

There was no one above me in this hierarchy. I was the commander in chief. And I was still a brand-new governor. I would succeed or fail on my own.

I began issuing orders: "Yes" . . . "No" . . . "Do this" . . . "Don't do that" . . . "This is what I want" . . . "We are not going to do that."

The generals, the police chiefs, and the rest of the team had a barrage of questions for me. The answers couldn't wait. "Are we calling up the Maryland Air National Guard or only the Maryland Army National Guard? How many guardsmen? One thousand? Two thousand? Four thousand? What about helicopters? Do we want tanks or just Humvees? What are the plans for protecting the vital infrastructure of Baltimore? What protection do the hospitals need? How do we coordinate the assistance of the police and fire departments and other agencies from out of town?"

I had to make about a hundred important decisions like that almost immediately. I relied heavily on the advice of my team, but the decisions were mine.

Around the same time, the Baltimore City Board of Education announced that public schools would be closed on Tuesday.

The mayor, at our urging, announced a weeklong, 10 PM to 5 AM curfew, beginning on Tuesday night. Major League Baseball made the decision to postpone Tuesday night's game at Camden Yards. Wednesday's game would be played but closed to the public.

I immediately moved my top executive team out of Annapolis to the city for the duration. Baltimore was where the action was, and Baltimore was where we should be. Until further notice, I said, we'd be working out of Schaefer Tower, the state-owned office building on Saint Paul Street downtown. I asked the lieutenant governor to remain in Annapolis running the governor's office and the daily business of state government.

At every turn, I was faced with critical decisions as the questions kept flying at me.

At one point I got to breathe for a second and thought to myself: *I am just eighty-nine days on the job. I am issuing orders to experienced law-enforcement and military officials on a mission that could well determine the future of my state and its largest city. Thousands of people are following my orders. Hundreds of thousands more are counting on me to make the right decisions.*

I'd never fought a riot before. I had barely gotten used to people calling me *Governor.* I was a small-business guy. They didn't teach a course at the National Governors Association's "baby governor's school" called *What to Do if Your Largest City Is On Fire.* But, thankfully, I had a strong team to work with. I believed in them and in myself. I knew how to make a plan and follow it. This was no time for indecision or hesitation. We had to act with clarity and confidence.

It was now 8:45 PM and time to tell the world what was going on: I had signed a state-of-emergency declaration two hours earlier and a huge mobilization, coordinated by the men and women in this building, was already well underway. "Today's looting and acts of violence in Baltimore will not be tolerated," I said in front of the large bank of media. "I strongly condemn the actions of the offenders who are engaged in direct attacks against innocent civilians, businesses, and law enforcement officers . . . People have the right to protest and express their frustration. But Baltimore City families deserve peace and safety in their communities."

The reporters pressed for details, and I laid out our plan. The city needed help, I explained, and the state was now delivering it. The state of emergency gave us the authority. The troops were rolling in. Operation Baltimore Rally was underway.

I didn't bring it up, but the reporters kept asking why the state of emergency hadn't been declared any sooner. I explained that my staff had been "trying to get in touch with the mayor for quite some time. She finally made that call, and we immediately took action."

Straightforward question, straightforward answer.

Rawlings-Blake would complain bitterly that I had intentionally thrown her under the bus with that comment. She used even more colorful language to one of my top aides. To which I can only say I didn't go out of my way to blame the mayor for the city's slow response. At the same time, when asked directly by the media, I wasn't going to lie for her either.

That would be a turning point in my relationship with Mayor Rawlings-Blake—and not a happy one. She would blame *me* for the verbal beating she took in the local and national media. Not her own unfocused response to the rioting. Not her dreadful comments about giving the rioters the "space" to destroy. She would blame me, the governor who acted decisively to save her city when she was too overwhelmed, too indecisive, and too frightened to get the job done.

What went wrong with the mayor? Before the riots, she'd been widely seen as a rising leader in the Democratic Party. Among her close friends and biggest boosters were powerhouse Democratic consultant Donna Brazile and Valerie Jarrett, one of Barack Obama's most trusted advisors. Rawlings-Blake served as the treasurer of the Democratic National Committee and was already being talked about as the leading prospect to replace five-term US Senator Barbara Mikulski, who had just announced she'd be retiring at the start of 2017. But Mayor Rawlings-Blake was struggling now, and it was obvious to almost everyone.

Right after the press conference ended, Alex handed my cell phone to me. Christie was calling. I was eager to speak with him. He too had confronted a major disaster in his first term as governor: the massive destruction of Hurricane Sandy in October 2012.

"I just watched your press conference," he said. "Great job. You're being decisive. You're being a leader. You've stepped in and taken command."

"Thanks," I said.

Christie being Christie, he wasn't shy about sharing his views.

"But that's not enough," he continued. "In addition to all that, it's really important that you let people see that you care. People are scared. You have to reassure them. You have to tell them that life will come back to normal, that law and order will return, that everything will be okay. Besides just being the governor, making the right decisions and directing the entire response, you also have to be the consoler in chief."

That makes a lot of sense, I thought.

"My advice to you," my friend said, "first thing in the morning, you need to go up to Baltimore and let people see you."

"Chris," I interrupted. It's never easy interrupting Chris Christie when he is on a roll.

"Chris," I said. "I'm not waiting till the morning. I'm going to Baltimore right now."

He seemed to like that. "My defining moment came three years after I became governor, with Hurricane Sandy," he said. "Yours is coming right now, three months in. But listen, I believe in you. This is why you were elected."

Christie wasn't just passing out advice. Before we got off the phone, he also offered practical help. "What do you need?" he said. "What can I do?"

"What help can you send?"

"As soon as I hang up the phone," he said, "I will have my state police superintendent call your superintendent. They'll work it out." They agreed to send 140 riot-trained New Jersey state troopers, who would leave a few hours later and would soon be on the streets of Baltimore.

After the call with Christie, I spent another hour at the MEMA command center, making sure everyone knew exactly what we were doing and how our plan of action was taking effect. Then I got back in the SUV and, with a far smaller caravan this time, left tiny Reisterstown for the twenty-five-mile ride into the burning city of Baltimore, the new wartime commander in chief heading to the front lines.

Honestly, I had no idea what lay ahead.

As soon as we pulled onto I-795, speeding toward the city, one of the troopers said to me, "Sir, the White House is calling. President Obama would like to speak to you."

He handed me the phone. I asked the troopers to turn off the ear-splitting siren so I could hear.

"Good evening, Mr. President," I said. He got right to it.

"I saw you declared a state of emergency for the situation in Baltimore," the president said to me. I assumed he was calling to offer federal assistance to the state of Maryland.

Boy, was I wrong.

"I'm calling to express my concern," he continued. "I'm concerned that your actions could potentially inflame an already tense environment. My strong advice would be that you exercise caution and restraint in the city. Because it is a volatile situation."

I told him that I was painfully aware of just how volatile the situation was.

It was fascinating how the Democratic president navigated his conversation with me, the rookie, white, Republican governor who had recently defeated his candidate for governor of Maryland in this overwhelmingly Democratic state and whose majority-black, largest city was now in flames. A lot of landmines there. Anthony Brown was more than Obama's political ally and choice for governor. The men were friends. They'd been close since Harvard Law School. Now, President Obama was in the slightly awkward position of trying to influence this unwelcome outsider.

I listened respectfully. He was polite and quite deft in his message delivery. But I had no intention of revoking the executive order, recalling the troops, or retreating to Annapolis. I was racing to save Baltimore from burning down, and the president was basically saying I shouldn't be going there. He couldn't stop me. I was the governor. But now he was tactfully pressuring me—not chastising me exactly, more like trying to keep me in check.

He kept saying, "Again, I would strongly recommend that you exercise caution and show restraint."

"Mr. President," I told him, "I can assure you that we are going to exercise caution and show restraint. But I'm also going to do whatever it takes to make sure that this violence doesn't continue and that we keep the people of Baltimore safe."

The president was never heavy-handed. He wasn't trying to boss me around. He was just letting me know that he was concerned.

"Mr. President," I said, "thank you, I can't tell you how much I appreciate the fact that you took the time to call. Thank you for your input. Good
night."

My detail leader flipped the siren back on, and we continued racing to
Baltimore.

CHAPTER 17

SHOCK TRAUMA

Keiffer Mitchell, Steve Crim, and I headed straight for Shock Trauma, which, come to think of it, was not a bad way of describing the critical condition that the city of Baltimore currently found itself in. In just the past few hours, 400 businesses had been destroyed. One hundred and twenty-seven police officers and firefighters were injured severely enough to be taken to local hospitals, including the University of Maryland Medical System's R. Adams Cowley Shock Trauma Center on South Greene Street.

Shock Trauma is one of the nation's leading institutions for treating severely injured and critically ill people. Its groundbreaking team approach saves lives every day.

Freddie Gray had been taken to Shock Trauma on April 12 with his life-threatening injuries. If anyone could have saved him, it would have been the incredible doctors and nurses there. And now, sixteen days later, Shock Trauma was overflowing with police officers and other first responders who'd been injured by rioters seeking to avenge the young man's death.

You go to Shock Trauma when you're in really bad shape.

I saw broken bones and serious burns. I met officers who'd been hit by bottles, bricks, and cinder blocks. Many of the first responders felt abandoned and scared.

"I came to see how you guys are doing," I said.

That simple gesture, the fact that the governor had shown up to check on them, had grown men and women openly emotional. "Thank you for having our backs, Gov," they kept saying to me. "Thanks for being here."

"I was in Iraq," said a gray-haired Baltimore city police officer who looked like he'd stared down some bad guys in his time. Now, he was lying in a hospital bed, his neck broken in the day's mayhem. "I never saw anything like this before. Rival gangs were working together. They were organized. They were communicating by cell phone."

He said he and a team of fellow officers had been forced into a corner at Mondawmin Mall by an advancing mob. "We had nowhere to go," he said. "We didn't have riot gear. Not enough shields or helmets. We couldn't use tear gas because we didn't have gas masks. We didn't have rubber bullets, and we couldn't fire our weapons. There was a gang up on the roof tossing cinder-blocks down on our heads."

It sounded like a war zone. I could hardly imagine the panic he must have felt.

"The mayor abandoned us," the veteran cop said to me. "She ordered us to stand down. We were sitting ducks out there. We needed to defend ourselves the way we were trained to." He started to cry.

I hugged him. Then, I went to the next officer, and I hugged him too. And the next one and the next one and the next one. There was no media inside Shock Trauma. No cameras. No microphones. This was no publicity stunt. I was there because I cared and because I was genuinely grateful for the dedication and bravery of those who had agreed to protect and serve the citizens of the state I'd been elected to govern.

The men and women of the Baltimore Police Department were put in an impossible position. On the one hand, their fellow officers were the ones being accused of killing Freddie Gray. Now, they were literally under attack and not permitted to respond. A lot of them were city residents. They hated seeing their city destroyed. They hated not being able to save it. They were desperately crying out for strong leadership.

Yes, there are some bad cops. We all know that's true. But by and large, the vast majority of police officers are dedicated, hardworking people who put their lives on the line every day for the rest of us. I have always believed that. Now, angry people were looking at them and only seeing them as racists and murderers.

As I was consoling the distraught officers at Shock Trauma, Keiffer excused himself to take a call. It was from his wife, Nicole, and she sounded panicked. She was at home with their two young children, as looters trashed a nearby hardware store and Rite Aid pharmacy. Nicole said she was hiding upstairs in a bedroom with young Jack and Kenna with all the lights turned off. Looking out a window, she had just seen several rioters running through their backyard.

"I need to check on my family," Keiffer said, promising to catch up with me as soon as he could.

"Absolutely," I told him. "Do whatever you have to. Let us know if they need anything. I hope everyone's okay."

Keiffer kept his wife on the phone the whole way home. By the time he got to their Bolton Hill neighborhood, things seemed to have calmed a bit, he told me later. The looters were mostly out of the stores. His own backyard looked clear. Keiffer's wife and children were still hiding upstairs with the lights off, watching the live riot coverage on TV. Keiffer asked his twelve-year-old son if he was okay. "Everything is gonna be all right, Dad," Jack told his father. "The governor is coming."

Shock Trauma was filled that night with people who felt deserted and overwhelmed. It was a diverse group: black, white, Latino, and Asian. Police officers, firefighters, and paramedics. Men and women, young and old. I personally spoke to as many of them as I could. Then, I made a point of thanking the nurses and the doctors too. After what they'd all been facing and would continue to face, at least they would know that they had a governor who was looking out for them and who would have their backs.

———————————

I couldn't stay at Shock Trauma all night. I needed to get over to Schaefer Tower, where my leadership team and much of my cabinet were waiting. I was already late to the all-hands meeting I had called at our new Baltimore command center. But as soon as I climbed back into the SUV for the short drive to Saint Paul Street, my comms guys were on the phone. Steve put them on speaker. "CNN keeps calling," Matt said. "They really want you to go live."

"I don't have time to do an interview with CNN," I snapped. "Don't you think we have more important things to do right now? I'm not doing it!"

"Just do this quick hit on CNN to let people know what's going on," Doug Mayer said.

"I'm not trying to get on TV," I insisted. "I'm trying to stop a riot. I'm trying to save the city."

As we made our way through the smoky streets, I kept refusing. Steve joined in, and all three kept pushing for it. Finally, I relented. "Okay," I said. "I'll do the interview. But we can't waste a lot of time on it."

I agreed to meet CNN anchor Don Lemon where he was set up on the street outside Baltimore City Hall, which happened to be on our way. "This has got to be quick," I warned the guys before I climbed out of the SUV.

As I stood on the sidewalk getting wired up for the interview, who should walk up to join us but the woman I had spent so many hours trying to reach, Mayor Stephanie Rawlings-Blake. I didn't realize until that moment that this was going to be a joint appearance.

Don Lemon spent most of the live interview trying to provoke me into complaining about the mayor's response to the riot. I certainly had my frustrations with the mayor, but I didn't see the point of broadcasting them at that moment live on CNN.

Three or four times, Lemon kept pressing me on why we didn't act any sooner. When I explained I had declared a state of emergency as soon as the mayor requested it, he tried to jam that as a wedge between us. I stayed positive, emphasizing that we had taken firm action and the situation on the ground was about to drastically improve. "I can assure you we have now taken over the situation," I said for what seemed like the tenth time. "This is not going to continue . . . We're going to get this under control. The city will be safe. And Marylanders will be proud of the effort once we get this cleaned up."

That's when I noticed Keiffer, standing on the sidewalk just to the right of the camera, gesticulating at me. He had finished making sure his family was safe and had caught back up with us outside City Hall. Listening to Don Lemon go on and on, Keiffer was obviously thinking the same thing that I was, and he was getting calls from Matt and Doug at Schaefer Tower. He was staring at me and slicing his extended right index finger across the middle of his throat, the universal signal for *"Cut if off! Now!"*

The CNN anchor wasn't done, even if I was. "How are you going to enforce the curfew tomorrow now that—" he demanded.

"We have to go," I said, glancing at the mayor and yanking out my TV earpiece. "Thanks for your time," I told the anchor.

Then, Rawlings-Blake also pulled her earpiece, as we both turned and walked right out of the live interview.

Twitter and Facebook exploded with complaints about Lemon's approach: "They are trying to stop the violence . . . You keep asking stupid questions . . . How many times are you going to ask the same question over and over again?" But maybe the mayor and I had finally found something we could agree on: Don Lemon had behaved like a jerk during that interview.

It was after midnight by the time I joined my executive team at Schaefer Tower. It had been an exhausting day. It had been only nine hours since our sudden turnaround in the Korean ambassador's driveway. So much had happened since then. We had no idea how long we'd be working out of our temporary digs in Baltimore. For the foreseeable future, this would be our round-the-clock home base.

We'd do whatever we needed to in the coming days. Walk the streets. Visit the churches. Thank the state and city police, the firefighters, the paramedics, and the guardsmen. Take helicopters to the command center at MEMA.

Every night, we agreed, we would sit down at the Baltimore Police Department command center for a joint progress report, assessing what we had achieved that day and making plans for the next one. Not a big meeting, just the principals: the mayor, her police commissioner, her chief of staff. Me, my state police superintendent, the adjutant general, my chief of staff.

Then, my team would typically head back to Schaefer Tower, where we would skip showers, forget to shave, catch five-minute catnaps, and become far too familiar with what quickly became known as our Riot Diet: an endless succession of pizza slices, candy bars, diet sodas, and the occasional stale donut. For better or worse, this was our twenty-four-hour command post for the foreseeable future.

Hundreds of state troopers had already moved into the city. So had the 1st Battalion, 175th Infantry Regiment, of the Maryland Army National Guard, whose uninterrupted history goes all the way back to the Revolutionary War. They built an instant tent city between Camden Yards and M&T Bank Stadium, where the Baltimore Ravens play. The armories weren't large enough to handle the 4,000 troops, the 1,000 additional police officers, and all the others involved in Operation Baltimore Rally. National Guard Humvees were already being seen patrolling streets all over the city, along with hundreds of heavy green military trucks, which in itself was a potent symbol of order being restored. Sometime in the middle of the night, I said my bleary goodnights.

The troopers drove me home to the governor's mansion, where I managed to say a groggy "good night, honey" to Yumi, snatch two hours of sleep, grab a fast shower, and change my clothes before I headed back to the city again.

CHAPTER 18

STREET CRED

Keiffer met me at the Baltimore Police Department's Western District station before the sun came up. As soon as I stepped out of the SUV, the troopers on my detail, Craig Ciccarelli and Thomas Scott, walked over to me with a bulletproof vest. "Sir," Thomas said, "we need you to put this on."

I recognized this was a volatile morning in Baltimore. People were already gathering in front of the station on West Mount Street. In the hours and days to come, I would be all over the city, interacting with all kinds of people everywhere. I understood that no one, not even a dedicated detail of highly trained state troopers, could 100 percent guarantee my safety. But I didn't want to confront the people of Baltimore like an armored warrior. I wanted to interact person to person. I hated what that vest symbolized.

"I'm not wearing it," I told the troopers.

They didn't like that, but they didn't put up a fight. They just figured they'd have to watch me extra closely. After a briefing from the city police station commanders and a round of thank-yous with the cops, we hit the streets. Next stop: North and Penn.

The burned and looted CVS was still smoldering. The firefighters were still on the scene, joined now by large contingents of city and state police officers and uniformed guardsmen. This was Ground Zero, a busy West Baltimore intersection that was now an international symbol of the city's darkest hours.

I wanted people to see that their governor was there.

I stood at the corner, breathing in the acrid smell of the smoldering buildings, offering thanks and promises to stop the violence and begin the process of rebuilding. "We're not going to have a repeat of last night," I declared emphatically. "It's not going to happen tonight."

People were salvaging what was left of burned or wrecked homes and businesses, dragging charred furniture and busted display cabinets onto the sidewalk. Everywhere we went, I saw sad scenes of human tragedy, dreams built over decades of hard work destroyed in a single night. I listened to people's stories, assuring them we would do what it took to bring life back to normal. Most of the residents I encountered were black. Quite a few of the merchants were Asian. The store owners were surprised to hear me say *anyeong haseyo* to them in Korean. All of them—residents and small shop owners, blacks and Asians—were victims of these destructive riots. Some had insurance. Most didn't. These were hardworking people. This was their city too.

An older woman was standing on a corner, just weeping. I went over to her and hugged her. I remembered what Christie had told me about being the consoler-in-chief and letting people know that things were going to be okay. The people of Baltimore were in pain. They needed to know they had a governor who cared and who was taking charge.

Across North Avenue, the mayor was holding a press conference, standing at a forest of microphones, surrounded by reporters and TV crews. I had no interest in joining her.

Instead, I spent the time walking and talking to regular people, asking how they were doing and what we could do to help. That's what I was there for.

For the most part, I would leave the interviews to others, especially General Singh. She was a perfect choice: a strong black woman with the forcefulness and firm posture of a natural-born leader. Standing in front of the cameras in her tan combat fatigues, she delivered a potent message to the people of Baltimore and beyond: "We are here. We mean business. We are going to get this done."

"I want to go to Freddie Gray's neighborhood," I said.

When he died, the young man was living with his sisters in Gilmor Homes in Sandtown-Winchester. The response I got from my troopers wasn't overly enthusiastic. "Not a good idea, sir," Craig said to me. "It's too dangerous."

"I think it's important for me to go there," I responded. The people in Sandtown-Winchester needed to know I was going to listen to their concerns.

I met first with Tessa Hill-Aston, president of the Baltimore NAACP, at the group's satellite office on Gilmor Street. I promised our initial chat would be just "the beginning of a dialogue."

"This neighborhood," she told me, "has been known for the police to just pick you up and throw you in the car, take you around the corner and beat you."

I listened to her carefully. "We're going to address the underlying causes," I said. "We will do that. But right now, we're going to deal with the immediate crisis."

That meeting was important. But what I'd really come for was a chance to walk these streets with Freddie Gray's neighbors. So that's what I did.

"I'm very sorry for your loss," I told the residents I spoke with. "I promise you, we're going to try to bring some peace to the neighborhood. We'll work on addressing some of these issues that you're concerned about."

It would be an understatement to say that people were surprised to see me. They looked almost shocked.

"Hey, that's the governor," I heard several people say. "What's he doing here?"

I faced no hostility. No one expressed anger or resentment toward me. They just didn't expect to see me in their neighborhood.

There were several young men about Freddie's age playing basketball on a nearby court.

"Hey, guys, what's up?" I said.

"Is that the governor?" one of them asked.

"I came down to see how you all are doing," I said.

I shook hands with each of them. One of the guys, Desmond Edward, passed me the ball. I took a jumper from the top of the key.

Desmond was quoted later in the *Baltimore Sun*. He said he'd never shot hoops with a governor before. "It was pretty good," he said. "A new experience. He can shoot."

I definitely liked the "he can shoot" part. It's good to know I still got game—and at least a little street cred.

———————————

Rumors were flying everywhere. Some were true. Some were half true. Some were concocted out of thin air. Security Square Mall was closed over rumors that looters were heading in that direction. That one turned out to be nothing. Word was also that the city's gang leaders and drug dealers didn't appreciate the occupying armies on what they considered *their* streets. That one was definitely true.

At scattered spots, small groups of protesters threw objects at police, now in riot gear. Nowhere near as rough as Monday, but Tuesday was still young.

At the White House, President Obama spoke publicly about the riots in Baltimore. This time, there was nothing equivocal about his language or his tone. He clearly denounced what he called the "senseless violence and destruction . . . They're not protesting. They're not making a statement. They're stealing. They're destroying and undermining businesses and opportunities in their own communities. They need to be treated as criminals." The president had completely changed his tune. Maybe I had gotten through to him. But as the afternoon gave way to evening, no one knew for sure: Would the streets erupt in violence again? Would the Baltimore curfew hold?

Back at Ground Zero, there was a large, public standoff around 10:15 PM. I wasn't on the corner for this one. I was back with my team at our Schaefer Tower command post, assessing our first-day performance, making plans for tomorrow, consulting with the chiefs and the generals, all while monitoring the live coverage on TV. This would be the first major test of the citywide curfew.

A couple of hundred demonstrators, many of them from out of town, remained outside the CVS store at the busy corner of North and Penn. They were face-to-face with police in helmets and riot shields, while announcements blared from a helicopter overhead. "You must go home. You cannot remain here. You will be subject to arrest." Other choppers shined high-intensity floodlights on the crowd. Some of my own people had been opposed when I first called for the use of helicopters. Now, everyone was very happy we had them in the sky, as their floodlights turned the night into day.

Around 10:30, some of the demonstrators began throwing rocks and smoke bombs. In long ranks, standing side by side, the riot-equipped city police held their ground. They didn't advance on the demonstrators, but they also refused to budge. Behind them was a huge presence of Maryland National Guardsmen, along with their trucks and Humvees.

That show of force alone did not disperse the crowd. They were dug in. There was one especially significant demonstrator. He seemed to be the chief violent instigator. The TV cameras were focused on him. He was pacing and yelling and throwing things, acting several degrees wilder and more frantic than anyone else on the street.

"You must go home," the announcements continued overhead. "You are subject to arrest."

The rabble-rouser picked up what looked like a bottle with a rag fuse, a makeshift firebomb, and hurled it toward the officers. It landed a few feet short. He then moved forward, standing almost face-to-face with the cops in their riot gear. Still, they did not move.

Then slowly, without any announcement at all, a Maryland National Guard Humvee inched toward the police line, approaching from behind. Watching on live TV, it was hard to tell if the guardsmen and the police officers communicated directly. But at just the right moment, the phalanx of officers methodically parted, creating a small separation just a couple of feet wide.

A uniformed guardsman reached out of the vehicle and snatched the man who had thrown the firebomb. In a single, swift movement, the man was lifted off his feet and yanked inside the National Guard Humvee.

The Humvee backed out and drove off. Not a punch was thrown. No one seemed to be injured. But the violent instigator on the street was no longer there.

"What just happened to that guy?" Doug Mayer asked at Schaefer Tower.

The answer came back from two or three of our people almost in unison: "He's just gone."

And he was.

That seemed to do it. Within minutes, the crowd began to dissipate. With the leader of the violence now missing in action, the energy of the mob seemed to fade almost immediately. These citizen-soldiers of the Maryland National Guard had delivered a strong message that was clearly received. *We have a job to do. We aren't standing down.*

Tuesday night was the turning point we had all been hoping for, a huge improvement over the night before. Our Schaefer Tower command center erupted in cheers and high-fives as the curfew successfully took hold.

Wednesday morning, Keiffer and I were back out walking in the neighborhoods. We stopped at the Avenue Market on Pennsylvania Avenue. Five or six rough-looking dudes were standing together, arms folded, glaring straight ahead.

"Gang members," Keiffer whispered to me.

"Yeah," I deadpanned, "I kinda suspected that as soon as I saw the neck tattoos."

They were eyeing me suspiciously. Not one of them suggested I sit down for a chat or that we go outside for some friendly hoops.

"Fuck the governor," the toughest-looking one said.

"What's he doing here?" I heard another one grumble.

One of the troopers shot me a look. "Let's keep moving, sir," he said. But I wasn't ready to leave.

"I know you guys have a lot of things on your mind," I said, not sure how they'd respond to that. But they began to speak. One of them mentioned the mayor closing community centers. Another brought up the lack of jobs and the poor city schools.

"We ain't too happy 'bout that," he said, shaking his head ominously.

"I understand," I told him. "And you know what? You've got the right to be mad about the schools and the community centers and some of the failures here in the city."

They talked about Freddie Gray. They talked about the police. They had some valid concerns and serious complaints.

"Look, I hear you," I said. "But this violence—this isn't helping anybody. These are your own neighborhoods that are getting burned down."

They nodded at that. But their facial expressions were unyielding, and I couldn't tell if I was really getting through.

"These ladies down the street, they don't deserve to have the windows broken out of their houses," I said. "And these guys who have the corner stores, they didn't deserve to get burned out. All this violence is hurting your own people. You've got to help do something about this. We can talk about all this other stuff. We can try to help fix some of these other things. But right now, we've got to stop the violence. And you need to help us. We're going to keep working on the things you're talking about that aren't right. But first we have to get the city back under control."

As we spoke, I felt like we might be turning a corner.

We'd started with a list of grievances and a whole lot of attitude. Now, they were listening to me, and I was listening to them. One of them said to me, "I feel you, Gov. I feel you." Another said, "We hear what you're saying, man."

Then came the moment I would not have predicted. "Can we get a selfie with you?" one of the guys asked.

I posed for pictures with them. Every one of them.

"Man, I can't believe the Gov talked to us," I heard one of them say as we left the market. "The dude even listened," added one of his friends.

CHAPTER 19

CALM AGAIN

Mayor Rawlings-Blake continued to be an issue. I probably should have expected that. Wednesday, we had our nightly meeting at Baltimore police headquarters. General Singh. Commissioner Batts. Colonel Pallozzi. The mayor. Her chief of staff, Kaliope Parthemos. My chief of staff, Craig Williams. And me. After just one night, the mayor was already itching to lift the citywide curfew. I didn't think we were close to ready yet.

"The bar owners say the curfew is killing their business," she said.

"I understand that bar owners are upset about losing business," I answered. "But would they rather have their businesses burned down?"

"And the gang leaders are really angry," the mayor said to me. "They're demanding that if we don't . . . "

"Did you just say, '*The gang leaders are angry*'?" I thundered at the mayor. She nodded.

"*So what?*" I shot back. "I don't care if the gangs or the drug dealers are upset because their drugs sales are down. Let me ask you something: Do you want the city to be more like Monday night with all the violence and the fires and the damage and the chaos? Or would you prefer the calm of Tuesday night? I'd rather have it be more like Tuesday."

She tried to raise the ante on me.

"The gangs are threatening that if we don't lift the curfew, they're going to march downtown and burn down the Inner Harbor."

"You tell them to go ahead and make my day," I said. "Tell them to come on down, I'll be waiting for them, and several hundred state troopers and National Guard soldiers will be waiting for them."

As I glanced around the room, people were staring down at the table or leaning back in their chairs, looking distinctly uncomfortable.

The mayor and her police commissioner kept pushing. "It is a city curfew," she said. "We instituted the curfew. I am the mayor. I'm going to have a press conference, and I'm going to say, 'I'm lifting the curfew.'"

I pushed back harder. "Well," I said to the mayor as all the others sat quietly in their seats, "you have every right to do that. But here's what I'm going to do immediately after your press conference. I'm going to say that the mayor has completely lost her mind, and as governor in a state of emergency, I am immediately reinstating a curfew. So if that's what you want—"

Despite the mayor's concerns and the gang leaders' threats, the curfew remained in place.

If the Baltimore riots brought out the worst in some people, they brought out the best in many more, even before the smoke had cleared. Church groups. Students from Johns Hopkins, Loyola, and Towson University. Volunteers from companies and industry associations. They all came out to help. The Governor's Office of Community Initiatives, led by my old friend Steve McAdams, organized more than 2,000 volunteers. We set up a Maryland Unites website and funneled donations to pre-vetted community organizations to fund rebuilding projects.

Countless good people from around the corner and around the world wanted to do what they could. They showed up with their tool belts and jumbo-size trash bags. No one had to ask them. They just got to work, beginning the long process of rebuilding Baltimore. Mission BBQ, the Glen

Burnie–based barbecue chain, rolled in trucks, donated food, and set up industrial-sized grills outside the stadiums to feed the thousands of soldiers who were camped there. Union tradesmen helped replace the doors on looted stores. Food banks popped up around the city. Under the watchful gaze of cops and guardsmen and first responders, this army of voluntary generosity commissioned itself to help pull the battered city back up on its feet.

That didn't mean our work here was over. Not even close. Things didn't let up a second for us. Over the next four days and nights—slowly but surely—I could really feel peace being restored in Baltimore and law and order taking hold.

It wasn't any one thing. It was everything together, a fully integrated response. Firm leadership at the top. A clear sense of where the lines were: Peaceful protesters were welcome but violent rioters would be quickly locked up. To me, it was crucial to make an overwhelming show of police and military strength. I didn't want there to be any doubt that we had all the force we needed. But if we showed enough strength, I figured we might not have to use it.

This was Ronald Reagan's idea, peace through strength, the very same concept I learned about as the chairman of Youth for Reagan. I hadn't forgotten. And all these years later, it came in handy again.

I'm proud to say that with 4,000 part-time citizen-soldiers in a hostile urban environment, along with 1,000 officers from across the state and around the East Coast, we didn't have a single incident of abuse, brutality, or misconduct in the streets of Baltimore. Not one.

Once we declared the state of emergency and took charge, no one else got hurt. No more buildings were destroyed. People were now coming out of their houses and stores and offering cold water to the police and the soldiers who were protecting them. Maybe some trust was even being restored.

On Thursday, the Reverend Al Sharpton joined Mayor Rawlings-Blake and the presidents of the Urban League and the NAACP for a rally that was half a call for activism and half a defense of Mayor Rawlings-Blake. Now was the time to "end the scapegoating," the New York–based activist and liberal MSNBC host told the packed congregation at the New Shiloh Baptist Church in West Baltimore. "Don't blame the mayor for what the last fifty years of mayors and governors didn't do," Sharpton declared.

The issues that sparked the violence were much larger than the Freddie Gray case, Sharpton argued, touting the importance of noisy protest. "Most folks don't want peace," he said. "They want quiet. They want people to shut up and suffer."

We were back together Thursday night at Baltimore police headquarters, the mayor's top people and mine. Twenty-four hours earlier, Rawlings-Blake had been pleading to end the curfew. Now, she and Commissioner Batts were making a very different request.

"Is there any way you can bring in two thousand more guardsmen?" Batts asked. He said his detectives had been picking up some ominous rumors: Gangs were receiving shipments of ferocious new weaponry; violent West Coast anarchists would soon be descending on Baltimore; roving hit squads were targeting city police; and some instigators were hoping to further inflame the city by staging "suicide-by-cop" encounters, purposely provoking the police into using deadly force.

Our state police investigators couldn't confirm any of that, and I was skeptical about much of it. I told the police commissioner and the mayor that I didn't believe we could deploy any additional Maryland National Guardsmen. Their request—and the panicked tone of it—was certainly a 180-degree reversal from the night before. It was then that Commissioner Batts said, "We have one other item, Governor."

I nodded.

"We have completed our internal police investigation of the Gray case," he said. "Almost an hour from now, we will be forwarding the results of the investigation to the state's attorney's office."

That certainly got my attention. "I'm not a lawyer," I cautioned the commissioner. "I'm not sure how much of that information I should be aware of now. I certainly don't need to know details from the investigation that would be inappropriate for you to divulge. But can you just tell me—the report you're turning over to the prosecutor, in your opinion, will it be likely to inflame the situation further or help to defuse it?"

The commissioner didn't waver this time. "Our internal investigation shows absolutely no wrongdoing whatsoever on the part of any of the officers," he said.

"And you feel confident that this is a thorough and fair investigation?" I asked.

"We had our very best, most senior people doing the investigation," Batts insisted. "We have confidence in the facts. This should ease tensions, I would think."

For the sake of the city, I was very relieved to hear this.

That's why we were all shocked when, twelve hours later, State's Attorney Marilyn Mosby announced that she was charging all six police officers with serious felonies, including second-degree murder, manslaughter, misconduct in office, and false imprisonment. An hour before the announcement, she had called Keiffer with a heads-up. We all gathered in front of the TV in our Schaefer Tower office to watch the state's attorney's press conference. As jarring as the charges were, the prosecutor's incendiary language was even more so. "To the people of Baltimore and the demonstrators across America," she declared, "I heard your call for 'no justice, no peace.'"

Was she announcing a sound prosecutorial judgment or leading a protest rally? Frankly, it was hard to tell.

Friday morning, I declared that Sunday would be "a day of peace and prayer" with special services at churches, synagogues, and mosques across Baltimore. At many houses of worship, this would be the first time the congregations would be together since the major rioting began. If peace was going to return to the city, I knew the faith community had a role to play.

Baltimore archbishop William Lori agreed to lead an interfaith service at Saint Peter Claver Catholic Church on Fremont Avenue, the border between the Sandtown-Winchester and Upton neighborhoods. Saint Peter Claver had long been known as the "mother church" of West Baltimore's African-American Catholic community.

In recent days, we'd been getting calls from other Baltimore neighborhoods—local politicians, clergymen, and community leaders—pleading,

"Don't forget about us just because we aren't in West Baltimore." There'd been some scattered outbreaks of juvenile delinquency in other parts of the city. People were understandably concerned that the unrest could spread. "We are vulnerable too," they said.

Friday afternoon, we dispatched additional state police officers plus Humvees and other heavy equipment from the National Guard to various other Baltimore neighborhoods. I walked the streets and met with local residents in Fells Point, Little Italy, and several other sections. My message to everyone: "Whatever affects some of us affects us all."

At our regular sit-down on Friday night, the mayor pushed again to lift the curfew. She was getting renewed pressure from the bar owners. Now the issue was Saturday night's boxing match between undefeated five-division world champion Floyd Mayweather Jr. and eight-division world champion Manny Pacquiao. The fight was being held in Las Vegas. But bar owners across the country, including in Baltimore, had paid as much as $5,000 to carry the action on live pay-per-view TV.

"The curfew will cost these business owners a fortune," the mayor said to me. I felt for the small-business owners, but I didn't want to fill the streets of Baltimore too quickly and have the violence explode again. Another round of protests was planned for Saturday, including a "massive national rally" led by former New Black Panther Party chairman Malik Shabazz, whose violence-tinged rhetoric often turned anti-Semitic.

"Let's see how the weekend goes," I said, holding the mayor off for another day or two. To me, it was still too early to pull the state police, the Guard troops, and the others out.

Here's another indication of how uncertain things still were as the weekend arrived. Saturday was Kentucky Derby Day. That was no particular issue for us. The derby was being run at Churchill Downs in Louisville, Kentucky, 600 miles away. But the 140th running of the Preakness Stakes, the second jewel in horse racing's Triple Crown, was set for May 16 at the Pimlico Race Course in Baltimore. Would we need to postpone the Preakness? Would the city's unrest still be an issue for the next two weeks? People were beginning to ask, and no one really knew the answer. It was all still one day at a time.

In fact, with the curfew and our strong presence remaining in place Friday and Saturday nights, things stayed calm. On Sunday, 250 people turned out for our "peace and prayer" service at Saint Peter Claver with Archbishop Lori presiding and at similar services at Southern Baptist Church, Fulton Baptist Church, and elsewhere. After ours, a large gaggle of media, national and local, waited for me outside.

"It's time to get the community back to normal again," I said. "It's been a very hard week, but we've kept everybody safe. Since Monday night, we haven't had any serious problems." It seemed like the right time, I said, for the mayor to lift the curfew. We'd gotten through Marilyn Mosby's announcement that she was charging six officers. We'd gotten through Saturday's protests—Shabazz's "massive" rally was a bust. Mayweather had won the fight by unanimous decision, and the bar owners survived.

"When I came into the city on Monday night, it was in flames," I said. "Stores were being looted, a lot of terrible things were happening. But since then, I've seen incredible acts of kindness. I saw neighbors helping neighbors. I've seen a community that cares about each other."

In her announcement that she was lifting the curfew, six days after the worst of the rioting began, the mayor sounded thoroughly relieved. "A lot of the unrest has been settled," she said after touring the reopened Mondawmin Mall.

The city was returning to normal, and the signs were everywhere. Most of the stores had reopened. People were out shopping again. The houses of worship were full. The children would be returning to school on Monday. Neighbors were out on the sidewalks. The needed repairs were beginning.

As soon as I left the church, I went straight to the tent city that had served as home base for the heroes of Operation Baltimore Rally. I wanted to thank each of them. I wanted to let them know that their mission had been successfully completed and that they were safe to pull out and return home to their families. These soldiers, police officers, firefighters, paramedics, and other first responders from around the state and the region had been there for us when we needed them. I was deeply grateful.

It would take months—*years,* probably—for Baltimore to fully shake off the pain of those terrible days. The mayor and I would continue to clash on how to secure the peace we had restored. Major divisions in the city still needed to be healed. There was much more to be done. The relationship between the citizens and the police department remained dangerously raw.

The Freddie Gray cases would eventually fall apart in court—a complete defeat for Marilyn Mosby. Despite her taunting rhetoric, the fiery prosecutor failed to win a single conviction. The first case, of Officer William Porter, ended in a mistrial. Then, Officer Edward Nero was found not guilty on all four counts, including two counts of misconduct in office, reckless endangerment, and assault. Two other officers were subsequently acquitted. In July 2016, following those acquittals, charges against Porter and the remaining officers were dropped. Mosby, the "no justice, no peace" prosecutor, was 0 for 6. Sadly, so were those who continued to seek the truth. They also failed to find it.

Unfortunately, the justice system has never fully answered the question that launched the Baltimore riots: What really happened to Freddie Gray? But thanks to the incredible efforts of our team, Baltimore was able to move past the violent self-destruction and pull itself back from the brink.

And what a baptism by fire for the brand-new governor of Maryland!

PART IV

HEALING

CHAPTER 20

DIRE DIAGNOSIS

The success of our Asian trade mission, two weeks of pitching the state as an international business hub to top officials in China, South Korea, and Japan, surprised almost everyone. Even Japanese Prime Minister Shinzo Abe seemed ready to facilitate Asian-trade opportunities for businesses in Maryland. But that surprise was nothing compared to the one that was waiting for me when I got home.

"Governor, I'm afraid we have some very difficult news to share with you."

When the doctor said those words to me in the examining room, I knew my life was about to become far more difficult. When I heard the potent phrases that followed—"cancer of the lymph nodes," "very advanced and aggressive," "stage three, possibly stage four"—I also had to wonder how much longer this life of mine was going to last.

It had been only five months since I had taken office, sixty days since the riots broke out in Baltimore. And here I was with a wife, three daughters, and now a young grandchild all counting on me and six million Marylanders expecting me to be their governor. But as I rode in stunned silence from my medical appointments back to the governor's mansion with "Live Like You Were Dying" in my ears, it wasn't my own suddenly shaky mortality that I was obsessing over. All I could think of this Friday of Father's Day weekend was, *How am I going to tell the people I love?*

This might sound strange, worrying more about breaking the news than about the threat of dying or whatever torment the medical professionals had in store for me. But that's what was preying most on my mind. How do you tell your wife that you have a late-stage, potentially deadly cancer? Directly, I suppose.

This was the woman I loved. She was a wonderful wife and mother. She had brought comfort and stability into my life. She had given me a family I never had. Though she'd never paid much attention to politics, she'd been at my side on the campaign trail. We'd celebrated our stunning victory together. We had so much ahead. And now this? I didn't want to hurt her. I didn't want to frighten her. I didn't want things to change.

As soon as I got to the governor's mansion, I led Yumi through the kitchen and into the room I call my *man cave,* my basement hideout with framed sports jerseys on the wall and a big-screen TV. No one would interrupt us there.

"Honey," I said, reaching across the sofa and holding her hands, "I have to talk to you about something pretty serious."

"Okay," she said, a slight catch in her voice. "What's wrong?"

Yumi knew I had just come from the doctor. After seeing the lump in Tokyo, she'd urged me to go. But she wasn't expecting such a dire diagnosis any more than I was.

"I have some scary news," I said. "The doctors told me I have cancer."

I waited a moment. In the silence, I could hear my own heart beating. I didn't know how much more to say. I didn't know how much detail Yumi wanted to hear. I only knew that I had to stay strong for her.

She blinked. "I thought they said everything was okay," she said.

"I know," I answered. "But they did more testing, and they found some things in here." I tapped my belly.

Yumi and I come from very different cultures. We have different ways of showing emotion. I'm not sure if it's because she's Asian, but she isn't quick to show hers. She almost never cries. For years, she'd made fun of me because I'm Irish and I get emotional. I cried on our wedding day. I cry watching a movie. This time, I didn't cry, but Yumi did.

I didn't go into great detail in that first conversation, but I did say, "It's all over my body, and it's spread."

She had a few questions: What is it called? When will we know? What kind of treatment do you need? I answered as well as I could.

"I don't know," I said to the last one. "They want me to meet with a cancer doctor. I'm not sure, but he'll try to come up with a plan."

As I spoke, I realized I was sounding more downbeat than I meant to. "We're going to be okay," I assured her. "I'm a fighter. I promise we'll get through this. I pray we will."

Yumi is a deacon in her church. The idea of prayer is what she grabbed on to. "God is going to get us through this," she said to me. "You're not going to die. You're going to get better. I know you are. God has a plan for you."

"I hope you're right," I said. "I'm sure you are. I love you."

I met with Dr. Arun Bhandari, a highly regarded oncologist at Anne Arundel Medical Center in Annapolis. I liked him a lot. He was a focused, kind, and caring man. But he didn't think he had the specialized experience to manage my treatment alone. "I want to continue to work with you," he said, "but I think you should go to either Johns Hopkins or the University of Maryland."

I set up interviews with the top doctors at both hospitals. The first was scheduled at the University of Maryland Medical Center in Baltimore, where I met Dr. Kevin Cullen, the head of the Cancer Center, and he introduced me to Dr. Aaron Rapoport. As soon as I had my first discussion with Rapoport, I told my scheduler Amanda, "Cancel the meeting at Hopkins. This is where I'm going to be treated. This is going to be my guy."

He was one of the smartest and nicest people I'd ever met, an Orthodox Jewish doctor with excellent credentials and a phenomenal human touch. His dad was one of the founders of Shock Trauma, where both Freddie Gray and the Baltimore police officers had been taken. The son was a world-renowned oncologist. He and Bhandari agreed to be a medical tag team, a Jewish guy from Baltimore and an Indian guy from Anne Arundel County treating the Irish Catholic guy with a life-threatening cancer. I liked the diversity. Each of us brought something unique. I especially liked the bedside manner of these doctors. They hadn't even known each other before, but they quickly became friends. No ego. No competition. No disagreements as far as I could tell. We were all united in beating this cancer.

"You have a lot of tumors, and they're all over," Rapoport told me that first day. "Diffuse, large, B-cell, non-Hodgkin's lymphoma is a rapidly growing, fast-spreading cancer, one of the worst in that way. The good news is it also responds very well to chemotherapy. So, the tumors tend to shrink quickly. But it's so advanced, it's probably also in your bones, which makes it more difficult. We'll need to do a bone-marrow biopsy, which will tell us one way or the other if it's spread into your bones. That will be the difference between stage three and stage four."

Without giving any precise odds, he made clear that a spread like that would drastically reduce my chances of survival. My cancer was so advanced and I had so many tumors, surgery alone would not be an option. Neither would radiation. The doctors said I would need a very intensive and prolonged course of chemotherapy. "Give me the most intense you have," I told him.

Most people with cancer get their chemotherapy as outpatients, hooked up to a drip for a couple of hours at a time. The chemo they had in mind for me sounded way worse than that. It would be administered twenty-four hours a day for four straight days. I would go home for ten days. Then, I would come back to the hospital for another round-the-clock, four-day blast. This would go on for five straight months.

The way the two doctors explained it, they'd be pouring massive amounts of poison inside my body. They would do everything they could to kill the cancer cells, without actually killing me. The treatment had to be intense and prolonged. Otherwise, the cancer would keep growing, and that would be all she wrote.

"You are going to go through hell," Rapoport promised me. "But I think we can get you back and healthy in the end."

"Do whatever you have to do," I told him. "My life is in your hands."

CHAPTER 21

SHARING IT

I didn't want to call our daughters and tell them on the phone. That felt awkward, almost cruel. Kim, Jaymi, and Julie were three grown women with successful lives of their own. But they were still our children, and I was still their dad. This news would be hard for them to hear.

As it happened, they were all coming over that night for the start of Father's Day weekend. I would be able to tell them together and in person.

All three of them cried. Jaymi, the middle one, the prosecutor and a softball player who usually acts like a tough girl—she was the one who cried the most. It all got to me, and as hard as I was trying to be the strong dad, I shed tears along with them. Who would ever want to be the father who makes his children cry? But they were incredible. It was as if my sharing that tough news drew us all closer together—one big group hug for Yumi, the girls, and me. "We love you," they said. "What can we do to help?"

As they tried to console me, I tried to console them. "It'll be okay," I said. "I promise you. We'll get through it together. We'll do whatever it takes."

The next morning, Saturday, I told the lieutenant his duties were about

150

to expand. I said the same thing to Craig, my chief of staff. Then I called my closest personal staff into the State House office and shared the news with them: Kara Bowman, my senior assistant; Amanda Allen, my scheduler; Steve Crim, my public-affairs director; Matt Clark, my communications director; and Doug Mayer, his deputy. Kara and Amanda had already been making appointments and fielding a bevy of calls from doctors and others. I needed Matt and Doug to set up a press conference for Monday afternoon and, with Steve's help, figure out exactly how to break this news to the world. These were people I worked with literally day and night. They were as close to me as family. They were all deeply rattled when I told them. There were more tears. These people truly cared for me, but they were also total professionals. And I knew I could count on all of them.

So Yumi knew. The girls knew. The lieutenant governor knew. My close personal staff knew. But there was someone else I couldn't wait much longer to tell. And it wasn't going to be easy. We'd invited my dad for Father's Day dinner on Sunday. He was excited to be with all of us in the governor's mansion to celebrate the holiday. Even at eighty-six, my dad was still a big presence. He loved to talk. He loved to eat. He loved to tell stories and to laugh. But soon after he got to the house, I called him aside to share the news one-on-one.

"I have to tell you something, Dad," I said in my best stoic-son tone of voice. "It's not the best of news."

This clearly wasn't going to be the Father's Day banter he had been looking forward to.

"I went to the doctor this week," I said. "Apparently, I have cancer. Lymphoma. It's pretty advanced. I'm gonna beat it, but it's going to be a struggle. That's what the doctors are telling me."

My whole life, I had never seen my dad look as he looked when I said those words. Every parent can imagine how he felt. From the day you lay eyes on that child, no matter what else you do, your primary job is to keep him or her safe from harm. And every parent, at some point, comes to the realization that it's not always possible. My father stared at me and cried. Not tears of joy this time. I could tell his heart was broken. He didn't know what to say. I'd just handed him his toughest Father's Day ever. As hard as Jaymi had taken the news, my dad took it even harder. Even though I was fifty-nine years old, to him I was still his little boy, and he felt helpless to protect me.

As enthusiastic an eater as my father usually was, he wouldn't touch a bit of his meal. He just sat in the chair and cried.

I kept hugging everybody and telling them it would all be okay. The fear I felt wasn't for me. Not yet. It was for them. It was what Chris Christie had told me during the riots: I couldn't just focus on making the decisions and solving the problems. I also had to be the consoler in chief. Now, I needed to do the same for my own family.

I knew that soon I'd also have to do it again for my cabinet secretaries, for the rest of my larger extended staff, for my friends and supporters, and for the millions of people who just a few months earlier had put the future of their state in my suddenly shaky hands.

I prayed that I was up to the task.

I wanted to be absolutely transparent about everything. The people of Maryland had put their trust in me and elected me as their governor. I owed them a candid and full explanation.

Vague rumors had already begun to circulate about my health. While I was seeing doctors and getting tests, I'd missed a couple of meetings, which wasn't like me. The *Washington Post* ran a story that wondered if I might have picked up some kind of bug on my trip to Asia.

I wanted to address the situation immediately.

But first thing Monday morning I was expected at Anne Arundel Medical Center for my bone-marrow biopsy surgery. *Was the cancer stage three or stage four? Was it in my bones or not?* To say I was nervous about the biopsy results would be a ridiculous understatement. But either way, I had to know. So I focused my anxiety on a more imminent threat: the twelve-inch metal implement that the surgeon was going to drill into my hip to core out a sample of my bone marrow.

"You will be put under full anesthesia," the nurse informed me, "and we'll be giving you some serious painkillers. So, after you wake up from the surgery, we want you to go home and just get some rest. No driving. No operating heavy equipment. And you shouldn't make any major decisions."

I told her not to worry about the driving. "The state troopers haven't let me drive since I was elected in November," I said. I promised I would avoid all backhoes and excavators. "But I am holding a press conference this afternoon."

The nurse looked shocked. "No, sir," she said. "I don't think that will be possible."

After trying and failing to talk me out of it, she left the prep room and summoned the surgeon from the operating room. Through his sterile face mask, he warned me sternly, "Governor, you are going to be in no shape to do any press conference today."

I told him I appreciated his advice, but I really didn't have much choice. "Before I check into the hospital to start twenty-four-hour-a-day chemo, I want to directly inform people what's going on."

"That's a really, really bad idea," the surgeon insisted. "You will be still recovering from the anesthesia, and we are going to give you Percocet or Vicodin. You are going to be in pain and pretty loopy from the meds."

I stared quietly at him as he pressed valiantly on until he realized I wasn't giving in. "They aren't going to ask you questions at this press conference, are they?"

Clearly, the surgeon hadn't attended many press conferences with the Maryland State House press corps. "Yeah, Doc," I informed him. "I'm pretty sure they will ask me plenty of questions."

He shot me one of those *you're crazy* looks, and then they wheeled me into the operating room.

After waking from the surgery and having a couple of hours to get my fuzzy head together, I headed to the State House, where I summoned my entire cabinet and more of our senior staff. I wanted to give them the word of my condition before the press conference.

I delivered the news to them as straight as I could give it. This team had put their hearts and souls into their new jobs for five months. Needless to say, this was a shocking development.

I told them, "I could not be more proud of this team. I have no doubt that you will all step up and make sure we don't skip a beat. I'm going to beat this cancer, and we are going to keep changing Maryland for the better." There were cheers, tears, and hugs all around.

A huge throng of media were waiting for me when I walked into the Governor's Reception Room on the second floor of the State House a few minutes later. It's a place for bill signings, formal receptions, and other serious business.

The reporters didn't know what they'd been summoned for, but they knew it was something important. The first lady stood to my left. The lieutenant governor was next to her. Also with me at the podium were Kim and Jaymi, their husbands Louis and Ben, and my little granddaughter, Daniella. My brothers Patrick and Tim were there. Cabinet secretaries and some of my staffers stood near the front of the room. Every seat was taken. Reporters and cameramen stood behind the rows of chairs. There were nearly a dozen TV cameras, several of them broadcasting live. I wore a dark gray suit, a white shirt, and a light purple tie. I'd been an underdog so many times before, but this time I knew the struggle I was about to describe wasn't just the fight of my life. It was actually a fight *for* my life, the kind no one can afford to lose.

I was as ready as I would ever be.

"I called this press conference today," I said, "to talk about a new challenge that I will be faced with. It's a personal one, one that will require me to once again be an underdog and a fighter, which is something I think I'm known for. A few days ago, I was diagnosed with cancer. It's an aggressive, B-cell non-Hodgkin's lymphoma. It's a cancer of the lymph nodes."

I looked out into the packed room. No one said anything yet. Hardly anyone even moved. I think they were *stunned*. I wasn't sugarcoating anything.

"I've learned over the past few days that this cancer is very advanced and very aggressive," I said. "When I embarked on our trade mission a few weeks ago, when we went to Asia, I had no idea of my condition. I've learned a heck of a lot more in the past ten days or so."

I was still piecing together all the details, I explained. "But I'm going to face this challenge with the same energy and determination that I've relied on to climb every hill and overcome every obstacle that I've faced in my life."

I just laid it all out there.

"The good news is that although the cancer I have is a very aggressive one and it's spread very rapidly, it's also one that responds very aggressively to chemotherapy treatment, and there's a very strong chance of success. Not only a strong chance of survival but a strong chance of beating it altogether and getting rid of the cancer."

I tried to put the news in terms a roomful of reporters could easily grasp, from the optimistic underdog they had all gotten to know.

"The best news is that my odds of getting through this and beating this are much, much better than the odds I had of beating Anthony Brown to become the sixty-second governor of Maryland," I said. When that got a laugh, I dished up some other betting analogies. "The odds are better than finally doing away with the rain-tax mandate. The odds are better than delivering tax relief for the families of Maryland. Better than the odds of passing a budget that doesn't include tax hikes and reins in state spending." I was on a roll. "Better than the odds of reducing tolls for the first time in fifty years.

"And definitely," I said, wrapping up my list, "better than actually having the *Baltimore Sun* name me as Marylander of the Year." That actually happened too.

"Over the coming months," I said, "I'll be receiving multiple, very aggressive chemotherapy treatments. Most likely, I'm going to lose my hair. You won't have these beautiful gray locks. I may trim down a little bit. But I won't stop working to change Maryland for the better. I'll be working hard and making the decisions that the people of this state elected me to make. I'm just like the more than seventy thousand people diagnosed with lymphoma every single year who fight it, beat it, and continue doing their jobs at the same time. With my faith, my family, and my friends, I know I won't just beat this disease. I'll be a stronger and better person and governor when I get to the other side."

Mostly, I maintained my composure as I said all that. My voice did crack a little when I told the reporters how I'd had to break the news to my family over Father's Day weekend "with the first lady, our daughters, and with my dad, Larry Hogan Sr., my role model. In the midst of this struggle, I was reminded once again how truly blessed and how truly lucky I am."

The media people had questions, just like I'd told the surgeon they would. Some were lighthearted. Some were deadly serious.

"Are your doctors Republicans?" one of the reporters wanted to know.

That got a small chuckle—or was it a nervous laugh? "They didn't tell me if they were Republicans or Democrats," I said. "But they did say they were huge supporters."

"How are you feeling?"

"This stuff has kind of spread," I said. "I have a lot of it in my abdomen. It's pressing up against my spinal column. It's difficult to eat because I'm kind of full, but I'm not terribly sick. It's just something I've got to go after before it gets worse."

"Do you know what stage it is, and how long is the treatment?"

I explained that I was waiting to hear the result of the bone-marrow test I had just come back from. "It's at least very advanced stage three, if not stage four," I said. "We'll find out the details of that probably this week. As far as the treatment, I want to be and they want to be as aggressive as possible." That would involve me spending time in the hospital, I said.

I said I'd be counting on the lieutenant governor even more than I already did. He'd fill in at some Board of Public Works meetings, and, when necessary, he would have the authority to sign official documents.

"Is it your plan to remain governor?"

I thought I'd made that clear. "Absolutely," I emphasized. "It's a tough thing to go through, and I'm going to miss a few meetings. But I'm going to have every capacity to make decisions. I'll be at a lot of meetings. You'll still see me at events. I'll be working most of the time, and my residence across the street is a hundred yards away."

As the questions kept flying, one of the reporters wanted to know if there were any circumstances "where you see the lieutenant governor taking over for you long-term?"

That was a softball. I'd like to think I hit it out of Oriole Park.

"I mean, if I *died,* I would say he probably is going to take over," I allowed. That got the laughter I hoped it would, easing the tension a bit. Then I quickly added, "But I don't foresee that happening."

That was a little dark, I suppose. But everyone seemed to understand that I wasn't planning on quitting or checking out for good anytime soon.

The State House reporters in Annapolis are a notoriously cynical crew. They don't tend to show a lot of emotion, except for the occasional flash of frustration at some politician who dares to duck a question from them. But as I shared my dicey diagnosis and spoke openly about the challenges ahead, I actually noticed that several of the reporters were wiping away tears. They seemed to appreciate my frankness as I bared intimate details of the toughest challenge of my life. Then, they did something I had never seen before, not from journalists. It was something that very nearly brought me to tears. As I stepped back from the podium, they got up from their seats and gave me a thunderous round of applause.

Reporters. Clapping for a politician.

I wasn't sure when I would ever see that again.

CHAPTER 22

HOGAN STRONG

My body was filled with cancerous tumors. I still had a vicious course of chemotherapy ahead of me, five or six months of four-day blasts of round-the-clock poisoning, which was more or less how the doctors described it to me. But I got my first flash of genuinely encouraging news since the initial diagnosis. According to the bone-marrow biopsy, my cancer was as advanced as it could be in stage three but was not stage four. Thank God it hadn't spread to my bones. I was hugely relieved at that. Even my doctors, I think, were a little surprised.

"Given the number and the size of the tumors," Rapoport admitted, "we are very thankful, praise God."

I was so lucky that golf-ball-sized lump had popped out in my neck in Tokyo. It had been like a warning light flashing on my dashboard. That lump may very well have saved my life. Without it, I would never have gone to the doctor when I did. The cancer would have kept spreading and reached my bones for sure.

"It makes my chances much, much better," I told the media on Thursday. For the past three days, they'd been pestering the communications staff for an update. Good news, bad news, whatever it was—I was committed to being forthright with them. I said, "It'll be easier now to go after this thing."

That was certainly true, up to a point. My chances were definitely better than they would have been. But this was still a highly aggressive, life-threatening disease. "It's up to you," Rapoport told me. "But I'm still recommending the most aggressive option. It's the worst to go through. But it's the most likely to be successful in the end."

"Give me aggressive," I said and kept saying, "the most aggressive you have."

Being governor requires constant multitasking. A thousand things always need to get done. I raced around trying to organize myself for the uncertain weeks and months ahead. Meeting with the cabinet members and senior staff. Signing an executive order saying that the lieutenant governor could step in for me should circumstances warrant, such as when I was under anesthesia for surgeries. Repeatedly reminding everyone that the hospital in Baltimore was only thirty-one miles from the State House in Annapolis. The University of Maryland Medical Center had Wi-Fi and cell service, and I could have as many visitors as I needed. "It's not like I'm disappearing for six months," I said.

Rapoport and Bhandari were itching to get my treatment underway. Those tumors inside my body wouldn't magically stop growing. I agreed we didn't want to press our stage-three luck. "We'll start first thing tomorrow," Rapoport said to me on Friday.

I understood the need to get rolling. Really, I wasn't trying to drag my feet. But our annual Change Maryland picnic was set for Saturday, the first since our scrappy grassroots organization had helped elect a new governor. I'd already postponed the picnic once because of the riots. At that time, everyone seemed to understand when I sent an email saying we should remain focused on helping families and communities rebuild in Baltimore. I urged everyone to volunteer in the city or donate to the relief effort. We couldn't reschedule the picnic again. Two thousand people were expected. This year's gathering was sure to be a bit of a victory lap. I really wanted to be there to thank my friends and supporters.

"Can't we wait until Sunday or Monday to start the treatment?" I asked Rapoport. "I've got all my friends coming to this picnic. They want to be there for me, and I want to be there for them." I was just hoping to hug my friends and let them know I was going to be okay. "Then, I'll go to the hospital," I promised the doctor, "and you can do whatever you want to me."

He wouldn't hear of it. "No, Governor," he said, "we cannot afford to wait."

"What's a couple of days?" I pleaded.

"No," he insisted. "I'm telling you. We have to get you in the hospital right now."

At that point everything got more real for me.

Even after hearing the diagnosis, even after the parade of medical specialists and the high-tech testing and the biopsy surgery, even after the State House bare-my-soul announcement, I don't think I had fully absorbed the urgency of my situation, not until I heard Rapoport say, *No, you can't wait any longer, not if you want to stay alive!*

"Okay, then," I told him. "I'm ready. Let's do this."

Early the next morning, the troopers drove Yumi and me into Baltimore. We entered the hospital through the basement and into a back elevator. The troopers led the way to my room. I had a port surgically implanted into my chest. That way, the doctors wouldn't need to keep sticking me with needles every time they wanted to administer a new round of drugs. There'd be a thin tube—a line—connecting the port in my chest to a metal pole holding a rotating menu of four or five different chemo drugs in plastic bags, pouring those ever-changing poisons into me. Whether I was lying in bed, sitting in a chair, or standing on my feet, that pole, which was mounted on a cart with wheels, would always remain at my side. The cancer-killing drugs would never be interrupted as they dripped into one of my main arteries twenty-four hours a day.

When air bubbles crept into the line, a monitor would start to beep, alerting the nurses to the problem immediately. Once we got started, they said, they would check on me constantly—my drug levels, my blood pressure, and my other vital signs. They had to be sure that my personal cocktail of chemo drugs was potent enough to kill the fast-moving cancer cells without also killing me. It was a delicate balance, and I was sure hoping they knew how to get it right.

The Change Maryland picnic went on without me.

The weather was terrible that Saturday. A huge storm blew through Anne Arundel County, almost a monsoon. The tents collapsed. There was an actual mudslide. But 1,500 people ignored the torrential rains and the tornado warnings and still showed up. I'm not sure whose idea it was, but somebody passed out wristbands to the people brave enough to come. The wristbands were lime green. Every kind of cancer has its own color now. Pink is for breast cancer. Orange is for leukemia. Lymphoma is lime green. Two words were printed on the wristbands: HOGAN STRONG.

Since I couldn't be there to see everyone, people also signed a huge get-well banner. A video crew went around, capturing messages for me.

"We love you!"

"We're praying for you, Gov!"

"That cancer doesn't have a chance!"

What a great way to start such a frightening journey, knowing that so many close friends and longtime supporters were all pulling for me. I actually felt lucky, despite where I was. I had an extraordinary support system in place. As I lay in my hospital bed with that line coming out of my chest, the metal pole at my bedside, and the first flow of drugs dripping in, the outpouring of love, all these people saying nice things to me, was always as close as my iPad.

It didn't make the time go any quicker, as the nurses kept switching the plastic bags on the chemo pole. I felt like a prisoner in that hospital room. But I didn't feel alone, and I wasn't in any real pain. Not yet. For the first few hours at least, my body seemed to be tolerating the drugs fairly well.

I went on my Facebook page on Sunday with quite an upbeat report. "I just made it through the first twenty-four hours of chemo," I announced.

"I am feeling healthy and strong. We are killing cancer cells left and right, and I have no side effects."

Clearly, I had no idea what was coming next.

Kara Bowman and Kyle McColgan brought thick binders into my hospital room, packed with cards and letters from people offering prayers, expressing sympathy, and saying they were pulling for me. Typewritten letters from elected officials and foreign dignitaries. Hand-drawn get-well cards from second-grade classes. People reaching out to me in every imaginable way. It was just a sampling of the tens of thousands of pieces of mail that I would eventually receive. As I lay there in my hospital bed, flipping through those binder pages late into the night, I began to tear up at the incredible sentiments that people were sending. At first, I thought I was just becoming emotional at their kind words. Then, I realized it was even deeper than that. I was slowly coming to grasp how very sick I was.

If all these people were pulling for me and praying for me, desperately hoping that I wouldn't die, maybe I really was in genuine peril here. I had been subconsciously trying to sidestep those thoughts, but it was also a reality I needed to face. For the first time, all alone in that hospital bed, I got scared. I literally cried out loud. My chest was heaving. My breath was short. I hadn't cried like that since my mom died. I had been trying to be strong for everyone around me. This was the terror I'd been holding at a distance. Finally, inevitably, the fear and vulnerability came crashing in.

Sleep was tough, and the constantly beeping monitor wasn't the only reason why. The steady drip of chemo drugs was starting to make me feel a little nauseous. I was also being pumped up with steroids, which was important. The steroids helped preserve the strength that the chemo drugs were sapping, part of the relentless tug-of-war that was occurring inside my body. But the steroids also kept me wired and manic, like someone was slipping me stiff doses of speed.

I lay in bed, hour after hour, wide awake, the line in my chest, the pole at my side, the rush of thoughts treating my mind like a NASCAR track. The monitor kept going off. The nurses kept coming in to change my drug bags, to take blood, or to check my vitals, and to ask me if I was feeling okay. "I'd feel a lot better," I told them, "if I could get some sleep."

I stared at my phone. I glanced at the clock. I tried to watch television. I solved most of the major issues facing the state of Maryland—in my mind, anyway. I played "Live Like You Were Dying" three or four times. I texted my staffers and then texted them again. Some would wake up in the morning to twenty texts from me about things I thought they should be working on. I could only imagine how they were responding to my digital onslaught: *Let's hope the gov gets well quickly so the rest of us can get some peace!*

I was not only in mental overdrive. I was also ravenously hungry. With all the fluids in me, I noticed I was swelling up. I don't know what I expected cancer to feel like, but I didn't anticipate all this. Partly because of the raging steroids, partly because the boredom was driving me nuts, I found myself thinking, *I'm not lying in bed for four days and nights like this. I really will go crazy. I've got to get out of this bed.* I didn't think I could bust out of the hospital entirely. The state troopers in the hallway would block my way or rat me out to the nurses. That's when I made my plan: I would grab my rolling chemo pole, head out into the hallway, and go have a look around.

CHAPTER 23

DOING LAPS

Our floor was a large rectangle—or, as I would quickly come to think of it, a long, four-sided track. I wheeled the pole beside me as I headed out the door and made my way into the hall. I was weak. I felt awful. I knew I didn't look so great. But lying in that bed seemed worse. *Take it one step at a time*, I told myself. Dragging that pole along in my sweatpants, polo shirt, and Under Armor sneakers, I had just discovered my new routine.

I wasn't the only one doing laps with a chemo pole. I met a woman in the hallway with a big smile on her face and a scarf around her head. Her name was Shelly Jones-Wilson. She came from West Baltimore, Freddie Gray's neighborhood. Shelly had the same kind of non-Hodgkin's lymphoma I had, though her treatment was further along. She became my first cancer buddy.

"You can never keep up with me," I teased her as I came up from behind. Shelly said she wasn't worried as we headed down the hall. I loved her sense of humor and her no-pretense attitude. "Bald is beautiful," I told her, and she warned me, "You think so? You might be joining the bald club soon."

I was the governor. She was a lady from West Baltimore. But that distinction didn't seem important at all. Not in here. We were two cancer patients, enjoying each other's company, encouraging one another however we could. Shelly was the one who shared a crucial piece of patient intelligence with me: "It's seventeen laps to a mile."

"I want to be just like you," I told her, and I meant it. She was an inspiration.

I met lots of other patients in the hallway and on other floors of the hospital. As the days went on, I wandered farther and farther afield, saying hello, introducing myself, asking how people were doing. I was happy to see all the traffic in the halls. The patients with the strength to get up hated lying around just as much as I did. And they couldn't have been any friendlier to me, welcoming me to the hospital, treating me like a fellow patient who just happened to be the governor of the state. As a born-and-raised people-person, I was in my element again.

"Hey, Governor," I heard a voice call to me as I walked the hallway one afternoon. The voice came through an open door of a room near mine. I stopped and stuck my head inside, where a young man was sitting up in bed.

"They call me the mayor," he said with a giant smile, holding out his hand to shake mine. "Nice to meet you."

His name was Jimmy Myrick Jr. He was there with his parents, Jim and Sharon. He had leukemia and Down syndrome. It took only a few minutes of conversation for me to recognize that Jimmy was one of the most incredible people I'd ever met in my life. Happy. Bursting with positive attitude. He was thirty-two years old, though he seemed much younger to me.

Jimmy had been active in the Special Olympics since he was eight, a champion swimmer and basketball player. He was a twenty-year Super Plunger at the annual Maryland State Police Polar Bear Plunge, one of those crazy people who jump into frigid Chesapeake Bay every January to raise money for the Special Olympics. He was a cheerleader with a team from the Maryland Twisters organization—and clearly a cheerleader in life.

Jimmy and I took some photos together and also some with his parents, who seemed so proud of him. I asked if we could post one of the pictures on our Facebook page.

"Sure," Jimmy said. "Go for it. Can I do laps with you?"

We did some laps together with Jimmy's dad pushing him in a wheelchair. As soon as that photo was posted on Facebook, the comments started pouring in, more than a thousand of them: "We know Jimmy from Special Olympics" . . . "We love Jimmy" . . . "He's in cheerleading with us" . . . "I see him every year at the Polar Bear Plunge."

When I told Jimmy about the buzz he'd been generating, a grin slid across his face. "Yeah," he said to me, "I'm kind of a big deal."

Some people might say Jimmy and I had little in common. The truth is we seemed to share a lot—and I don't just mean life-threatening cancers. It was an experience I would have over and over again. "Jimmy," I told him early on, "you're pretty famous. I see why they call you the mayor. Everybody loves you."

Yumi spent a lot of time at the hospital. So did Jaymi, who used up all her leave from her job at the Saint Mary's County prosecutor's office to be with me. Kim was working and taking care of little Daniella, but she and Louis also came by to visit. Julie popped in from Ann Arbor when she was home. Old friends dropped by.

I knew I'd be stuck in the hospital on and off for months to come. But I still had a state to run, and I intended to run it. I had my laptop, my iPad, and my phone. The Wi-Fi and cell service both worked fine, as my harried staff could well attest to. I certainly wasn't wasting time sleeping. I did have my doctor visits, spinal taps, PET scans, and laps around the floor. I kept meeting other patients and their families, especially on the pediatric oncology floor. Yes, I'd have ten days back in Annapolis between each of my marathon hospital stays. But I couldn't and wouldn't wait to get the job done. I still had many hours a day to be the governor.

One of my assistants, usually Kara, Kyle, or Amanda, was always there directing traffic, taking calls from the cabinet members and senior staff, bringing papers in and out, shuffling people in to see me, saying, "He's with the doctors right now, but he'll be back in half an hour. Can you wait?" My chief of staff, Craig, frequently was there with other top staffers going in and out.

We held meetings in my room. We met in the patient lounge. With larger groups, we went down the hall and commandeered the doctors' conference room. It was just the right size for sub-cabinet meetings and security-team briefings. I sat there in my loose-fitting hospital clothes connected to my chemo pole, working with my team. Honestly, it wasn't all that different from our sessions at the State House, though I didn't usually hang around the governor's office in sweats and tennis shoes. I am not sure how many other governors have ever run their states like this. But, you know what? It worked. Stuff got done. We did the state's business until I had to excuse myself for a medical procedure, a chemo bag change, or a meeting with Rapoport. Then I came right back in and finished whatever it was we were doing. I always had eight or ten agenda items tugging at me, same as usual. During the riots, we'd moved our command center to the Schaefer building in downtown Baltimore. Now, we were at the University of Maryland Medical Center, eight blocks away. I had a great team to lead, and I led them.

From what I was hearing, my staff, the hospital staff, and the public were all amazed.

During the riots, a lot of people said I displayed leadership, quick decisiveness, and the ability to handle a crisis under stress. Cancer was turning out to be a chance to demonstrate my determination. It showed I don't have any quit in me, not an ounce of it. That's what got me this far. And I figured that would get me through this too.

"I can't believe you're still working!" people kept saying to me.

"Governor, don't you want to take it easy for a while?"

"You need all your strength to fight this disease."

What they didn't understand was that the work was therapeutic for me. If I sat there feeling sorry for myself or worrying that I might die, it would have been a lot tougher than staying busy all day and night, working and solving problems. It was my obligation. But it was also my choice. Yes, this was a huge personal challenge that I didn't expect to be facing. But as I told anyone who asked me, "I'm going to work through this just like all the other people who get cancer do. I'm too busy to worry about the cancer. I've got a state to run."

I got some eye-rolling when I talked like that. Some people certainly thought, *He's kidding himself. But, you know, if it helps him deal with the situation—well, okay, then.* The doctors. The nurses. The other patients. The troopers. The staff. My family and my close friends. I loved all of them. Somehow, together, I knew we would get through this.

By then, the lime-green Hogan Strong wristbands were popping up everywhere. Yumi and Jaymi started wearing them. So did Orioles players Adam Jones and Manny Machado. People all across Maryland, I was told, were flashing these lime-green bands. The demand was steep. Folks saw it as a morale-boosting and awareness-raising opportunity. There were Hogan Strong bumper stickers and t-shirts. Route One Apparel, a College Park company started by a University of Maryland junior, quickly launched a Hogan Strong t-shirt line, promising $5 from each sale for lymphoma and leukemia research. "We're rooting for your full recovery, Larry Hogan," said owner Ali von Paris.

All of these supporters had watched my press conference. They'd read about my plight. They'd met me on the campaign trail or seen me at the riots or taken a selfie with me somewhere. Somehow, they felt connected, and they cared. I certainly wasn't expecting an outpouring like this. But damned if my illness hadn't inspired its own merchandise line!

It quickly spread beyond Maryland. On the presidential campaign trail, a voter in Rochester, New Hampshire, asked Chris Christie about the lime-green band on his right wrist. It was for a "dear friend," he said, "a guy with incredible courage and understanding for what it means to be a leader." Then Christie added, "I'm hoping I'm going to be able to cut this thing off once the doctors give Larry the good news that he's in remission."

Somehow or another, almost everyone is touched by cancer—as a patient, a family member, a loved one, a neighbor, a coworker, or a friend. There are a heck of a lot of cancer survivors out there. In every one of these cases, support from others is vital. All I knew was that a whole lot of people in Maryland and beyond were hoping and praying for me to survive. If you don't think that makes an incredible difference, I'll bet you've never had the experience of needing to fight for your life. At times like that, we need all the help we can get.

_____

Each time I was sprung from the hospital and sent back home to Annapolis, I immediately crashed. My 120-hour steroid-fueled hospital marathons thoroughly wiped me out. Once I was off the steroids, I could finally sleep again. But my ten-day returns to the capital were anything but a vacation. I had lots to keep me busy there. Meetings in my office. All the public events I could drag myself to. And the doctors had a whole other course of torture waiting for me, directed by Bhandari. He bombarded my body with an entirely different set of drugs, including massive doses of one called Neulasta, which stimulated my bone marrow to produce more white blood cells. That was important. My body was desperate for an immunity boost. But those Neulasta shots were horrible. Every bone in my body hurt like hell, from the tips of my fingers to the tips of my toes. I was happy to be out of the hospital, but now I felt like I'd been hit by a truck. In some ways, the outpatient treatments were worse than the inpatient chemo. Everything hurt. As the time went on, I stiffened. It got harder for me to move.

"You guys really aren't going to let up on me, are you?" I said to Bhandari.

"We want you to get well, Governor," he said.

How could I argue with that?

Working made me feel better, at least mentally. I quickly fell back into my office routine. Meetings with staff and the leaders of the Legislature. The Board of Public Works. Answering questions from the media: "Yes, I'm feeling okay . . . Yes, I'm getting my work done . . . No, the state is not on the verge of collapse." Coordinating with the lieutenant governor, the cabinet, and the rest of my team, who really stepped up. And then gearing up for each new trip back to the hospital.

In the weeks and months ahead, I would make some major decisions with long-term impact on the state. I would approve the Purple Line light-rail project for Maryland's Washington suburbs, the largest public-private transit project in North America. I would greenlight a long-awaited overhaul of the Baltimore city transit system. I would order the closing of the violence-plagued Baltimore City Detention Center.

That stuff I said at my first cancer press conference about continuing as governor really was turning out to be true.

After my first round of chemo, I said to myself, *That wasn't so bad. I can take this a second time.* It was a little worse the second time. I thought, *That was kinda bad, but I can take it a third time.* And so on. Each round got harder, and each one took its own special toll. I didn't like complaining about the physical ravages of chemotherapy. One thing about being around a lot of cancer patients: Sadly, there are always others who are worse off than you. I knew plenty of those people, and they showed amazing courage. That reality has a way of quieting your own self-pity. My self-imposed attitude was *Hey, Doc, just throw it at me. I don't care what it is. I'll get through it somehow.* But yes, I'll admit it now. The treatments were pretty bad, and they kept getting worse.

After my third stay in the hospital, I was shampooing in the shower. A whole clump of my hair came off in my hand. Then, another one and another one. I hated seeing those beautiful gray locks chasing each other in circles down the drain.

I got out of the shower and stared into the mirror. I looked like I had been to Chernobyl. The chemo made the hair follicles completely let go. I decided to just shave the rest of my head. I had no choice. Yumi almost fainted when she saw me. Soon enough, I'd lost every hair on my body, and I mean every single one. The eyelashes were a killer. I had no idea how important eyelashes are for keeping dirt and dust out of your eyes. I thought they were just for flirting. Who knew?

When I first lost my hair, Doug and Matt, the consummate communications professionals that they are, both said to me, "People will be shocked when they see you bald for the first time. We should probably put out a photo."

That made sense. Somehow, I needed to get control of this. But I didn't want to circulate a shot of me looking all hairless and forlorn lying in a hospital bed. That was just too depressing. I had a better idea. "I'll put on my best power suit," I said to Matt and Doug. "And a pair of Ray-Ban shades. I will be the most bad-ass governor anyone has ever seen." We took the photo right outside my office door, next to the sign that says, "Larry Hogan, Governor."

My arms are folded. I'm leaning back. My eyes are behind the Ray-Bans. That photo went viral immediately, with 1.4 million people seeing it on our social media, and it was shared everywhere. It sent the exact message I was hoping for: "Cancer, you messed with the wrong dude. This one isn't going down without one hell of a fight."

I'm not the most vain person in the world. But it was hard not to notice how terrible I looked. I was putting on weight at a ferocious pace, in part because of the steroids. Because of the cancer treatment, I was quickly on my way to a forty-pound, full-body ballooning. My head swelled up, unevenly. My skin was discolored. And now I had no hair. I couldn't hide out at home the way some cancer patients choose to. It wasn't just the mirrors in the governor's mansion that were judging me. I was out making speeches, attending large meetings, holding major press conferences, being interviewed by reporters, and showing up on television nearly every night. I didn't have to guess if people were thinking, *That guy looks horrible.* The evidence was everywhere.

Back at the University of Maryland Medical Center, the traffic never let up, and not just in the hallways. The president of the hospital was stopping by. So was Kevin Cullen, the head of the cancer center. Former governor Bob Ehrlich came to visit. Other patients and their families dropped by constantly to say hello. *Jeez,* I thought, *it's busier in here than in my office.* Keiffer Mitchell brought fresh-squeezed orange juice. Besides being my senior advisor, Keiffer had a side business making and selling fresh juice at a farmers market in Baltimore. I'm not saying the man had found his true talent, but Keiffer squeezed some excellent juice. Jaymi, who loves to eat as much as I do, had been smuggling in pizza, chicken wings, and Five Guys burgers—at my direction, I should probably add. That might have had something to do with the weight gain!

Yumi was constantly on me to eat healthier food. She tried to enlist Rapoport in her campaign. "Would you tell my husband he has to eat healthy?" Yumi asked him one day.

"No," the doctor said. "I'm going with the governor on this one. Whatever he can eat, I want him to eat. It's important that he gets food down.

With these drugs, we need to keep weight on him. He doesn't have to eat vegetables if he doesn't want to. If he wants milkshakes and pizza, that's what he can have."

Yumi was appalled. "Vegetables are good for him," she insisted. But finally, in the long nutritional debate between husband and wife, I had a respected doctor on my side. "I told you Dr. Rapoport is a genius," I said to Yumi.

CHAPTER 24

BEING BLESSED

Some of the best advice I ever received came from a five-year-old.

The governor of Maryland gets the use of skyboxes at Camden Yards, M&T Bank Stadium, and FedEx Field, where the Baltimore Orioles, Baltimore Ravens, and Washington Redskins play. It's one of the cool perks of the job. For the Redskins' home opener September 13 against the Miami Dolphins, I invited some cancer patients from a group called Cool Kids Campaign to join me in the governor's box.

I wasn't feeling great. Those outpatient treatments were really slamming me, as much as the inpatient blasts were. But we all headed down to the field before the game, where the children and their parents got to shake hands with some of the players. The players couldn't have been friendlier, answering questions and posing for photos with the kids. Then, we went back upstairs to the box to fuel up on stadium hot dogs. A couple of the Redskins cheerleaders—*team ambassadors,* they are called—stopped by. There was one boy, the youngest one, whose name was Andrew Oberle.

Andrew had a different kind of cancer than I had. His was T-cell acute lymphoblastic leukemia. He'd already been through two years of treatments to make his bone marrow behave right. Andrew was five years old and not the least bit shy. He came over to me after the cheerleaders left and said, "*Gubba-nuh*, my mommy helped me write a list for you now that you have cancer." I was about to get some sage advice from the tiniest, most adorable person in the suite.

"At first, you're not going to like your doctors," Andrew said. "But they're there to help you. You will learn to like them."

I told him I would try to remember that. He kept reading.

"It's okay to cry," he said.

"Good."

"Find your hugging person," he continued, adding, "Mine is my mommy."

Andrew read the ten items on his list, all excellent advice. But the one that I remember best was "Make sure they give you the numb-numb cream before you get the pokey."

I knew those weren't technical medical terms, but I also knew exactly what Andrew meant. "I'll insist on it," I promised him. "No pokey without the numb-numb cream."

The Dolphins beat the Redskins that day 17 to 10, but Andrew and I agreed to stay in touch. The next time I was in the hospital, I repeated the story and joked with the nurses. "Hey," I said, "how come I don't get any numb-numb cream before you give me the pokey? You guys just keep sticking me."

"We only do that with the kids, Governor," one of them said with a smile.

I'll bet Andrew would call that a lame excuse.

———

All along, the doctors kept complaining that I wasn't protecting my compromised immune system carefully enough. They had a point. But I have always loved meeting and engaging with people. It's what I thrive on. I'll bet I've shaken a hundred thousand hands in my life and probably taken nearly as many selfies. Hugs are like fuel to me.

As more and more people heard about my battle with cancer, lots of them were eager to talk to me. I wanted to talk to them too. Each time I came out of the hospital, I promised the doctors I'd be more careful. Each time, I wasn't careful enough—not as far as Rapoport was concerned.

"Governor, my wife showed me your Facebook page," he said to me when I went in for my next four-day chemo marathon. "I couldn't help but notice that you seemed to be shaking hundreds of hands. You really cannot continue doing that."

"Yeah," I began to explain. "I was just—"

He cut me off. "No. I'm serious."

"I'm using hand sanitizer," I protested.

"That's not good enough. You have a severely weakened immune system. You're really going to get sick."

"All right," I relented.

But everywhere I went, people were reaching out for me. I tried giving elbow bumps instead of handshakes, which felt like a poor substitute. Too impersonal. I'm just not an elbow-bump kind of guy.

I took a group of cancer kids with me to Camden Yards. Again, we were out on the field to meet the players. Everyone was shaking hands and saying hello and sharing hugs and taking selfies. I was trying to be good. "I'm sorry," I said half a dozen times. "I can't shake your hand."

Orioles outfielder Adam Jones, who was still wearing a lime-green Hogan Strong wristband, must have overheard me. Without saying a word, he ran into the dugout and came out with two brand-new Baltimore Orioles batting gloves.

"Here, Governor," he said. "Put these on. Then you can shake all the hands you want to."

I slipped on the gloves and spent the rest of the afternoon shaking hands. At a Baltimore Ravens game, I repeated the trick with a pair of wide receiver's gloves. Those worked too, but it was unbelievable how sticky receivers' gloves are. I'm not sure how those receivers could ever drop a pass! Each time I shook another hand, it was hard to pull away. Our hands were almost glued together. But nobody seemed to mind.

On Thursday morning, September 24, I completed my fifth four-day round of inpatient chemotherapy. The pattern was holding. Four days in, ten days out, each new round more horrible than the one before. My body was weaker. I felt sicker. My insides were that much more in turmoil. By round number five, I was really ravaged.

Cardinal Donald Wuerl had reached out to my office to invite Yumi and me to an audience with the pope during his North American tour. Pope Francis had been in Cuba and was now visiting Washington, DC. He addressed a joint session of Congress that morning, the first pope ever to do that. Then, he was heading to the offices of Catholic Charities of the Archdiocese of Washington and flying up to New York later that afternoon.

I was at the absolute worst part of my entire cancer battle. I wasn't sure I could pull myself out of bed, let alone head to Washington. But if ever there was a time I needed to meet the Holy Father, this was it.

I didn't look good. I didn't feel good. I was in pain. The chemo had been so brutal, I was hardly able to pull myself out of the SUV. Walking into the building, I really thought I might fall over.

As soon as Yumi and I got into the small reception room, Cardinal Wuerl walked the pope over to meet us. "Your Holiness," he said, "this is Governor Hogan."

"Holy Father," I said, "it is such an honor to meet you."

It was obvious that the pope had already been informed of my story—who I was, what I was battling, all of it.

I'd been a Catholic all my life. I wouldn't call myself a varsity Catholic, but I was definitely on the team. He took both my hands in his hands, and he looked me in the eye. He had glittery eyes and a beautiful smile. For that intense moment, it was as if Yumi and I were the only people in the room, the only people anywhere.

"Holy Father," I said, "I'd like to ask for your blessing for all of those afflicted with cancer."

He put his hand on my bald, sweaty, swollen head. He prayed in Latin. With the fingers of his right hand, he traced a sign of the cross on my forehead.

Then in English he said, "God bless you." He handed a rosary to me and another one to Yumi, blessing both of them.

I had met five presidents, but this was my first pope. It was a hugely moving experience for me, having the pope bless me as I stood in for the cancer patients of the world. I really wasn't prepared for the emotional punch of it.

As Yumi and I walked slowly out of the Catholic Charities building, all I could think of was how blessed I was—and how badly I needed to get home and go to bed. But just as I flopped into my seat in the SUV, Kyle said Amanda had been frantically calling from Annapolis. President Obama and Vice President Biden, it seemed, were unable to see the pope off that afternoon from Joint Base Andrews in Maryland. The White House was hoping that I could join Secretary of State John Kerry at 4 PM at Andrews to represent the president and vice president.

It was an incredible honor. I understood that. But I also understood I was in no position to accept it. I said to Kyle, "I honestly don't think I can do it. I don't know if I have the strength to stand out in the sun at Andrews. When do they need to know?"

"Now," he said. "They've been calling since you went in to see Pope Francis." The Swiss Guard, who provide security for the pope, make the Secret Service look almost lackadaisical. There had been no way for Kyle or even my state troopers to interrupt my audience with the Holy Father.

I thought about it for another second, before saying, "I don't know how I'm going to do it, but I have to do it. Tell the White House I would be honored." This was going to bring a whole new meaning to *Hogan Strong*.

It was already after lunch by then. I had just enough time to get back to Annapolis, crash for a couple of hours, grab another shower, change my clothes, and get to Andrews in time.

Yumi and I met John and Teresa Kerry at Andrews, along with some Air Force generals and officials from the State Department and the Vatican. We waited in a small holding room until Pope Francis was about to arrive; then we all walked out toward the tarmac where the pope's official plane, *Shepherd One*, was waiting for him.

There were bleachers, which were filled with students from Washington-area Catholic schools, dressed in their uniforms. Everyone was excited about seeing the pope. But as we walked out to the tarmac, the school kids started chanting, "Hogan Strong! Hogan Strong!" That hit me like a steroid shot, a much-needed boost of energy in the afternoon sun.

"We're all praying for you," the secretary of state whispered to me.

We took our position at the far end of the red carpet, where the mobile steps led up to the papal plane. I could feel the afternoon sun beating down on my head. A few minutes later, the pope arrived. As he made his way past the generals and the State Department people, my chemo fever was raging. I could feel balls of sweat, not drops, sliding down my back.

As the pope approached us, I said to him, "Holy Father, thank you for the blessing this morning on behalf of cancer patients around the world."

He stopped sharply, right in front of me. Again, he looked me in the eyes. The pope put one hand on my right shoulder, his other hand on my left shoulder, and gave both shoulders a gentle squeeze.

His English was a little weak, but his meaning was strong and clear.

"I pray for you," he said, his hands still on my shoulders. And then he repeated with emphasis, "I pray for *YOU.*"

He wasn't just uttering a general prayer for all the world's cancer patients. He made it sound as if he was seeking divine intervention specifically for *me.* I'd spent my time in Catholic school. I had been around a lot of Catholic ritual over the years. This was unlike anything I had ever experienced or felt before.

Being in the presence of the pope twice in one day and having him bless me the way he did—I wasn't quite sure how to react or what it might mean for my ultimate recovery. But even a J.V. Catholic like me knew this much: It certainly can't be a bad thing when the Holy Father prays specifically for you.

I got through my final four-day round of twenty-four-hour-a-day chemotherapy, number six, in mid-October. It was, as predicted, the most gruesome of them all. Not fundamentally different from the others, but several screw turns worse. Since my body kept being weakened, even the same treatment felt more wrenching and intense. All I could think of was what a relief it would be when I was finally finished—this phase, anyway. Although I didn't complain to anyone, I knew I couldn't take much more.

Was all this torment worth it? Were we killing all the cancer cells? I'd been getting regular scans. Each time, the hospital techs pumped me up with a contrast agent and rolled me into a big, twisted metal machine with safety warnings everywhere. The scans seemed to take forever. I had to lie perfectly still. The techs were constantly saying to me, "Breathe. Hold your breath. Okay, you can breathe again."

The contrast agent, I was told, makes the tumors glow. Originally, I was lit up like a Christmas tree. But as time went on, the glowing colors began to dim. Instead of big tumors, the scans were showing smaller ones. Instead of forty-some, it was thirty, then twenty, then ten. Rapoport seemed encouraged, but he wasn't very explicit about what any of this meant. In understated doctor-speak, he kept saying, "We're encouraged by the progress. We're seeing some shrinkage. God willing, we will continue to." That's about as far as he would go.

Finally, I heard that my tumors were "ninety-five percent gone." That sounded wonderful, but it was still far from definitive. Even at five percent, highly aggressive, fast-moving cancer of the lymph nodes can quickly roar back. I still had to wait. Even after the final round of chemo, no one knew anything for sure. I was hoping for an instantaneous report. But the doctors said they would order another round of scans thirty days after my chemo was finished. They couldn't make a definitive determination before then.

Those were the longest thirty days of my treatment. I tried not to count the passing days and hours, as I ground through my painful outpatient visits and was weaned off the steroids. I tried to keep my mind on my work. Thankfully, I had a few diversions along the way.

On Saturday, October 24, the University of Maryland Children's Hospital was holding a benefit concert at the Joseph Meyerhoff Symphony Hall in Baltimore. It was a great cause, one that had become even more important to me over the past few months. Of course, I wanted to be there for the kids, for the hospital, and for the wonderful doctors and nurses who had been taking such good care of me. But I also had another reason: The headliner was Tim

McGraw. His song "Live Like You Were Dying" had been there for me when I needed it most. I even had the lyrics printed out on my desk at the State House.

Before the show, I had an opportunity to meet Tim backstage. I don't know what I expected, but the world-famous singer seemed genuinely interested in the cause he was there to support. That afternoon, he had paid a visit to the hospital, touring the wards, meeting some of the children, and saying "thank you" to the doctors, nurses, and other employees. He was very nice and the exact opposite of a stereotypical superstar.

I told him "Live Like You Were Dying" had become my theme song as I fought my own battle with lymphoma. I explained how I listened to the song constantly. "Whenever I feel down," I said, "or like I need a kick in the ass, I play your song." I paused and looked him in the eyes. Was he understanding how much it meant to me? "I just want you to know how much your song inspired me," I said.

Tim nodded slowly, his big black cowboy hat dipping forward. He said he really appreciated hearing all that.

"You know," he said to me, "that's not my best-selling record. I've had bigger hits. But that song seems to really touch a lot of people. Every time I sing it, I think of my dad."

Tim's father, Tug McGraw, was a Major League Baseball player, a solid relief pitcher for twenty years with the New York Mets and the Philadelphia Phillies. He was known for his easy outspokenness and his self-deprecating sense of humor. He set the tone early in his career when he was asked if he preferred the new AstroTurf at the Houston Astrodome to real grass. "I don't know," he said. "I never smoked AstroTurf." It was Tug who coined the phrase "Ya Gotta Believe," which became a rallying cry for decades of Mets teams. In the 1980 World Series, Tug struck out Willie Wilson of the Kansas City Royals to hand the Phillies their first world championship ever.

Tug McGraw was hospitalized with a brain tumor in 2003 and told he had three months to live. He died nine months later on January 5, 2004.

The Children's Hospital fundraising concert drew a sold-out crowd. I got a chance to welcome the 2,000 people who attended. So did two of the hospital's young patients, Desiriah Brown, age five-and-a-half, and Logan Reich, thirteen. Desi was being treated for the childhood cancer neuroblastoma. Logan had gone for surgery after severely fracturing his arm in a trampoline mishap.

In my brief remarks, I shared some of the Tim McGraw story with the audience. "When I first got my diagnosis," I said, "the first thing I did after talking to the doctors was go play his song on my iPad, and I keep the lyrics sitting on my desk. So it's an honor for me to meet him. I thank him for being an inspiration."

Then, I quickly got off the stage to let Tim do his show. And it was a great one.

I was up on the balcony, looking down at the stage, as the concert came to a close, and the people roared their approval with a standing ovation. Tim came out for a second encore and final song of the night.

He walked back to center stage in his trademark black hat and faded jeans. Then, without any warning, he pointed up at me in the balcony, and said, "This song goes out to the governor. He's a good man, and he's had a tough fight, and I want to dedicate this song to him."

The band started playing, and Tim began to sing. I recognized the words immediately. It was the opening verse of the song that had helped save my life.

> *I was in my early forties*
> *With a lot of life before me*
> *And a moment came that stopped me on a dime.*

I mouthed the words as Tim McGraw sang them. In the crowd below, I could hear people singing the same words out loud.

> *I spent most of the next days,*
> *Looking at the X-rays,*
> *Talkin' 'bout the options,*
> *And talkin' 'bout sweet time.*

Tim was down in a crouch now. His voice was packed with emotion. He was giving it everything he had. By then, people were looking up at me and pointing. On the balcony next to me, others were openly crying, not even wiping the tears from their cheeks. Soon, I had tears running down my swollen face as well. By the time Tim got to the chorus, it seemed like all of Symphony Hall was singing along.

> He said, "I went skydiving.
> I went Rocky Mountain climbing.
> I went 2.7 seconds on a bull named Fu Manchu.
> And I loved deeper,
> And I spoke sweeter,
> And I gave forgiveness I'd been denying."
> And he said,
> "Someday I hope you get the chance
> To live like you were dying."

The love in Symphony Hall that night was unmistakable. I swear, you could almost reach out and squeeze it. And it wasn't just coming from the stage. When Tim McGraw got to the end of the song, people were clapping and cheering and crying all at once. I threw my fist triumphantly in the air, knowing there was nothing that could stop me now.

What a night it was!

Then, just as we were leaving, the singer's tour manager rushed up to me. She was holding a guitar in her hand. "Tim asked me to give this to you," she said. "He wanted you to have it."

Right away, I noticed some writing on the front of the guitar. The manager held it up so I could read what was written there.

"To Gov Hogan," it said. "Live Like You Were Dying, Tim McGraw."

(Top) Big sis:
When I grow up, I
want to be like Terry
(Bottom) Running mates:
Helping elect Dad to
Congress in 1968

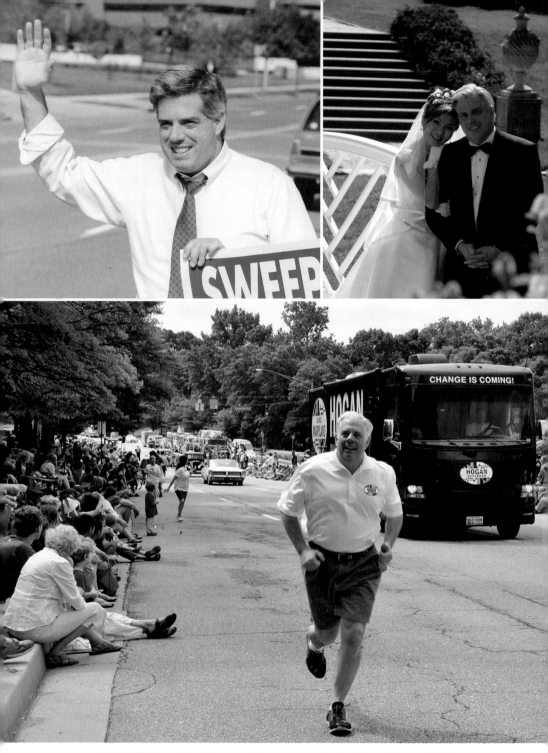

(Top Left) Long odds: Trying to defeat career politician Steny Hoyer in 1992
(Top Right) True love: The happiest day of my life, May 1, 2004
(Bottom) Double time: Actually running for governor

(Top Left) Party man: Celebrating my Republican primary victory, 2014
(Top Right) Diner duo: Campaigning with Chris Christie at the Honey Bee in Glen Burnie
(Bottom) Snow day: Inaugurated as the 62nd governor of Maryland

(Top Left) Rescue mission: Landing in riot-torn Baltimore with Keiffer Mitchell
(Top Right) In command: Letting the cops and guardsmen know I have their backs
(Bottom) Neighborhood walk: We are here to save the city

(Top) Tough news:
It's late-stage lymphoma
(Bottom) Hogan strong:
Yumi, Jaymi and I, showing
off our new wristbands

(Top) Sweet song: Singing along with Tim McGraw at Baltimore's Symphony Hall
(Bottom Left) New look: Cancer doesn't have a chance this time
(Bottom Right) Holy father: Pope Francis blesses me and prays for cancer patients everywhere

(Top) Modern family: son-in-law Louis Velez, me, Yumi, daughter Jaymi, granddaughter Nora, and son-in-law Ben Sterling. Granddaughter Daniella, son-in-law Taesoo Kim, daughter Julie, granddaughter Ada, daughter Kim and grandson son Cam *(Bottom)* Rescue pups: Who could say no to Chessie and Anna?

(Top) Front lines: Touring the new field hospital at the Baltimore City Convention Center
(Bottom) Precious cargo: Yumi and I on the tarmac at BWI awaiting
the arrival of 500,000 COVID-19 test kits from South Korea

CHAPTER 25

CANCER-FREE

On the morning of November 16, Rapoport came into the examining room with my latest scans. Dr. Cullen, the head of the cancer center, was with him. I was hopeful, but I'd also been trying to prepare myself for whatever the news might be. I'd brought Yumi with me. I knew this was the moment of truth.

"Governor," Rapoport said to me, "our prayers have been answered. There is no sign of cancer in your body. You are one hundred percent cancer-free and in complete remission."

Just like that. No buildup. Very matter-of-fact. "This is wonderful news," he added, "and the best outcome we could have possibly hoped for."

A wave of relief crashed through my body, ten times stronger than the steroids. The feeling was incredible. Until I heard that word, "cancer-free," I never knew what real relief felt like.

I hugged both doctors. I hugged Yumi. I think I may have gone out into the hall and hugged the troopers and the nurses. I was so relieved. But I wasn't entirely out of the woods just yet, as Rapoport made clear. Apparently, six rounds of massive, inpatient chemo weren't quite enough. He said we needed to talk about continuing my medical treatment. The additional treatment would be less intense, he said, but would go on for another year. This was a different kind of chemotherapy. "It can significantly decrease the chance of the cancer returning," the doctor said.

I didn't even wait for the details. He didn't have to ask me twice. "Whatever it is," I told him, "let's do it." After everything I'd been through up till now, I was more than ready to seal the deal. He and Bhandari would explain more later, he said.

Before Rapoport left the room, I had something I needed to say to him. I was sure he knew what I was thinking, but I really wanted to say it out loud. "Doctor," I said, "I just can't thank you enough. You and the nurses and the staff and your entire team have been incredible. Thank you for saving my life. And I know we are going to make sure this cancer never comes back."

He was a religious, Orthodox Jew, and he liked to quote Hebrew scripture. But this time he didn't call on any specific verse. He simply said, "From your lips to God's ears."

Later that same day, I was back in the Governor's Reception Room. But as I addressed many of the same reporters, aides, cancer patients, family members, and well-wishers I had faced five months earlier, my message was far cheerier this time. Coming out of cancer is a whole lot sweeter than going in.

Which was strange because I looked and felt so horrible. Each four-day round of twenty-four-hour chemo, each new bag of cancer-killing poison flushed into my arteries, each assault from those outpatient marrow-building drugs—each one of them had torn me down even more. And I was really showing the wear. It was ironic but true: Here I was, about to make this celebratory announcement about my supposed healthfulness, and I looked like I was dying. But good news is good news, regardless of how bad I looked or how bad I felt. I was going to deliver it with all the exuberance it deserved.

"Incredibly," I declared to the cameras and to the world, "as of today, I am one hundred percent cancer-free."

My aides had laid out some of the tens of thousands of get-well cards and letters I'd received since June, when I announced that my body was riddled with dozens of tumors and millions of voracious cancer cells. All those incredible well wishes still put a warm glow over me. Among the family, friends, and supporters who packed the room this time was one of my littlest heroes, cancer survivor Andrew Oberle, who had given me all that sage advice about the pokey and the numb-numb cream and my need to find a hugging person. Andrew's list with all the helpful advice had earned a spot on my desk, right beside the Tim McGraw lyrics. Since that day, Andrew and I had become pen pals, writing each other words of encouragement. In front of everyone, this brave little boy walked right up to the podium while I was talking and gave me the most wonderful hug. He also handed me a new card. On this one, he had scribbled "Way to go Governor Hogan!" He signed it "Your pal, Andrew." I knew I'd find a place on my desk for this card, too.

"I am so incredibly thankful to so many people who have stood by me in the fight," I said, hardly able to contain my emotions. "Such acts of kindness have kept me strong and my spirits high, and they are undoubtedly among the reasons I'm on the road to recovery."

The patients, especially. "It's because of these fellow patients that I will remain committed to raising awareness, encouraging research that will one day lead to a cure for this terrible disease," I said.

I wasn't out of danger yet. I wanted to be completely clear about that. I explained that I would keep getting scans and would immediately begin a course of follow-up treatments that would have its own physical challenges.

I hoped I would soon be feeling better, I said. Who knows, I added, I might even get some of my hair back, though that would turn out to be wishful thinking! Kind of like when I said five months earlier that I'd probably lose some weight!

From mid-June, when I was first diagnosed, until mid-November, when the doctors declared me cancer-free—what a head-spinning ride it had been. Torture in the hospital and more torture when I was out. You've heard the expression "pick your poison"? No sane person would choose either of those, unless together they promised a road back to health. Thank God I'd gotten this far. But even though the cancer was out of my body, clearly I wasn't done yet, not even close.

For me, cancer was not going to be a five-month, in-and-out journey. I had another full year of "preventive maintenance" ahead of me.

It would be a different kind of chemo than I'd been getting before, my doctors explained to me, though undeniably potent in its own unique ways and with a whole new set of side effects. It was all designed to keep those cancer cells from roaring back.

Even as I moved through my next phase of treatment, I didn't want to overlook my progress so far. The cancer was out of my body. We were just trying to keep it out. I took what victory laps I could. I got a nice pre-Christmas present from the presidential campaign trail. My buddy Chris Christie was campaigning in New Hampshire for the Republican nomination. He'd been wearing his lime-green Hogan Strong wristband ever since they first came out, before he'd even formally announced for president. I'd seen it on TV every now and then, when he was in a debate or sitting for an interview. If I looked closely, I could always catch a glimpse of lime green.

The minute he heard my good-health news, he immediately called to congratulate me. "You can finally get rid of that wristband," I told him.

But Christie being Christie, liking to do things his way, had another idea. "I'm not taking it off," he said. "You have to come to New Hampshire and cut it off."

Which is how on Sunday night, December 21, I came to be in Peterborough, New Hampshire, riding with Christie on the second day of his four-day bus tour of the first-in-the-nation primary state. Standing in front of a town hall meeting of New Hampshire voters, I took a pair of scissors and snipped off his no-longer-needed green wristband. "We're in the season where we're counting our blessings," Christie said. I was certainly counting mine.

Like me, Yumi had also gotten deeply attached to the patients. Even though I was out of the hospital, she kept going back to visit some of the kids she had gotten to know. She was so heartbroken when she lost a couple of them. There was a beautiful young girl named Juliana Carver who really touched our hearts. Juliana had been diagnosed with alveolar rhabdomyosarcoma (ARMS) in 2007 when she was five years old. Now almost fourteen, she'd been fighting the disease ever since. Juliana came up to Yumi one day and said, "I heard you're an artist."

"That's true," Yumi answered. "I am an artist."

"I want to be an artist when I grow up," Juliana said.

"Maybe I'll come visit you in the hospital," Yumi told the girl with a smile, "and we can do some art together."

On Yumi's next visit, she brought colored pencils and large pads of paper. She and Juliana sketched together. They met several other times. Tragically, Juliana died. I'm not sure whether their visits could officially be called art therapy, but I will tell you this much: Yumi got as much out of their time together as Juliana could possibly have.

"These kids have such long stays in the hospital," Yumi said to me after returning from one of her visits. "When they are under stress, the art helps them pour their emotions out. It takes their minds off what they are going through."

Out of that relationship with Juliana and the other children came an art therapy organization called Yumi CARES (Children's Art for Recovery, Empowerment, and Strength). Yumi and her friends are raising money to provide professional art therapists, art supplies, and other support for hospitals. Kids are putting their emotions down on paper, which is so much better than keeping everything bottled up inside. The boys and girls, some too young to do it any other way, are expressing feelings they could never express with words.

My sister, Terry, and her entire family came to Maryland to spend Thanksgiving with us. Fresh from my final round of inpatient chemo, I loved having them around. Terry and her husband, Bob, along with their children and grandchildren—they always lifted my spirits whenever we spent time together. During the holidays, everyone seemed fine. But after the first of the year, I got a very worried call from my niece, Becky, who was crying on the phone. Becky told me that her mom didn't seem right. Becky was really concerned. Terry was walking and talking and looked okay—but something was definitely wrong. She was forgetting things she should remember and was sometimes saying things that made no sense. Terry had seen a clip of me on the national news and told her family, "Lar was just here," as if I had been standing in the room with her. That was one of those worrying incidents, which seemed to be getting worse.

It took many visits with different doctors at different hospitals to finally get an answer. I flew down to Charlotte to see her and the family. The diagnosis could hardly have been more troubling. My sister had a rare, degenerative, always-fatal brain disorder called Creutzfeldt-Jakob disease. The United States has only 350 cases a year. Symptoms, which can include memory loss and behavior and vision problems, usually begin around age sixty. Patient lifespan is measured in months, not years. There is not much treatment, and there is no cure. In just a couple of months, my sister went from perfectly fine to frequently confused to totally out of it and needing to be hospitalized. I got a call at the end of February that Terry had taken another turn for the worse. Soon, she was receiving palliative care at a hospice.

Devastating news like that gives life perspective. Compared to what my sister and her family were going through, my battle with lymphoma was suddenly feeling like a walk in the park. Terry, we all understood, had very little time left.

I decided to give a new award—the Governor's Courage Award, we named it—to the Special Olympics athlete who made the biggest impact of the year. I decided I would present the first annual Governor's Courage Award to one of my favorite pals from the hospital, "the mayor," Jimmy Myrick Jr.

I was hoping to do it at the Polar Bear Plunge in January, where thousands of people would be jumping into the frigid waters of the Chesapeake Bay. But it turned out that the normally gung-ho Jimmy wasn't feeling well enough to plunge.

Some of Jimmy's Special Olympics teammates agreed to accept the prize on his behalf. Then I followed up by visiting him in the hospital. He was so excited. He had watched a video of the award presentation. And now Jimmy was getting his plaque directly from his pal, the governor.

Jimmy was also excited because he'd gotten some other good news. "Governor," he told me, "they're gonna let me go home." I could not have been any happier for him.

Jimmy left the hospital, going home on February 1. Almost immediately he got an infection. His weakened immune system wasn't able to fight it. On February 12, 2016, Jimmy died. He was thirty-three. It was a terrible blow. My heart was broken. The world truly was a better place because of Jimmy's big heart and his zest for life.

Hundreds and hundreds of people packed Saint Christopher's Catholic Church in Chester for his funeral. It was an honor that Jimmy's family asked me to speak. Everyone in the church loved Jimmy, and so did I.

I told the story about the way he and I became buddies and how much he'd meant to me as I fought my own cancer battle. And then I said, "We're going to change the name of the Governor's Courage Award. From now on, every year we'll be giving the Jimmy Myrick Jr. Courage Award."

I could see his parents in the front row crying. So were at least half the other people in the church. Jimmy's life will continue to be an inspiration to others.

I had a PET scan on February 29, confirming that my own illness hadn't yet returned. As soon as I said goodbye to my doctors and nurses, I scooped up Yumi, our three daughters, and our granddaughter. We headed straight for Baltimore Washington International Airport and boarded the next flight to Charlotte. Thankfully, we were able to spend some time with Terry, who was in and out of consciousness by then. She wasn't in pain, but it was excruciating seeing my older sister that way. Since my mom had died thirteen years earlier, Terry had been the emotional heart of our family. We stayed with her for four days, before flying back to Maryland, where the Legislature was still in session. Terry died two days later, on March 5. She was sixty-seven.

"My heart is broken," I wrote on my Facebook page. "My only sister passed away this morning. Mary Theresa Lazarus was the best big sister anyone could ever ask for."

We all flew back to North Carolina to be with Terry's family and attend the funeral. The whole family was at Charlotte's Saint Thomas Aquinas Church on March 12. Yumi and our daughters. My dad. My four younger brothers. Everyone's spouses and kids. Without telling me they were coming, four of my young staffers from the governor's office, Kara, Amanda, Kyle McColgan, and Kyle Gilbert, all piled into a car and drove all night to be there with us. That really meant a lot to me.

I'd spoken at funerals for fallen police officers and firefighters, military heroes and former governors. It was always difficult for me because I get so emotional. But giving the eulogy at my own sister's funeral was much, much harder than any of that. I just spoke from the heart. The memories all came rushing forward from our earliest days in Landover Knolls, when watching her made me dream of one day growing up to be a teenager. I was choking up almost from the minute I started talking. I wasn't at all sure I would be able to make it through, especially as I looked out at my niece, Becky, and my nephews, Keith and Kevin, and my brother-in-law Bob.

I loved my sister and looked up to her my entire life. She knew me longer and better than anyone. Losing her wasn't just painful. It was almost hard to grasp. It was terribly difficult for my brother-in-law and my niece and nephews. For me, after losing my mom and now my sister, I truly knew the meaning and the feeling of loss and grief and a broken heart.

Not until the beginning of October 2016, sixteen months after I was first diagnosed, nearly a year since my cancer was declared in remission, would all my treatment, including the preventive-maintenance follow-ups, finally be completed. There'd be days I didn't think it would ever end. Some lasting damage from the chemo will never go away. The doctors will continue to watch me for several more years. I will keep going back for regular PET scans. But what a great feeling it was to finally be told, "That's enough." My prayers had all been answered. Hogan Strong had kept me strong, and along the way we helped raise money for cancer research and raise awareness to help a lot of people.

I posted a photo on Facebook of my final chemo session, me smiling and flexing my arms. "100 percent cancer-free and in complete remission," I wrote proudly. "I could never have made it to this point without the amazing support of my family, friends, and staff, along with an incredible team of doctors and nurses . . . My heart, my thoughts, and my prayers go out to all the other victims of cancer and their families. I plan to make the most of every single day I am given, and I won't stop fighting until a cure is discovered for this terrible disease."

When I returned to the mansion that afternoon, several dozen of our staffers were waiting for me out front. They asked if I'd take care of one lingering piece of personal business, cutting off all the Hogan Strong wristbands they'd been wearing since my treatment began.

"I'd be honored," I told them.

With a small pair of scissors, I went from one person to the next, snipping off every one of them.

"It's been a heck of a year and a half," I told everyone. "I really could not have made it without all of you. Everybody worked so hard and picked up the slack while I was goofing off. The love and support and well wishes from everybody here were incredible."

I was truly fortunate to have a team like these folks looking after the people of Maryland and also watching my back.

I knew exactly how to celebrate.

On Sunday, November 6, I joined more than 20,000 runners at the third annual Across the Bay 10K. The group run, which started on the western side of the Chesapeake Bay Bridge, was designed to highlight the natural beauty of Maryland. People organized teams and raised money for their favorite charities. My assistant Kara had helped organize the Hogan Strong group, supporting lymphoma research.

I wasn't the fastest runner that morning, not by a long shot. But I don't believe there was anyone on that bridge who was any happier to be there. I was alive. I was healthy. I had a whole new appreciation for the amazing life I had. I was helping a cause I cared about. I had on some very cool shades and a black track suit with lime-green lymphoma trim. I was running with people I loved, who had been there for me, and doing it for people who were going through battles just like mine. It didn't matter to me if I was the last one to reach the finish line on the Eastern Shore side of the bridge. Just being in the race was all the prize I could have ever wanted.

Without the support of my family, my staff, my friends, and the endlessly generous people of Maryland, I'm not sure I ever would have made it to this point. And from the time I was first diagnosed, I had one other loving supporter constantly at my side: my dog, Lexi.

That may sound strange, talking about a dog that way. But pet lovers will understand. All my life I'd heard people say that a dog is a man's best friend. Never before had I fully l appreciated how much I counted on Lexi.

Lexi was a frisky little Shih Tzu. For the past sixteen years, she had always been there for me. I'd adopted her in 2000 as a ten-week-old puppy, meaning she'd been in my life slightly longer than Yumi had. Way back then, Lexi was my secret weapon with Yumi's girls. If I had a dog as precious as Lexi—really, how bad a guy could I be? Fifteen years later, when I headed home from my chemo stays at the hospital, Lexi was waiting at the governor's mansion for me, wagging her tail and licking my face.

No dog lives forever, and we all knew that at her age Lexi's time was running out. As 2016 had rolled along, and my cancer battle had too, she'd been creakier on her feet and noticeably slower getting around. We both were. That year, as Christmas neared, it was obvious: Lexi didn't have much time left. We had a full house with all the family. She seemed happy to be with everybody, though she could barely walk by then. She rolled up in a little ball under the Christmas tree, quietly following all the action around her. Everyone got the chance to say goodbye.

We all knew this was our last time with Lexi. And I think she could tell it was her last time with all of us. She died in my arms two days after Christmas. We weren't sure if we would ever have a dog again.

PART V

UNITING

CHAPTER 26

DONALD WHO?

When Donald Trump rode the golden escalator down into the Trump Tower lobby on June 16, 2015, and announced he was running for president, I didn't pay much attention. I was five months into my term as governor of Maryland. I'd weathered the Baltimore riots and the state's Democratic Legislature. Two weeks earlier, I'd found that lump in my throat during my trade mission in Tokyo. It was a couple of days after Trump's announcement that the doctors shocked me with the news that I had those forty to fifty cancerous tumors.

So, when the New York real-estate developer and reality-TV host declared he might like to run the country—well, let's just say I had other things on my mind. Frankly, at the time, most people thought Trump's candidacy was a publicity stunt to help him negotiate a more lucrative contract for *The Apprentice*. It wasn't that I thought a political outsider from the real-estate industry had no business running for office. We had mirrors in the governor's mansion, didn't we? It was just that no one believed Trump's candidacy was serious. The media didn't. The political pros didn't. I didn't. And let's not forget, at that point neither did Trump.

On July 15, weakened from chemotherapy and watching my hair already starting to fall out, I endorsed Chris Christie for president. It wasn't just out of loyalty because he had supported me. I genuinely liked and respected him. He was smart. He was tough. He was experienced. Like me, he was a right-of-center Republican governor of a Democratic northeastern state who knew how to get things done. There were a bunch of talented candidates in the race, but Christie was the one who clearly deserved my support.

In the months that followed, Trump's campaign continued to surprise just about everyone. He was the only one the media focused on. He rose in the polls. He dominated the early debates. His catchy slogans seemed to strike a chord with certain people: "Build the Wall!" "Who's going to pay for it? Mexico!" "Lock her up!" The insulting nicknames took on lives of their own: "Pocahontas!" "Little Marco!" "Low-Energy Jeb!" "Crooked Hillary!" "Lyin' Ted!" One by one, the sixteen other more qualified Republican candidates were pushed aside by the celebrity billionaire from New York. After finishing second in the Iowa caucuses to Cruz, Trump romped in New Hampshire, winning the February 9 Republican primary by 20 percentage points. I was with my friend Christie that night in New Hampshire. He dropped out of the race the next day.

Two weeks later, Christie left a phone message, asking me to call him in Fort Worth, Texas. When he didn't hear back from me right away, he left a second message: "Want to talk to you about Trump. The sooner, the better." I was tied up in meetings and didn't have a chance to call him back immediately. Half an hour later, I heard the announcement that shook the presidential campaign: The New Jersey governor had just become the first major Republican officeholder to endorse Donald Trump.

To nearly everyone's disbelief, Trump was now roaring toward the Republican nomination. Of course, the reporters in Maryland would start asking me about Trump. The truth was I didn't like anything I was seeing on the presidential campaign trail on either side. Nine months from election day, the campaign was already so mean-spirited, so bitter, so unrelentingly personal that it was hard to see how this tortured process was ever going to produce the kind of leadership that America really needed.

"I am completely disgusted with national politics in both parties, Democrat and Republican," I said on March 8 when the reporters asked if I'd be following my friend Christie onto the Trump campaign. "I'm not paying much attention. I'm trying to focus here in Maryland."

All that was true, and it really was how I felt. I didn't like what I was seeing, and I didn't want to get dragged into any of it. I wanted to do the job I had been elected to do and stay as far away as I could from the divisive politics of Washington, even if the nation's capital was just a short drive west on Route 50. And if Trump really was going to be my party's nominee? Well, that would bring up some issues I would have to confront eventually, the main one being, Was I going to give him my support? I was a lifelong Republican. And Trump was now a Republican too, after a lifetime of supporting mostly Democrats and being registered as both a Democrat and an independent. But we were very different kinds of Republicans. I had worked passionately for Ronald Reagan in 1980 and 1984. Trump had supported Jimmy Carter in 1980 and Walter Mondale in 1984, and had even published full-page newspaper ads in the *New York Times* in 1987 attacking Reagan for being too hard on the communist Soviet Union. When I ran for governor, my platform focused on ending the angry rhetoric and divisive politics. My entire term in office was about bringing people together to find bipartisan, common-sense solutions. Yes, Trump and I were both outsiders who wanted change. We were both fed up with Washington and politics as usual. But we could not have been any more opposite in our approaches. Trump was using inflammatory, angry rhetoric to divide the country. Because people were so frustrated and angry with Washington, that strategy seemed to be working for him.

"I'm not a Trump fan," I told an AP reporter on March 24. "I don't think he should be the nominee. At this point in time, I have no idea who the candidates are going to be or who I'm going to vote for . . . It's a mess. I hate the whole thing." Of course, that quote got some pickup, a Republican governor talking like that about the Republican front-runner for president.

I wasn't exactly sure yet how I was going to handle all this. As far as I was concerned, Hillary Clinton was the last person who should be elected president. Honestly, it seemed to me that both parties were about to choose unacceptable nominees. I knew this much already: I was nowhere close to endorsing Donald Trump.

In late March, Princeton University was playing the Naval Academy in baseball. Christie and his wife, Mary Pat, came down to Annapolis to watch their son Andrew, who was the starting catcher on the Princeton team. The family came by the governor's mansion for brunch.

"Donald wasn't too happy about you," Christie said after we'd been sitting around a while. "He called me. He said, 'What the hell is up with your boy Hogan?'"

As Christie recounted the call, he tried to explain in terms that Trump would understand. "'Look, Donald,'" Christie recalled saying about me, "'he's a freshman governor in one of the bluest states in America, where you are not too popular. If you ask me, he's probably doing exactly what he should do.'"

"'Okay, I guess that makes sense,'" Christie said Trump told him. I guess to Trump, the business guy, my lack of support must have seemed like a reasonable business decision.

I was eager to know how Christie was feeling about all this. He'd gotten some grief in the media for his half-hour blank stare after Trump won four of the five primaries on Super Tuesday. Some people even likened Christie's press-conference demeanor to someone in a hostage video. "You're getting blown up over your press event with him," I said. "Chris, I just don't understand. Why did you do it?"

"He's not so bad," Christie said with a laugh. "One-on-one, he's a much different person than he is onstage. That's just the persona of Trump. You'd really like him."

"I don't know about that," I said.

"Look," Christie said. "Do I think he's the best-prepared candidate ever to be president? No. Do I think I would have been a better candidate? Yes, that's why I ran. But you and I both know that Hillary should not be president. So I think I should do everything I can to help make Donald a better candidate."

"You probably can make him a better candidate," I told Christie.

Trump kept winning. Though Cruz grabbed four of the seven primaries in late March and early April, Trump got more delegates. When the Maryland primary came around on April 26, I didn't endorse anyone. I couldn't find anyone I wanted to endorse, and I didn't vote for Trump in the primary either. He certainly didn't need me. That day, he got 55 percent of the Republican vote in Maryland and easily won the other four states—Connecticut, Delaware, Pennsylvania, and Rhode Island—in the so-called Acela Primary. At that point, there was no catching Trump.

Asked again and again in a press conference on April 29 about the presidential campaign, I gave the same answer I had been giving.

"I said I was not going to get involved, and I would not endorse any candidate and that I was going to stay focused on Maryland," I told the reporters. It seemed to me like they had completely lost interest in any issues having to do with Maryland or my job as governor or anything the administration might be doing. Uncharacteristically annoyed, I ended the press conference with, "Does anyone have anything to ask other than Trump?"

The media weren't the only ones trying to bait me on Donald Trump. The Democratic Party came at me with all guns blazing, seeing a chance to link a highly popular Republican governor with the locally unpopular Republican presidential candidate. Democratic congressman John Delaney, who was then angling to run against me in 2018, pulled a juvenile stunt in Annapolis to get some attention at my expense. He hired a mobile billboard to drive in circles around the State House. On one side of the truck there was a huge unflattering photo of Trump and the question "GOV. HOGAN: WILL YOU SUPPORT TRUMP AS THE REPUBLICAN NOMINEE?" And if you happened to catch a glimpse from the passenger side, you'd have seen that same blowup of Trump's mug and the message "SILENCE IS AN ENDORSEMENT," with the signature line: "Because everyone in Maryland will lose if Trump wins—Congressman John Delaney."

I just ignored Delaney, and he went away soon enough, eventually launching a hopeless campaign for president in 2020 after his pollsters told him he had no chance of beating me in 2018. In early May, the Democratic Governors Association tagged me as one of the "Silent 9" Republican governors who'd been insufficiently vociferous in their disavowals of Trump. The politics of this were obvious enough. My opponents figured that, wherever I came down, this was a loser for me. If I backed Trump, I'd be aligning myself with a figure who was polling in Maryland at 29 percent. And if I did not support Trump, I'd be alienating some of the hard-core Republican base voters who had supported me from the start. Either way, the Democratic operatives figured, I would damage my political standing in Maryland and hurt my chances of being re-elected in 2018.

After Trump won the Indiana primary on May 3, the Republican race was essentially over. John Kasich and Ted Cruz both ended their presidential runs. The bombastic New York real-estate developer became the party's presumptive nominee.

I was already sick of being asked all the time to comment on whatever Trump said or tweeted, which was usually something mean-spirited, insulting, or outrageous. "My thoughts are pretty clear," I told the State House reporters on June 9. "I've talked about it ad nauseam for four or five months. My thoughts haven't changed. I have nothing more to add."

When WJZ political reporter Pat Warren pressed me about the Trump campaign, I told her the same thing: "I'm not involved in it. I don't care to be involved in it. I'm not going to endorse anyone and would rather focus on things here in Maryland."

But did I think Trump was fit to be president? "Well," I said, "I just said I'm not going to talk about Donald Trump anymore. I have nothing to do with Donald Trump."

On June 14, when he renewed his call to ban Muslim immigrants after a mass shooting in Orlando, I said, "I don't know what his position is. I don't care about Donald Trump. I don't listen to Donald Trump."

What else could I say about Donald Trump?

I didn't like his kind of politics, in substance or in style. I wouldn't be campaigning for him. I had no plans to attend his coronation at the Republican National Convention, which was set for July 18 to July 21 in Cleveland. But would I vote for him in November? I had never been asked that question, not in so many words, as I was barraged by reporters almost daily over the past few months. By June, I could feel that final question closing in.

I knew that whatever I said, it was going to make a lot of people angry. I'd already been getting hostile Facebook messages from Democrats demanding I strongly attack Trump and from Republicans demanding I endorse "our" candidate. I was keenly aware of the potential conflict between personal values and party loyalty. And I also knew the price that conflict could entail. My mind raced back to the Watergate summer of 1974 when I was eighteen and my father faced a similar defining choice of his own.

Was I the independent, bipartisan leader many Marylanders thought they had elected? Was I my father's son? Was I the kind of person who could make the difficult choice, even if it carried real risk for my political future?

"Will you support Donald Trump?" I was asked by a reporter at a press gaggle outside Prince George's County Community College on June 15.

"No," I said.

"No?"

"No," I said emphatically.

"If he puts Chris Christie on the ticket?"

"I've said it over and over and over again. I'm not a supporter of Donald Trump. I'm not gonna endorse Donald Trump. I'm not gonna get involved in the campaign. I'm not gonna go to the convention."

"What about voting for him in November?" a reporter finally asked for the first time.

"No, I don't plan to," I said.

It was the "no" heard everywhere.

So who would I vote for then? Hillary? No, not her either. "I guess when

I get behind the curtain, I'll have to figure it out," I said. "Maybe I'll write someone in."

Now, there was an idea I could get my head around. If only I could think of the right person, a write-in candidate of decency and integrity. Someone who believed in reaching out and welcoming people in. Someone with a common-sense attitude and hard-earned experience. Someone who was more my kind of Republican.

CHAPTER 27

ACTUALLY GOVERNING

One of the redeeming facts of American life is that no matter what craziness is happening on the national political scene, things are still getting done in our nation's state capitals. State governments, even the most dysfunctional ones, have urgent jobs to do. Our children need to be educated. Public safety needs to be preserved. Vulnerable citizens need to be cared for. Floods, tornadoes, and hurricanes need to be responded to. Highways need to be prepared. These are not abstract responsibilities. They are crucial to the day-to-day operation of modern society and real people's lives. If the work of state government isn't accomplished, people suffer and politicians get tossed out.

Which is one of the reasons that governors, no matter their party or their ideology, are usually more pragmatic and more effective than senators and congressmen. Governors can't just argue in committee hearings and make fiery speeches pandering to narrow special-interest groups. To govern effectively, especially in states with divided government like mine, the governors depend on the power of compromise. I'm the CEO of a $46 billion operation with 60,000 employees. I can't just argue. I actually have to govern.

Tragically, in Washington, DC, in recent years, common-sense governing seems to have completely broken down. Both parties are to blame. And look where it's left us—with acrimony, gridlock, and a complete inability to solve the biggest problems facing the nation.

Contrast that with Maryland. As the country was becoming more divided and Washington even more dysfunctional, we were taking care of important business for the people of our state. As a Republican in charge of the state with veto-proof Democratic majorities in both the House and the Senate, I managed to get things done. Our administration had a long list of agenda items for our sophomore year—some hugely complex, some quite straightforward. And we were accomplishing them, even as I continued with my grueling outpatient chemo treatments.

One proud achievement was working with the Legislature to produce what became the Justice Reinvestment Act of 2016, one of the most comprehensive overhauls of any state's criminal-justice system. We cut Maryland's prison population more than any state in America, promoted a more rational system of punishment and rehabilitation, and delivered a whole new range of services to crime victims, all while saving the taxpayers a ton of money.

These were practical steps, supported by liberals and conservatives alike. Encouraging treatment over incarceration for nonviolent drug offenders. Reducing the maximum sentences on some less serious crimes. Changing how the state handled parolees, separating the technical violations from the more serious abuses. Some of these changes might sound arcane to outsiders, but they had real impact. Here's one example anyone could get behind: The new system dealt more intelligently—on a case-by-case basis—with elderly and severely ill inmates. Too many of the state's prisons were starting to look like nursing homes or hospital wards. And that was hugely expensive. Freeing up these resources allowed us to focus on the genuinely dangerous criminals who actually threatened the public.

This was long before Kim and Kanye met with Donald Trump in the

Oval Office to push for prison reform, long before Trump's "First Step" program brought similar changes on the federal level. I'd like to think we helped spark some of that.

Our Justice Reinvestment Act required real give-and-take with the Legislature. But many important improvements I could make on my own by taking executive action. In June, we launched a statewide Customer Service Initiative to help residents and businesses dealing with all state agencies. The improvements included better customer-service training for state workers and proven, business-tested methods for measuring how well our employees performed. When people contact state agencies, whether they're renewing a driver's license, applying for getting any kind of permit, or seeking assistance with a problem, they have a right to a prompt, friendly, helpful response. "Marylanders expect the best possible customer service from their state government, and that is exactly what they deserve," I said when we launched the initiative.

One of the most encouraging aspects of the Customer Service Initiative was how enthusiastically most state workers jumped in. The vast majority are dedicated civil servants and really want to serve the public effectively. They just needed the right leadership and encouragement.

And then I rallied to the defense of summer vacation.

Really.

On a picture-perfect summer day—sunny, mid-eighties, low humidity—I headed out to the boardwalk in Ocean City and issued an executive order directing all public schools in Maryland to quit starting classes before Labor Day. For years, school districts voted to bring students back earlier and earlier, chipping away at the traditional summer break. The school year would remain the same 180 days it had always been, but school boards had been stretching out the school year over more months. An overwhelming majority of parents and teachers and nearly all kids hated that.

The September school start, I said that day on the boardwalk, would be a benefit "not only for families on vacation this week but also for the teachers and the students working here in Ocean City." State Comptroller Peter Franchot, a Democrat, stood at my side in the sunshine and pointed out the genuine economic benefits. One study calculated that a post–Labor Day start would pump $74 million a year into the state's economy.

I got some predictable grumbling from a few county school-board members who said I was usurping their scheduling authority. Some of the more partisan legislators denounced me, even though most of them had voted shortly before I took office to support the September start, back when they thought a Democratic governor would get the credit. The chance to do something like this—to make a stand that improves people's lives, even a little—is one of the true pleasures of being governor. And everywhere I went after that, parents and students came up to me to say, "Thanks for letting summer be summer."

———————

As the national Republicans gathered in Cleveland to nominate Donald Trump as their 2016 candidate for president, I was 516 miles away drinking beer, eating crabs, and catching up with thousands of Marylanders at the fortieth annual J. Millard Tawes Crab and Clam Bake in the Eastern Shore town of Crisfield. It's a big thing here in Maryland. That was where I belonged and where I preferred to be.

"The people of Maryland elected me to be their governor," I explained that day. "I don't have any obligation to play politics in Cleveland."

The seafood festival, which takes its name from a late Maryland governor, is always a down-home, grassroots kind of event. I'd been attending for decades, though I had to skip the previous year because I was getting chemo.

"This is way better than sitting in the hospital," I said as I sampled the steamed crabs, fried clams, corn on the cob, and juicy red slices of watermelon.

As the Republican conventioneers pretended to be enthusiastic about Trump, I wasn't only munching seafood and sipping cold beer, I was also doing my day job. I announced the innovative Congestion Management Project, a long-awaited plan to ease the constant backups on Interstate 270 in Montgomery County and several other especially traffic-clogged roads.

"There's a convention?" I joked as I stood on the side of that unintentional parking lot in Bethesda. "I'm focused on Maryland like I said I would be. I have no interest in the convention. That's why I'm not there."

Any Maryland driver knows what a traffic nightmare this stretch can be. I said we'd earmarked $560 million for the improvements, $230 million of it targeted to I-270. On weekday mornings, more than 250,000 vehicles travel that stretch of interstate near the Capital Beltway. "This highway is simply not equipped to handle that kind of volume," I said.

But this would not be a typical road construction project. The issues this time were too big for that. We needed fresh thinking. "We are calling on the most creative minds in the transportation industry to step forward as we continue our investment in critical infrastructure projects."

And if we don't get the brilliant ideas we're hoping for?

"We are not going to award the contract," Maryland Transportation Secretary Pete Rahn jumped in to add.

———————————

I had already said I wasn't voting for Donald Trump, and I certainly would never vote for Hillary Clinton. The Maryland vote was a foregone conclusion. With Maryland so solidly Democratic, my vote wasn't going to make any difference in the outcome of the presidential race. But maybe I could still make my choice mean something.

On October 28, I went to the Pip Moyer Recreation Center on Hilltop Lane in Annapolis, one of the seven early-voting locations in Anne Arundel County. I signed the register and walked up to the booth. Then, as promised, instead of voting for any of the listed candidates, I wrote in a different name.

I wrote in the name of my eighty-eight-year-old father: Lawrence J. Hogan Sr.

I'd never voted for a write-in before in my life. But I liked the symbolism, skipping two candidates I considered unacceptable and choosing someone honorable and decent who stood for something I believed in. A man who had demonstrated to the world, in the darkest days of Watergate, how to put the national interest in front of party loyalty and had paid a personal price.

The reporters had been asking since the summer who I was planning to vote for. Until I actually did it, I didn't tell anyone. But that afternoon, Doug Mayer put out a statement that summed up exactly how I felt: "As he has said for many months, the governor is extremely disappointed in the candidates from both major parties and decided to write in the name of the person who taught him what it meant to hold public office with integrity, his father, Larry Hogan Sr."

I understood that my ballot wouldn't have any practical impact. I wasn't expecting any election-day groundswells for my dad. In Maryland, votes for unofficial write-in candidates aren't even counted individually. They go into a pile marked "other" at the state board of elections. But I was okay with all of that. I was proud of my vote.

I wasn't the only Republican politician who skipped Trump and Clinton. My friend Charlie Baker, the governor of Massachusetts, told reporters in Boston that for the first time in his life, he had left his presidential ballot blank. Former president George W. Bush and his wife, Laura, said they didn't vote for either of the major-party nominees. Mitt Romney wrote in the name of his wife, Ann. John Kasich wrote in John McCain.

CHAPTER 28

EVERYTHING CHANGED

Donald Trump didn't need Maryland to get elected president, which was fortunate for him since he got walloped so badly in our state. When the votes in our state were counted, the New York billionaire walked away with a paltry 34 percent. Hillary Clinton got 60 percent and all of the state's ten electoral votes. As far as I know, my dad's final vote tally remained at one. Maryland was definitely not Trump Country. But on election night, as the final states reported and Trump moved past Clinton in the electoral college, I said to Russ, Doug, Ron, and the rest of my political team something that might have sounded overly dramatic at the time: "Life as we know it has changed."

It was even truer than I realized.

While Trump was running for president, he'd been a factor I needed to manage, but more of a distracting sideshow than a daily reality. But now that

Trump had actually won and was going to be the president, that distraction would multiply tenfold. It was something about which I would always need to be mindful. Every day in every way, I'd have to work that much harder just to keep those around me focused on Maryland.

Never mind that I hadn't supported him. Never mind that our politics and our temperaments couldn't have been any more different. As far as the media and my opponents were concerned, almost everything I did or said in Maryland suddenly had to be seen through the distorted filter of Donald Trump.

With the incoming president consuming so much of the newsprint and the airtime, it was far harder to talk about the issues that really affected Maryland. It was definitely more of a struggle keeping people focused on our own agenda. At every single press conference, reporters were repeatedly grilling me about the latest eruptions from Trump-land.

What about the Women's Marches the day after the inauguration? What about the travel-ban protests at airports across the United States? What about the latest crude, insensitive, or racially taunting tweet? It was always something with this guy, and for some reason the media believed I was required to weigh in on all of it. Given who Trump was, there was an endless supply of inane and disruptive outbursts. A man who ran as provocative a campaign as he did wasn't going to be a typical president.

I knew this much: If I spent all day reacting to his tweets, I'd have very little time to work on my real job, getting things done for Maryland.

There was something else I knew, something that was hard not to take personally: In a state that Hillary Clinton had just won by 26 points, my re-election as governor was beginning to look like a very steep climb. The Trump squeeze—and that's exactly what it felt like, a squeeze—was politically painful for me. The coalition that elected me included lots of Democrats and independents along with Republicans. It was that broad bipartisan support that was keeping my poll numbers up in the 70s, some 40 to 50 points higher than Trump's. I had managed to get through my first two years in office battling overwhelming odds, taking on a political monopoly and getting things accomplished that no one believed were possible. For most of the past year, my achievements had been complicated by the Trump campaign. But I had been able to ignore that, stay on message, and continue to get things done. Now, with Trump as president, I could no longer ignore the guy. His polarizing actions in office could destroy any chance I had as a Republican of winning re-election in 2018.

I knew what was coming. Democratic operatives in Annapolis and Washington, DC, would do everything they could to tie the unpopular Trump around my neck like an albatross. That's how the politics of division get played these days, and there was little I could do to stop it, no matter how much I hated those divisive tactics on either side. I wouldn't attack Trump personally, but I would speak up clearly when I strongly disagreed or when something directly impacted the people of Maryland. Otherwise, I'd refuse to take the bait.

This is exactly the path I followed. In my State of the State address on February 1, I didn't mention the name Donald Trump a single time. Instead, I called on the Legislature to create tax credits to boost manufacturing jobs, and to forcefully confront the growing scourge of opioid addiction. I called on Republicans and Democrats in the Legislature to join me in these efforts, though some of the Democrats seemed highly resistant to cooperating with the governor from "the party of Trump," as they were now referring to me.

"We have not been defined by party or ideology but by our common purpose and our united obligation to solve problems, to make progress, and to bring real and lasting change to Maryland," I said that day to the joint session of the state senate and House of Delegates. "We have already accomplished a great deal. But together, we can and we must do more."

We weren't hearing much talk like that from anyone down the road in Washington.

Instead of arguing about Trump, I just wanted to keep the momentum going in Maryland. In the two years before Trump became president, we had cut our unemployment rate nearly in half. We now had more businesses open than at any other time in state history. We had gone from forty-ninth to the top ten states in economic performance. We were the biggest economic turnaround in America. And I was laser-focused on keeping that progress going.

———————

Though Donald Trump had been a factor in my life for at least a year by then, I had never met the man or anyone else in his family. That was about to change.

On February 26, 2017, after Trump had been in office for a little more than a month, the new president and First Lady Melania Trump were hosting the annual Governors' Dinner in the East Room of the White House. Forty-six of the nation's governors were expected. I was certainly wondering how that would go. Before the big event, I spoke to Christie at the Republican Governors Association.

"You should be ready tonight," he warned me. "When you are with Donald, there is a good chance he's gonna bust your balls."

"Well, that wouldn't surprise me," I said. "But I think I can take it."

"Just be yourself and give it right back to him," Christie said. "He respects that."

"You know me, Chris," I told him. "What else would I do?"

So, when Yumi and I went through the receiving line, I was fully prepared to get a load of grief from the president. I knew how prickly Trump could be to anyone who wasn't 100 percent supportive. I knew that in Trump's eyes I could easily get labeled an enemy.

He and Melania were standing side by side at the head of the line in the elegant reception room, saying hello to the various governors and their spouses, when Yumi and I made our way up.

"Mr. President," I said as the White House photographer started snapping pictures. "It's an honor to meet you."

"Are you kidding me?" Trump roared out. "It's an honor to meet *you*. I can't believe how popular you are in that blue state of yours."

What was *this*? Trump was being *really nice to me*!

He turned to Melania. "Honey," he said, "do you know how bad I lost in Maryland? I got, like, 35 percent of the vote."

Thirty-four, actually. But who's quibbling?

"And this guy?" Trump went on, motioning at me. "They love him. His approval rating is seventy-something. Incredible!"

It almost seemed like begrudging respect. Trump had been a reality TV star. He appreciated blockbuster ratings. One thing was for sure: He pays close attention to popularity polls.

But if I was expecting some tension at the White House dinner, the evening didn't entirely disappoint. That's where Jared Kushner came in. At one point, I was having a lovely conversation with Ivanka Trump. The president's daughter was even more beautiful in person than on TV. Smart and charming. She could not have been any more friendly. I told her we had good friends in common, the Cordish family. David Cordish is a wealthy investor and developer from Baltimore whose holdings include the Live! Casino & Hotel in Arundel Mills near BWI Airport. David's son Reed, a former Princeton tennis player now in the family business, had married Ivanka's best friend.

The Trump and Cordish families had known each other for more than a decade. Donald Trump had sued David Cordish for hundreds of millions of dollars in 2004 in a casino dispute. But they settled their lawsuit, and the former litigants became fast friends. The way I heard the story, David was lamenting to Ivanka that he wanted his son Reed to meet a nice girl and settle down. Ivanka suggested a fix-up with her friend Maggie Katz, who was newly single. To tighten the circle even more, Reed Cordish had just gone to work at the White House as assistant to the president for intergovernmental and technology initiatives, working closely with Jared Kushner.

Small world, huh?

"Jared," Ivanka called to her husband in her distinctive, soft voice. "Come over and meet Governor Hogan."

He walked up and shot me one of the coldest stares I've ever received. "Uh, yes," he said. And then: "I know who Governor Hogan is."

I ignored the chilly greeting. "Jared," I said, "I was just telling Ivanka that I'm friends with the Cordish family."

"Yes, I know," he answered flatly. "They told me that you did not support my father-in-law in the primary."

"Jared, I was strongly supporting Chris Christie in the primary," I said. I could see Jared cringe upon hearing that. "But just to be honest, I didn't support your father-in-law in the general, either."

I told him that I wanted the president and his administration to be successful but that I was staying focused on my job as governor. "Unlike most of the people in the cabinet and on the president's staff, you won't hear me personally attacking the president."

Ivanka continued to be delightful. But those last words didn't matter. Jared and I were pretty much done.

The next morning, Chris Christie wanted a report on how things went with Trump at the White House. "Did he rough you up?" Christie asked.

Not at all, I assured him. "The president was pretty nice. He was impressed with my poll numbers."

I was already aware of Christie's own run-ins with Jared Kushner and the Kushner family. As the United States attorney in New Jersey, Christie had sent Jared's father, Charles Kushner, to prison for tax evasion and campaign-finance corruption. Jared had recently gotten revenge by having Christie booted from the Trump transition, which Christie had chaired. Jared seemed to be blocking the New Jersey governor from key White House appointments. By this point, the hard feelings definitely ran both ways.

"I think you might be right about Jared," I told Christie. "That's one more thing you and I have in common. He apparently can't stand me either."

On Easter Sunday, 2017, my brother Tim took my dad to lunch on the water, enjoying soft-shell crabs. They had a long, lazy afternoon. Then, Dad came to the mansion and had dinner with Yumi and me. Ever the big eater, he asked for a second dessert. Then the three of us retreated to the man cave in the basement.

My dad settled into the leather recliner. Yumi was next to me on the couch. As always, she made sure my father's wine glass was full. As we chatted, CNN was on in the background. A report came on mentioning the late North Korean dictator, Kim Jong-il. "You know," my eighty-eight-year-old father said, "I met with him when I was in Pyongyang."

My father started telling the story. How not too many Americans got to go to North Korea. How he traveled there with a delegation of former members of Congress. He talked about how tightly the government controlled everything. How the entire visit was staged like an intricate show. It was a vintage Larry Hogan Sr. story: funny, opinionated, a little larger than life.

"They had people singing and dancing for us," Dad said. "Everybody looked happy. They had actors going by in boats on the lake with smiles on their faces. But we wanted to talk to real people. So we tried to sneak out at night, but they tracked us down and dragged us back. They had government watchers following us wherever we went."

"Where did you stay?" I asked my father.

"They put us up at—"

He started to answer, but he just stopped mid-sentence.

"Dad?" I said.

He was looking right at me, but he wasn't saying anything.

"Dad?" I asked. "Are you okay?"

I glanced at Yumi. She looked alarmed. I got up and went over to his chair. "Dad, are you all right?"

He was slumped in the recliner, unable to move, unable to talk, with a stricken look of terror in his eyes.

I ran down the hall to where the state troopers were. They called 911 and rushed back to the man cave with me. Within a minute or so, the Annapolis paramedics were there, struggling to lift my dad onto a gurney. Big as he was, it wasn't easy. I could tell he was trying to talk, but nothing was coming out.

The paramedics rushed my dad to the hospital, where the doctors quickly determined that he'd had a massive stroke. My brothers got there soon after with my stepmother, Ilona. We were with him in the emergency room most of the night.

The doctors ran every test imaginable. They had no encouragement to offer us.

The oldest of my four brothers, Matt, was getting married in Costa Rica the following weekend. And we were all looking forward to being there, including my dad and Ilona. Now, with Dad in the intensive-care unit, the plans were a big question mark. It was too late to cancel the wedding. "You guys all go," I said to Ilona and my brothers. "I'll stay here with him."

Dad died on Thursday, April 20, four days after the stroke. We had the funeral on April 29 in Annapolis when everyone was back from the wedding.

Saint Mary's Church, a couple of blocks from the State House, was completely packed. Four governors came. So did plenty of other political people, past and present, Republicans and Democrats, including Congressman Steny Hoyer, whom I'd almost beaten and who still held my father's old seat. Chris Christie came down. My dad had touched a lot of people, that was clear. Archbishop William Lori said the Mass. I delivered the eulogy.

I told the story of my father's role in Watergate, what that meant for the country and what it meant for my dad. "It was his defining moment," I said from the altar of the ornate Catholic church. "It is that very moment in history which he is most remembered and most admired for." I told about his early days, his service in the FBI, his surprising run for office, and his dream of seeing his name on the governor's office door—a dream he'd realized in an unexpected way forty years later.

Just like my mom, Dad had gone out on a high note, having lunch with one son and dinner with another. He was in the governor's mansion, where he knew he belonged, holding a wine glass and telling a story, surrounded by family, when he ran out of time.

"Larry Hogan Sr. was my hero and the man that I am most proud of," I told the mourners that day. "He stood up and fought, even when the odds were stacked against him. He spent his entire life fighting valiantly for the things he believed in, and that, I believe, will forever be his legacy."

CHAPTER 29

TOUGH SELL

You get to do a lot of fun things when you're the governor, and I don't just mean the predictable ones—living in the mansion, attending White House dinners, and skipping the TSA lines at the airport. Since I took office, I've gotten to hang with the greatest Ravens, Redskins, and Orioles. I've gone backstage to meet some of my favorite country artists. I presented the title belts to three world boxing champs at the MGM National Harbor—and the Woodlawn Vase to Triple Crown winner American Pharoah at Pimlico after the Preakness. I even got to dance and sing a duet of Patsy Cline's "Crazy" onstage in Salt Lake City with Marie Osmond. As I told Seth Meyers when I appeared on *Late Night*—yes, I did that, too—I was hoping that last one might lead to a lucrative Nutrisystem endorsement deal!

On Memorial Day weekend of 2017, I was asked to be the honorary starter at NASCAR's fifty-eighth annual Coca-Cola 600 at Charlotte Motor Speedway. I wasn't quite sure what all my responsibilities would be, but I knew that waving the flag to start the race before 100,000 people and a national TV audience would be pretty cool. Sharing the honors that day as the grand marshal was actor Channing Tatum. Female fans may remember Channing from his role as a stripper in *Magic Mike*. He was promoting his latest film, *Logan Lucky*, where he played a guy plotting to rob the Charlotte race track.

The night before the race, Channing and I were speaking at the NASCAR Hall of Fame. "I know some of you may be wondering why the Maryland governor is the official starter of tomorrow's big race," I said to the crowd of race crews and sponsors. "Well, NASCAR has really been making an effort to attract more women fans. Which is why they recruited Channing Tatum to be the grand marshal. But to tell you the truth, it wasn't working as well as they had expected. That's when they decided they needed to reach out to me for reinforcement."

The crowd loved it. All of the women in the room were laughing, frankly a little too hard, I thought. So was "Magic Mike," who said, "Thanks for the help, Governor," as he shot a glance at the heavy-set, nearly bald, middle-aged man with whom he was sharing the stage. "I really appreciate you backing me up."

But I couldn't spend every weekend dancing with Marie or hitting all the races on the NASCAR circuit. I had my own important race to run. We'd achieved the impossible four years earlier: an underfunded, barely known Republican businessman winning a governor's race in deepest-blue Maryland, pulling off the upset of the year. But now I was a successful incumbent. Surely, if we did it once, we could do it again.

Couldn't we?

"It will be an uphill battle," my new campaign manager, Jim Barnett, said to me as we began making plans for my 2018 re-election campaign. "There is less than a fifty-fifty chance we can win."

And that was coming from *my own campaign manager*!

He wasn't alone in his negative assessment. Doug Mayer, Russ Schriefer, Steve Crim, and Ron Gunzburger, my senior advisor for the past four years, weren't quite as negative—but almost. It wasn't impossible, they agreed, but everything would have to go just right. And that hardly ever happens in politics.

At first, this deluge of pessimism didn't make sense to me. I felt like we had everything going for us. Sure, Maryland was a tough Democratic state. But I had all the advantages of incumbency. Raising money is never easy, but this time I knew as an incumbent I could raise boatloads of it. Our team had done a great job. I had a record worth bragging about. We'd been getting national attention lately for turning the state around. I'd quelled the Baltimore riots and beaten late-stage lymphoma. We'd cut more than 850 regulations. We'd slashed tolls at every single facility across the state. We had the biggest economic turnaround in America. We'd repealed the damn rain tax. The Democrats in the Legislature were still taking shots at me, but they'd ended up supporting a big chunk of my agenda.

And then there were my job-approval numbers. They were still up in the stratosphere, higher than any other governor in Maryland history and higher than any governor in America with the exception of my friend Massachusetts governor Charlie Baker. Since I'd been in office, my job-approval rating had gone from 57 percent to 63 percent to 68 percent to 70 percent. The pollsters kept saying, "It can't go any higher." Then, it would jump again. At the start of the re-election campaign, that key measure was up in the thin atmosphere at 73 percent.

I mean, really. With numbers like those, how hard could it be to win a second term?

Very, very hard, the smart people around me all seemed to agree.

First of all, only one Republican governor had ever been re-elected in the history of the state. No one had done it since Theodore McKeldin in 1954. My old pal Bob Ehrlich had learned that lesson the hard way, getting beaten *twice*—in 2006 and 2010—after his surprise victory in 2002. And what insightful lesson did the one-term Republican governor take from his two subsequent drubbings by Democrat Martin O'Malley? It had nothing to do with any mistakes or limitations of his own. Ehrlich concluded that no Republican candidate, no matter how smart or how driven, could ever again be elected to statewide office in Maryland. For Republicans, he said, the state had simply become unwinnable.

As the re-election campaign began to take shape in late 2017, I was being eyed by the state's political pundits as the next Ehrlich, lucky to win once, highly unlikely to do it again. In their view, my victory four years earlier was a fluke, a result of low Democratic turnout, a lackluster opponent in Anthony

Brown, and an unpopular sitting governor in Martin O'Malley. Not too many people seemed to think electoral lightning was going to strike again, however high-flying my poll numbers might be. Maryland was still Maryland, and this time I would have no O'Malley to kick around. The Democrats would do everything they could to wrestle power back from the Republican interloper. Really, all the Democrats had to do, the professionals agreed, was turn out the vote and keep saying one word: "Trump."

As we sought to continue the transformation of Maryland, the man in the White House hovered over my race like one of those mammoth floating Baby Trump balloons with the orange skin, tiny hands, full diaper, and amber wave of mane. And Trump kept doubling down on the things that kept his popularity in Maryland so low. The divisive rhetoric. The unhinged tweets. The insults. The constant immigrant bashing. The stubborn embrace of Vladimir Putin, Kim Jong-un, and other despots. Always trying to separate people instead of uniting them, as we'd been doing in Maryland. Trump had his fans here, as he did everywhere, and they would stick with him no matter what. Many of these base Trump supporters also backed me, even though I'd never hidden my feelings about the president.

As our campaign got rolling, Trump's job-approval rating in Maryland was at 29 percent, a full 44 points below mine. I had the approval of 60 percent of African Americans and 67 percent of Democrats. He barely registered there. But liking someone and voting for that person are two entirely different things. And when the pollsters asked Marylanders if they would vote for my re-election, there were an awful lot of *nos*, even from those who had a favorable opinion of me and approved of the job I'd been doing. At that point, only 47 percent of Marylanders said they would vote to re-elect me.

Strange times.

"The governor's great," the pollsters kept hearing people say. "But, no, I won't be voting for him. I'm not voting for any Republicans this time. We are going to send a message to Donald Trump." Forty-eight percent of likely Maryland voters said they planned to vote against every single Republican on the ballot to send that message. That's how much they loathed the man in the White House.

Jim, Doug, Ron, and Russ, as well as our pollsters, data folks, and other veteran campaign people said they'd never seen anything even close to this before, a 26-point drop-off between the job-approval and re-elect numbers—and all because of Donald Trump. The Democratic nominee for governor, whoever that turned out to be, would do everything possible to link me with the unpopular Republican president, my advisors warned me. The Democrats wouldn't be running against Larry Hogan or Hogan-Rutherford in 2018. They'd be running against "Trump-Hogan."

On April 24, I was pleased to sign several bills protecting Maryland's animals. One bill encouraged pet adoptions. Another increased enforcement against animal cruelty. And one bill was aimed at puppy mills. On that day, Maryland became the second state in the country, after California, to ban pet stores from selling puppies and kittens bred at commercial mills. Some of those mills have unspeakable records of animal cruelty. I wanted our state to do everything we could to discourage that. But before the bill signing in the second-floor Reception Room, I stopped by the Lawyer's Mall outside the State House, where several dozen grateful animal lovers were waiting with shelter dogs who needed good homes.

You can probably guess what happened next.

When Lexi had died sixteen months earlier, Yumi and I had both decided that we would not get another dog. Not anytime soon. But my resolve started to melt away the moment I began cuddling a couple of those puppies. They nuzzled against my neck and shoulders. One of them nibbled on my chin. I said hello to every single one of them.

"If puppies could vote," I said with a laugh, "I'd get a hundred percent."

Among the dogs outside the State House that morning were four little Shih Tzu puppies and their mom. They came from the BARCS animal shelter in Baltimore. I couldn't help it. I fell in love with the whole family, which had been rescued from West Baltimore where the riots had been. I couldn't imagine sending them back to the shelter. I told Yumi that we really needed a puppy. It took a little convincing, but we ended up rescuing all five of them, the four little puppies and their mom.

My granddaughter Daniella got one of the puppies. My press secretary,

Shareese Churchill, got a puppy for her two little girls. Her parents adopted another one. Yumi and I adopted the littlest puppy of them all and her mom too. But what should we name them? We needed help deciding. Thousands of people offered suggestions. We got a lot of good ones before we finally settled on two. The mom, Anna (for Annapolis), and Chessie (for Chesapeake) the puppy went from the streets of West Baltimore to the shelter to the governor's mansion. It was a real doggy Cinderella story.

Puppy power strikes again!

There was some talk I might draw a pro-Trump conservative Republican challenger, primarying me from the right. But no one like that showed up this time. My approval among Republicans was 87 percent. So that was one less thing to worry about. We would have beaten any primary challenger. But a Republican-primary battle would have wasted campaign dollars and would have surely inflamed some in the party base, possibly making some of those voters stay home in November. I easily could have gotten a couple of black eyes along the way. The Democratic candidates were the ones I had to be ready for, and they were already lining up.

Given the registration advantage and the big blowback against Trump, nine Democrats were itching to get a crack at me. The three strongest were Rushern Baker, the Prince George's County executive; Kevin Kamenetz, the Baltimore County executive; and Ben Jealous, the darling of the party's progressive wing and a firebrand who'd been national president of the NAACP. They were all formidable. Baker and Kamenetz ran large counties and had solid constituencies already in place. Jealous was a nationally known civil rights leader with a strong media profile.

Jealous snagged primary endorsements from Senators Bernie Sanders, Cory Booker, and Kamala Harris and from his childhood friend, comedian Dave Chappelle. The candidate's rousing oratory and his platform of free college tuition, legalized marijuana, and a fifteen-dollar minimum wage seemed to connect with Democratic voters. Tragically, Kamenetz had a heart attack and died on May 10, six weeks before the June 26 primary. Boosted by that vacuum in the race and an energetic troop of progressive volunteers, Jealous won the Democratic primary with 40 percent of the vote, 10 points ahead of Baker. Then, the real race began.

Ben Jealous had spent all his money to win the primary. He needed to pause and reload. This time, unlike in 2014, we had the money advantage. We decided to define our opponent before he had a chance to define himself. As we did with Anthony Brown four years earlier, we came out fast with a Facebook video, describing Jealous as "Too Extreme" and "Too Risky," an out-of-the-mainstream politician Marylanders could not afford. We honed in on his budget-busting government-paid health care plan. "Even the *Washington Post* called Jealous's programs pie-in-the-sky," the video said. The Republican Governors Association stepped up with two defining TV ads of their own. We didn't have to beg for their help this time.

Jealous objected, insisting he'd been unfairly portrayed. "Larry Hogan, you have no idea," he declared as soon as the video went up. "Your attacks that came out this morning are sad, dude." Though we had never met, Jealous would often refer to me as "dude" or "brother." But he failed miserably to offer any alternative definition of himself.

If the former NAACP president wasn't the extremist we were making him out to be, who was he? What was his vision for Maryland? I suppose he and his campaign team were too busy scrambling to raise money in Hollywood to develop a message. But thanks to our early burst of ads and their failure to effectively shoot back, an image of Ben Jealous was already taking hold with voters. Defining him was made easier by the fact that few in Maryland actually knew him. He didn't have a long career in the state. Though his parents met in Baltimore, he was born and raised on California's Monterey Peninsula, two hours south of San Francisco, before heading off to Columbia University in New York City and then a Rhodes Scholarship in England.

"If you liked Martin O'Malley," I said, shaking my head, "you're gonna love this guy because he's talking about tens of billions of dollars in tax increases."

Clearly, this was going to be a spirited campaign.

But even before things really got going, Jealous managed to create a giant mess for himself without any help from us at all. On August 8, he called a morning press conference in Towson to announce endorsements from several elected officials. Referring to some of the recent back-and-forth about his expensive social-welfare plans, Erin Cox of the *Washington Post* asked Jealous if he considered himself a socialist. With his new endorsers visibly cringing behind him, he responded to the reporter, "Are you fucking kidding me?"

It wasn't a preposterous question that Erin Cox asked. Jealous had been a chief surrogate for the 2016 presidential campaign of Bernie Sanders, who called himself a Democratic socialist, and Jealous had lately been pushing Medicare for All. The candidate's comment went instantly viral. It wasn't just the public vulgarity that struck people. It was Jealous's hair-trigger response. The Republican Governors Association tweeted out a clip of the f-bomb and called Jealous "unhinged." The state Republican Party sent a missive that read "Ben Jealous for governor? Are you f—ing kidding me?" Doug Mayer, speaking for our campaign, drew a sharp contrast with the high-minded, unifying tone we'd tried to strike in Annapolis, adding a subtle dig at Trump: "The governor believes in raising the level of political discourse in our state and in our country, and cursing at reporters asking questions is the exact opposite of that. We need more people in public office who understand that words and tone matter, not fewer. We already have plenty who don't in Washington."

By early afternoon, Jealous was apologizing on Twitter "to @ErinatThePost for my inappropriate language in response to her question earlier today. As a former journalist, I know how important it is for a free society to respect reporters and answer their questions honestly." Belatedly, he offered a cleaned-up response to her query: "I'm a venture capitalist, not a socialist. I have never referred to myself as a socialist nor would I govern as one."

He'd have saved himself some trouble if he'd answered that way the first time.

Our campaign had a core message: "Independent Leadership that Works" was the way we summed it up. It was the idea that politics didn't have to divide people. That we could bring everyone together around a common-sense set of principles to keep the state on the right path and to get things done. Job and business growth. Social tolerance. Fiscal responsibility. Education. The environment. And we could do all that without being harsh or giving away the store. In that way, we positioned ourselves in direct contrast to Democrat Ben Jealous and Republican Donald Trump, both of whom seemed to be pushing the politics of division. I was the man in the middle who could talk sense to both sides. I didn't care what was a so-called "Republican idea" or "Democratic idea." I simply cared about what was a good idea. That's where the "independent" part came in.

Our message sounded familiar, but the campaign we built around it was almost the exact opposite of our 2014 theme. For one thing, I had a day job now as governor, a very busy and demanding day job that also included a lot of night and weekend work. I had never been a part-time governor, and I wasn't about to start now. Four years earlier, I'd been able to take a leave of absence from my business for most of a year while I ran for governor full-time. Full-time cruising the backroads of Maryland in my trusty campaign bus—I wouldn't and couldn't do that now, fun as that might have been. With the race in high gear, I just had to work twice as hard, twice as fast, twice as smart—whatever it took to give my all to both jobs, governor and candidate. Leaving after a cabinet meeting to hit a campaign event. Squeezing a political speech between a sit-down with the senate president and a briefing with the state police. Until November, there would be no such thing as a day or even an hour off, not that I'd had too many of those over the past four years. But now, it would be pedal to the metal until the end.

Fortunately, I wasn't an underfunded outsider anymore railing at those in charge. Though the other party still controlled the Legislature, I'd been the governor for the past three-plus years. This time, I was running on *my* record, not just criticizing someone else's. The state was a much-improved place now. Everyone could see we were open for business again. Our economy had jumped from forty-ninth out of the fifty states to number eight in the nation. We funded education and transportation at an all-time record high. We eased some of the problems with Obamacare to ensure nobody would lose health coverage, and we protected and cleaned up the Chesapeake Bay to the best water-quality levels in a generation. Without the rain tax! At every campaign stop, I drove that message home. A large percentage of Marylanders liked all that, as the polls kept telling us. Now all we had to do was convert the love into votes—and continue to prove that I was no Donald Trump.

Raising money was easier now. Donors are much freer with their check-books when they think you have a chance to win. But this would also be a far more expensive campaign than the last one. We'd need a larger staff to help spread the message. We had an opponent who could raise big piles of money from national Democrats and his Hollywood friends. He could also expect massive infusions from the Democratic Governors Association, the teachers union, and various political action committees with names like Maryland Together We Rise. Sooner or later, most likely sooner, I knew the other side would be pummeling me with TV attack ads. We had to answer each one—or, ideally, predict and get out in front of them.

CHAPTER 30

GIVING PERMISSION

The Jealous campaign, along with the state and national Democratic Party, kept trying to paint me as the second coming of Donald Trump. I was blamed for every crazy tweet and for Trump's positions on the separation of immigrant families, Obamacare, Chesapeake Bay funding, and Russian president Vladimir Putin, none of which I happened to share.

I didn't answer most of those ridiculous shots, which would have allowed the Jealous team to set the terms of our debate. I stuck to my own economic message and kept reminding voters how much better off Maryland was since the Hogan-Rutherford Administration took office four years earlier.

We still delivered a few jabs, mostly on Facebook, and we usually crafted them with edgy humor. They were designed to drive Ben Jealous off his game. One of our Facebook videos was called "Ben Jealous's 7 Seconds of Silence." It featured a clip from an interview he'd done with Ryan Eldredge from ABC 47 television, where Jealous responded blankly to a question about the Eastern Shore of Maryland. The silence was uncomfortable to watch. It made Jealous look like he didn't know how to answer.

When asked by reporters about the awkward silence, he said his response was delayed by "word replacement," a technique he used in his lifelong battle against stuttering—not because he lacked knowledge about the region or the topic. Most people weren't buying it.

Just like in the Brown race, the spot psyched out our opponent, who was running a blisteringly negative campaign while we kept our television messages completely positive. It seemed to be working again.

One thing was certain: If we were going to win this race, we had to give people permission to vote for me, especially those who were appalled by Donald Trump or were saying they were going to vote against me to send him a message—a majority of voters in Maryland. It wasn't about driving up my favorability or job-approval ratings. There was no way my popularity could go much higher. But a lot of people—suburban women, African Americans, younger voters—had trouble voting for me even though they thought I was a good governor. They were locked in place by their anger at Donald Trump. We had to help them overcome that reluctance, maybe even make them feel guilty about punishing me for something I had nothing to do with. "If we lose suburban women," Russ reminded me starkly, "we will lose this election."

The answer? Role models. The testimonies of real people, explaining in TV commercials why they were voting for Larry Hogan, especially people you wouldn't necessarily expect. What could be more positive than that?

Russ produced a series of unscripted thirty-second spots, just pointing the camera and letting people talk. In one ad, a Montgomery County woman named Sandra called herself a Democrat for Hogan. "He's been huge on transportation," she said. "He's done a lot for the environment. He cares genuinely about women's issues." And then the kicker: "Since Hogan has been reaching across the aisle, I think voters can reach across the aisle." For suburban women wondering if they could vote for me in spite of Trump? Permission given!

The ad that really struck people featured the street-corner Baltimore voice of Arthur "Squeaky" Kirk of the Ruth M. Kirk Recreation and Learning Center in the Franklin Square neighborhood. "In this community right here is a disconnect," Squeaky said. He explained that he met me before the last election. I'd promised, win or lose, I would help his organization, and I actually delivered.

"A lot of times, he's here and nobody knows," Squeaky said in the spot. "We operate, man, off of friendship. So it is what it is. We making it work. A white Republican governor. He act like a regular human being to me."

For black voters who really approved of the job I had done but didn't think they could vote for a Republican? Permission given!

Though the ads feel almost random—just people talking about how they feel—great care went into our choice of message and messengers.

We had the money this time to do some cool things with data analytics, a level of depth and sophistication that can't be gleaned from a standard political poll. Instead of simply interviewing a randomly selected 800 people across Maryland, we questioned tens of thousands, probing what these likely voters were thinking, where they got their information, and what might move them. We spent hundreds of thousands of dollars on this data gathering, probably more than any statewide race in the country. It let us target voters with persuasive messages right down to the individual level.

Since suburban women were such a key target for us, we went even deeper there. For months, we ran an ongoing focus group of two dozen undecided female voters, mostly Democrats or independents, who seemed swayable even though they weren't currently supporting the Hogan-Rutherford ticket. What issues did they really care about? What scared them about our opponent? Were national events influencing their state and local choices? How could we convince them it wasn't fair to vote against me because of Donald Trump?

These women were amazingly frank and open, even when we didn't like what they had to say. Sometimes, if you listen carefully, you can learn some fascinating things. We learned a lot from these women, knowledge that would pay real dividends.

As September rolled around, I was feeling more confident, despite all the early warnings from my campaign team. Ben Jealous had some things going for him. He had raised a lot of out-of-state PAC money from a handful of donors. He had the teachers union, civil rights activists, and visiting progressives from New York, California, and Washington, DC, all revved up by the excesses of Donald Trump. But we were getting our own message out. With subtly contrasting styles and images, we were reminding people why they liked me in the first place and reminding them that I wasn't Donald Trump, without ever mentioning his name.

Jealous was still having trouble redefining himself. And he never quite seemed comfortable as a political candidate. He stumbled in his press conferences. At unscripted moments, he sounded nervous and ill at ease. He was a stirring orator with a fire-and-brimstone delivery that could shake a room. But as the campaign heated up, his shortcomings became more obvious. One of his biggest was how he got rattled under pressure and couldn't answer questions well.

Politics is a strange business, and here's further proof: Despite being locked in this months-long battle, the two of us had never actually met. Normally, a challenger wants as many debates as possible. Four years earlier, I was dying to draw de facto incumbent Anthony Brown into the debate arena. Jealous didn't seem eager to debate at all. There was some back-and-forth between our two campaigns, negotiating the particulars. But his side kept coming up with excuses why no plan was ever acceptable, rejecting all the many dates we offered. Our attitude was, *Anytime, anywhere . . . how 'bout this afternoon?* They just kept refusing. After continued pressure from the media, the Jealous campaign reluctantly agreed to just one debate.

I showed up Monday, September 24, at the Maryland Public Television studios for our carefully negotiated face-to-face. I was standing at the podium, ready to go, when my opponent rushed into the studio, disheveled, sweaty, and nearly late. He walked right past me and didn't say hello. Before the cameras came on, I walked over to him, shook his hand, and wished him luck, the first conversation we'd ever had. He seemed a little startled. But once the debate began, he performed much better than I expected. Feisty. Well coached. Constantly bringing it to me, though I did a lot of the bringing too. He wasn't as good on the comebacks, but he had his attack lines well memorized.

The hour got off to a predictably combative start as Jealous challenged my biggest strength, the state's much-improved economy. "You taking credit for an economy that's slightly better, years after the end of the recession, in some places, not all, is like taking credit for the sun rising, sir," he said to me. "Let's run on your record, not on mythology."

Apparently, I'd finally been elevated from "dude" to "sir."

I accused him of misrepresenting our impressive job-growth numbers. "Not a single word you said was true," I charged.

He fired back, saying that if I wanted to see the facts, I should visit his website, *benjealous.com*. "I'm not going to go to *benjealous.com*," I chuckled dismissively.

Linking me with unpopular people was a big part of the Jealous campaign strategy. On debate night, it wasn't just Donald Trump. Jealous also reached back to the 1988 presidential race and conjured up the name Willie Horton, a rapist and killer who was featured in a racially tinged law-and-order ad that George Bush used against Governor Michael Dukakis. Jealous's point, I believe, was that I was now for mass incarceration in Maryland, a connection I didn't quite grasp. "From Willie Horton to Donald Trump, your party plays by the same playbook," he asserted. "You lie and you scare people."

Actually, I corrected him, we'd *reduced* the Maryland prison population by 9 percent. Again, I scoffed at him. "Willie Horton and Donald Trump don't have much to do with this," I said. After yet another attempt to link me to Trump, I joked that just about the only thing I had in common with Jealous is that we *both* voted against Trump.

Since Jealous kept tying me to Trump, I figured I might as well tie him to California, where he was born and raised. "He must be thinking of his home state of California," I said at one point. Jealous did have an emotional comeback on that one. "If you're wondering why I didn't grow up here, sir, it's because my parents' marriage was against the law," he said. His mother is black. His father is white.

Going into the debate, most people had low expectations of Jealous. He certainly surpassed those expectations. I still won, but it wasn't a knockout.

I'll give the man credit. He went toe to toe with me and threw some pretty good punches.

It might have been his last hopeful night of the campaign.

Soon enough, we were launching another humorous social-media zinger. On October 8, we highlighted Jealous's many embarrassing gaffes, including his tendency to misstate which office he was seeking. "What exactly is @BenJealous running for?" we asked on Twitter with a Facebook link to the video evidence. "President? Governor of Virginia? We're not entirely sure."

As the soundbites made clear, our California-born opponent had spoken about how he was going to remove me "from the White House" (instead of the State House) and become the first black president (instead of the first black governor of Maryland). Just that past weekend, he had said he was going to be "the next governor of Virginia!"

He called a press conference the next day, accusing me of mocking his speech impediment. He said he had struggled with stuttering since he was a boy, and now my comments would encourage bullies to pick on other stuttering children.

"I need to draw a line," Jealous thundered. "He's gone beyond the pale, and he needs to stop."

As for the governor-of-Virginia stumble, he said, "It was the end of the speech, and I didn't even notice it. Honestly. It's just the way your brain works. I was told like fifteen seconds later. I was like, 'Oh!'"

We responded by compiling a bunch of other crazy comments Jealous had made that had nothing to do with stuttering. "Whether it was dropping the f-bomb to a reporter, saying he is running for governor of Virginia, or promising to raise taxes, Mr. Jealous can't simply disown his words every time he gets in trouble with voters," our campaign communications director Scott Sloofman responded.

We kept running full speed all the way to the end. At many of the rallies in the closing weeks, the crowds loudly chanted: *"Four more years! Four more years!"* To which I often responded: "Four more beers! Four more beers!"

I kept pushing myself and my staff kept pushing me. Working as the governor. Campaigning hard. Giving speeches. Raising money. Still recovering from cancer. When I say I was tired as we neared election day, those words don't begin to describe how exhausted I felt. Night after night, day after day. No breaks. No time off. No vacation. No weekends. Not enough sleep. Never a proper meal. It was amazing that I never said anything really stupid from fatigue. By the end, my brain was turning to mush. Our deputy chief of staff was Allison Mayer, who is married to Doug Mayer, our deputy campaign manager. Our finance director was Allison Meyers. Speaking at my very last fundraising event—our 378th—I thanked "Allison Mayer, our finance director, and her team for all of their absolutely incredible work."

"For five years I have busted my ass for you," Allison Meyers said, glaring at me, "and you don't even know my name?"

"Allison," I pleaded, "of course I know your name. It's just that I can barely even stand up. I can't even remember my own name."

Earlier in the day, I'd addressed Kara as "Kyle." They were two of my closest assistants, and they didn't look anything alike.

"We gotta get the heck out of here," I said to Kyle. It was definitely Kyle. "I'm done."

Normally, I like to stick around at these events to the bitter end to make sure I have spent time talking to and thanking every single person. This time, as soon as I finished my remarks, I went straight for the SUV, leaned the seat back, and didn't utter another word the whole way home.

CHAPTER 31

BLUE WAVE

The Democrats promised a massive anti-Trump turnout on election day, vowing they would ride that upsurge of motivated new voters to victory in the Maryland governor's race and recapture a state that was rightfully and historically theirs.

Voter turnout, the Jealous campaign had been saying for months, was their superpower for burying me. No Republican in Maryland, including me, had ever topped 900,000 votes, they accurately pointed out. So, if they could gin up close to a million of their supporters, they figured they could topple a high-profile Republican incumbent weakened by voter hatred of Donald Trump and post another big W for the Democrats on the national political scoreboard.

It *sounded* plausible enough. Plausible enough to worry about.

Give the Democratic Party and the Jealous campaign credit: They delivered many Democrats to the polls. More people voted on November 6, 2018, than had ever cast ballots in a Maryland governor's race in history: 2.3 million overall, 600,000 more votes than the 1.7 million four years earlier when I beat Anthony Brown. And that included more than 400,000 new Democrats who hadn't cast a ballot the last time around.

When the Jealous team caught sight of the long lines outside the polling stations in traditional Democratic areas like Prince George's County, Montgomery County, and the city of Baltimore, they got a late blast of optimism. They had done exactly what they said they needed to do. They had turned people out. They put bodies into voting booths. All that was left now, they excitedly told themselves, were the back slaps, the high fives, and the victory speech from their famously rousing orator candidate to a packed hotel ballroom.

The smell of Democratic victory was in the air. Or so they managed to convince themselves.

To watch the election results come in, I decided we should return to the scene of our triumph in 2014, the Annapolis Westin. We expected a larger crowd than we'd had four years earlier. Campaign staffers. Volunteers. Cancer survivors. People I'd met at the Baltimore riots. People from our administration. Friends from childhood and my dad's campaigns. Men and women who'd been with me since the early days of Change Maryland. Others who just wanted to celebrate how the state was being turned around. The Capitol Ballroom wasn't really large enough for everyone. It was going to be uncomfortably crowded that night, but we'd make it work. Was it nostalgia? Superstition? I don't know. I just liked the idea of being back there again where the magic happened. It somehow felt right.

This time the polls all had us ahead. The election-eve predictions were considerably more optimistic than they'd been when I ran against Anthony Brown. *Politico,* Fox News, the *Washington Post*—they all had the Maryland governor's race in the "likely R" category. I'm not sure if famed prognosticator Nate Silver was making up for his past sins four years after he'd so confidently predicted my humiliating defeat or if he was showing newfound respect. But his FiveThirtyEight blog declared the race a "solid R."

Still, given how wrong the so-called experts had been in 2014 and the massive Democratic turnout, what did they know, anyway?

All across the country, the signs were bleak for Republicans. After two years in office, Donald Trump was proving to be the least popular American president of modern times. On this night, he was also a very heavy anchor dragging down blue-state Republicans. His job-approval number was in the 30s, a good 40 points below mine. He still had his ardent supporters. Nothing he could say or do seemed to alienate them. But since his election in 2016, the president had done little to reach out to those who didn't already back him. Suburban women were a particular weak spot, all the political analysts said. His bullying demeanor, his Twitter outbursts, and his hard-core views were repelling crucial female voters in places like Chester County, Pennsylvania; Orange County, California; and Montgomery County, Maryland. He'd doubled down on the harsher parts of his agenda and turned up the volume on his divisive rhetoric. Trump was doing the exact opposite of what Ronald Reagan did, who worked to expand the Republican tent. If Trump kept going the way he was going, it seemed the entire Republican party might eventually fit into one of those little pup tents.

Would Democrats gain a majority in Congress in this mid-term election? Which party would pick up governorships in the thirty-six states voting that day? And what about legislative and local races? They set a course for the future. How much impact would Trump really have? All those questions would be answered in the next few hours. For Republicans, this had the makings of a long and difficult night.

I felt like we'd done what we had to in Maryland, pressing a positive, inclusive message of our own. Emphasizing the improvements in the state's economy. Reaching out to independents and Democrats. Making a special effort with voters—women, African Americans, union members, Asians, Latinos, young people—who are often suspicious of Republicans. Working ourselves ragged until the final hours. And reminding everyone over and over again that I was not Donald Trump. Truthfully, Jealous hadn't been quite the powerhouse opponent for which we had prepared ourselves. He campaigned hard. He took his shots at me. But in the face of our inclusive message and the complaints that he was too extreme, he never really found his footing and he never made the case for why a change was needed. Despite the late swagger the Democrats were feeling from the long lines at the polls, I arrived at the

Westin in an optimistic mood. People were already gathering in the ballroom. Yumi and I headed straight upstairs to the suite.

Kara and Kyle were with us along with our campaign chairman, Tom Kelso, and our campaign manager, Jim Barnett. Russ Schriefer, Doug Mayer, and Ron Gunzburger were in the suite too, followed later by our family, the lieutenant governor and his family, and key members of our finance committee. As I looked around the room, I thought to myself, *This is the inner circle—so where's my dad?* I was struck with a brief pang of melancholy. *He should be here,* I thought. *He really should be here.* When I'd started this journey, it hadn't occurred to me that he'd be gone before I was finished. The overcrowded room still seemed a little empty without my dad and my sister, who had also been there the last time.

We waited for the returns to come in, and I did what political people usually do in the early hours of election night. I stared impatiently at the TV, paced around, and kept asking our campaign team what, if anything, we were hearing. There wasn't much. The news channels all had wall-to-wall election coverage. They'd been on for hours already. But since the polls were just beginning to close across America, the anchors, field reporters, and studio pundits didn't have any actual news either. What they had, from Fox to CNN to MSNBC to the local channels in Baltimore and Washington, was endless speculation, prediction, and analysis. They talked about the turnout, which was heavy all around. They weighed the "Trump effect," which they all agreed would be a drag on Republicans. And they wondered aloud just how big the night's "blue wave" might be. Then, they repeated their points all over again.

I used the news lull to think about what I should say in my victory speech, assuming I got the chance to deliver one. I had a long list of people who needed thanking, but I also wanted to define the election with some overarching theme.

The victory, if we won it, would mean something special. This time, I wouldn't just be a Republican winning in a state that was two-to-one Democratic. I'd be only the second Republican governor to ever be *re*-elected in the history of Maryland, joining Theodore McKeldin in that very exclusive club. And I'd be doing it on a night when Republicans weren't supposed to win much of anything, especially in deep-blue Maryland.

That's when it hit me.

"Everyone's talking about red states and blue states and a big blue wave," I said to Russ and Doug. "They keep mentioning that blue wave."

"Yeah?" Russ asked noncommittally.

"What if I say I rode that blue wave with a purple surfboard?"

"That's awesome," Doug responded.

"You should definitely say that," Russ agreed.

It wasn't a line anyone wrote for me. But I thought it said something, the idea of not being a captive of any political party or any rigid ideology. Not red. Not blue. Something different. Bringing red and blue together. Thinking for myself. Doing what was best for the people of Maryland. Not marching in lockstep with anyone, not even the president of the United States. Weaving the tumultuous waters as circumstances required, somehow managing to stay on my feet. That image of the purple surfboard pretty much captured what I believed in and what was actually happening to me.

The pundits were right about the blue wave. From Maine to California, Republicans were taking a pounding everywhere. By the time the night was over, Democrats would win a majority in the US House of Representatives, eventually wrestling forty-one seats away from the Republicans and ending the GOP monopoly in Washington. Republican Governor Scott Walker lost in Wisconsin. Republican Governor Bruce Rauner lost in Illinois. And Democrats grabbed five open governorships that had been in Republican hands—Maine, Michigan, Kansas, Nevada, and New Mexico. The Democrats also overturned 350 legislative seats, taking control of seven legislative chambers—the Colorado Senate, the Connecticut Senate, the Minnesota House, the Maine Senate, the New York Senate, and both the House and Senate of New Hampshire. In red states where the Democrats didn't win, they tightened past margins and ran well ahead of where Hillary Clinton had two years earlier.

The news for Republicans was bad all over. Except in Maryland.

Actually, let me put a finer point on that: except in the Maryland governor's race.

As the results came in from the state's twenty-three counties and the city of Baltimore, our data whizzes carefully crunched the numbers in the war room hidden away downstairs. Every now and then, one of them would rush in with another update. Compared with the bleak news being reported for Republicans across the country, the news could hardly have been more different for our campaign. Category by category, we were capturing the votes we needed for victory and then some, easily topping the pollsters' predictions and our own stunning performance four years before.

At 9:07 PM, barely an hour after the polls closed, the Associated Press declared that the Hogan-Rutherford team had won a second term in Maryland. And this was no squeaker. By the time all the votes were counted, Boyd Rutherford and I would capture 55 percent of the vote, compared to 43 percent for Ben Jealous and his running mate, Susan Turnbull—a 12-point thumping on the most difficult night for Republicans in years. Yes, hundreds of thousands of extra Democrats got out and voted, just as Ben Jealous hoped they would. Unfortunately, from his perspective, a large percentage of them voted for me.

We won 31 percent of all Democrats, two-thirds of the independents, and damn near every single Republican. We got one-third of the votes in Baltimore City, up from 22 percent four years earlier. In heavily Democratic Montgomery County, we got an unheard-of 45 percent.

In our two-to-one Democratic state, I ended up earning more votes than any other candidate for governor, Democrat or Republican, had ever received in the history of Maryland.

Those Democrats and independents were especially key to our victory—and proof that the right kind of Republican candidate really could get voters to cross party lines, even with venomous anti-Trump resentment, even in a year when Republicans were getting battered everywhere. The Democratic voters we pulled away from Jealous gave us a crucial boost. We won overwhelmingly with suburban women. The female focus groups, the Sandra-from-Montgomery-County commercial, and our other outreach to women had obviously made a difference. By the end, everyone seemed to understand that I was definitely not Donald Trump.

Maybe even more remarkable, I ended up with 30 percent of

the African-American vote—a white Republican running against an African-American Democrat who was former national president of the NAACP. I'm not sure if there's an official category for that in the Guinness Book of World Records, but I can promise you no one else has ever matched it. "Squeaky" Kirk delivered!

So did the memories of how I had responded decisively to the Baltimore riots when the city's mayor was so overwhelmed.

Mileah Kromer, a political science professor at Baltimore's Goucher College, explained the victory as succinctly as anyone: "He cleaned up among Republicans, he bested Ben Jealous among independents and pulled away enough Democrats," Kromer told the *Washington Post*. "That's the Hogan coalition."

Apparently, the Jealous campaign thought the AP jumped too quickly in declaring a winner, firing off a last-gasp tweet to their supporters: "Stay in line. Keep voting." Given how far ahead we were, I'm not quite sure what they were holding out for. I'm glad I didn't wait for Jealous's concession call before heading downstairs to address our supporters in the ballroom. I'd have been waiting for a very long time.

People were ecstatic when I got downstairs and walked into the ballroom in my dark gray suit and shimmering purple tie. Yumi was at my side in a canary-yellow suit. Our entire family was there, filling the large stage. The room was jammed with our campaign team and the big crowd of supporters and volunteers who had worked their hearts out to make this victory possible. What a victory party it was!

"They said it couldn't be done in Maryland," I began. "But thanks to you, we just went out and did it."

Then I was ready to set up the money line.

"Four years ago," I said, "you helped us pull off the biggest political upset in America, and I became only the second Republican governor elected in Maryland in fifty years. And tonight, in this deep blue state, in this blue year, with a blue wave—it turns out I can surf!"

People were already standing and clapping.

"And we had a purple surfboard!"

They loved it. The room erupted in cheers.

"Thanks to you, I just became the second Republican governor ever re-elected in the entire 242-year history of our state. Thank you for making that possible."

In the spirit of bipartisanship, I wanted to reach across the aisle again. "Let me just take a minute to thank Mr. Jealous for running a spirited campaign and giving Marylanders a real choice," I said. "While we disagreed on the issues, he has my respect. I sincerely wish him well in his future pursuits."

Quoting a still beloved Democratic president, I gave a special shout-out to those Democrats who crossed party lines in our race. "Tonight," I said, "hundreds of thousands of Democrats reaffirmed the wisdom of John F. Kennedy, who said, 'Sometimes party loyalty demands too much.'" I was an undeniable recipient of that exact sentiment.

"The people of our great state voted for civility, for bipartisanship, and for common-sense leadership," I said. And I was so proud that they believed that was what they found in me.

We had a stunning victory, a genuine landslide on a night when such a thing seemed completely and utterly impossible. But unfortunately, the victory was ours alone. It was a tough night for many of our friends around the state and across the nation.

The Trump effect was devastating for my fellow Maryland Republicans. In 2014 I'd had the longest coattails of any Republican gubernatorial candidate ever. We helped elect Republican county executives, state senators, and house members, as well as county commissioners and courthouse and local officials all across the state. But nearly all those gains were wiped out in one night by the negative reaction to Donald Trump. Before the election, state party leaders boldly spoke about the "Fight for Five" campaign, their effort to flip five seats in the Maryland state senate to deprive Democrats of the supermajority that allowed them to override all my vetoes. Through fundraisers, rallies, mailings, and TV commercials, I worked hard for every one of the candidates. I raised $9.6 million for the previously nearly bankrupt Maryland Republican Party. But still, they all lost, including attorney and military veteran Craig Wolf, the Republican who challenged Maryland's Trump-fighting attorney general, Democrat Brian Frosh. None of our efforts could overcome the anti-Trump backlash at the polls. In all, the party lost three key county executive races, eight general assembly seats, and countless other county and local seats across the state.

Anne Arundel County Executive Steve Schuh and Howard County Executive Allan Kittleman, great leaders who ran great campaigns, both lost their seats to Democrats. In Baltimore County, my good friend state insurance commissioner Al Redmer, lost his race to progressive Democrat Johnny Olszewski. This meant that, in addition to the Legislature, all of Maryland's most populous jurisdictions would be controlled by Democrats.

At some point much later in the evening—I don't recall the exact time—Kyle came toward me holding his cell phone over his head. I was in the middle of a wild celebration in the ballroom, sharing this huge moment with the people who'd helped to make it come true.

"Ben Jealous's staff is calling," Kyle shouted to me.

"What? What did you say?" I yelled back over the noise.

"I think Ben Jealous is finally calling to concede," he shouted again.

"I'm sorry," I said. "I can't possibly take a call in the middle of this craziness. There's too much noise. I can't even hear."

Ben Jealous and I never did get a chance to connect, much like during most of the campaign.

So what did all of this mean for the future? Well, there was an entire state and national press corps just itching to figure that out.

CHAPTER 32

PURPLE
SURFBOARD

The day after the election, the reporters pressed me for an explanation of the big blue wave. I assigned responsibility right where it belonged, at the feet of Donald Trump. "We had President Trump say the election should be about him, even though he's not on the ballot," I said. "In Maryland, that's exactly what happened. It was a repudiation of the president, who lost this state by nearly thirty points."

The AP VoteCast exit poll certainly seemed to bear this out. Two-thirds of Maryland voters said the president was a factor when they decided who to vote for, and two-thirds said they had an unfavorable view of him. Only a third of Marylanders believed the country was headed in the right direction, compared with more than two-thirds who said it wasn't. Finally, a stunning 77 percent of Marylanders agreed Trump had the wrong temperament to be our president.

I was running about 40 points ahead of the president—and not just with Democrats and independents. I was far outpolling him even among Republicans and conservatives, in every single region of the state.

Almost immediately the speculation began about the possibility of me running for president in the 2020 Republican primaries. People saw me as both a center-right Trump critic and a Republican who had crossover appeal in a general election. Maybe I should consider running against Trump in the Republican primaries, people began to say. Given the fervent support he still had among base primary voters nationwide, that prospect would certainly be a long shot. But in the weeks after the election, that topic had gone from a faint whisper to a growing "what if" that political insiders and media pundits were tossing around on the cable shows and in the bars on Capitol Hill.

I did nothing to stir the waters. I said nothing to encourage speculation that I would consider challenging the president in a primary fight. Those vague rumbles built up organically, in part because of the lack of plausible alternatives: popular Republican officeholders who were willing to speak out against the president and could also attract Democratic and independent votes. Who else fit all three parts of that bill? Hardly anyone. For big-tent Republicans deeply frustrated with the president, there weren't many cheerful stories that came out of the mid-terms and zero first-string Republicans lining up to run against Donald Trump.

The ones who had the inclination to do it were simply too scared to oppose him or saw it as a futile effort.

They'd seen the president's sky-high approval ratings among likely Republican primary voters. They knew how vicious and personal Trump could be on Twitter to anyone who dared to even criticize him, much less run against him. Truly, no one of much stature was lining up yet. But once political experts absorbed the election results in Maryland, some of them began looking directly at me. Which, I'll admit, was flattering.

A week after the election, the right-leaning Niskanen Center held a conference in Washington, DC. "Starting Over: The Center-Right After Trump," the gathering was called. I was asked to deliver the opening remarks, not the kind of gig that usually goes to the governor of Maryland. I got the distinct impression that some people in the audience weren't just there for my wisdom. They were also looking for a fresh horse to ride. The group's president, Jerry Taylor, made a point of mentioning that I'd just been re-elected with significant support from women and African Americans, groups that Republicans have struggled to attract. "He lays a path that we might want to pay attention to," Taylor said of me.

I told the crowd that I, like they, was "completely fed up with politics as usual—and, quite frankly, I still am, maybe today more than ever. Compromise and moderation should not be considered dirty words. I believe it's only when the partisan shouting stops that we can truly hear each other's voices and concerns."

When I finished my speech, Jerry thanked me in front of the crowd and presented me with a book about New Hampshire, site of the nation's first presidential primary every four years. "We all hope you'll be making a visit there soon," he said.

I'm not sure if the group considered my words encouraging or not, but the talk continued to build. Conservative commentator Bill Kristol, who attended the event, had been trying for months to recruit a strong Republican candidate to take on Trump. All of a sudden, he was mentioning my name. Some nights, the cable shows could talk of little else.

All this buzz was miles ahead of where I was. I was just beginning my second term as governor. I had a lot of work to do in Maryland. I had taken no steps—*none!*—to launch a presidential campaign, especially one as daunting as a Republican run against Trump would be. But everywhere I went, people were asking, "So, are you gonna do it? Are you gonna run against Trump?" or saying, "We hope you run for president!"

I told everyone the truth. I had no such plans. I didn't even have any plans to make plans.

But my mind wasn't empty as those questions came up. I did have some lessons I'd learned from my own life and my four years of being governor. I had strong feelings about the country I cared deeply about and how toxic its politics had become. I wanted a seat at the table for influencing the tone of the debate and the future direction of the Republican Party. After my landslide victory in November, a lot of people in the nation were suddenly paying attention. I knew that, come January, when I'd be sworn in for my second term as governor, I would have a big inaugural speech to give outside the State House. I told myself that might be a perfect opportunity to lay some things out.

Every year that I'd been governor, I'd hosted a series of small holiday parties the week before Christmas for the people who helped me do my job—the cabinet members, the governor's staff, the women who worked at the mansion, and the state police officers from the executive-protection detail.

This year was no exception. We were almost four years in by now. Everyone was excited we'd just won another four. I worked closely with these people every single day. They looked after Yumi and me in every way imaginable. They really were family to us.

At this year's state trooper party, I got a surprise. We were exchanging our usual twenty-dollar gag gifts, poking gentle fun at each other's foibles, reliving memorable moments from the year. I thanked them all and said how much I cared about them and appreciated everything they did for me and my family. I wished everyone a Merry Christmas and Happy Holidays.

A couple of the troopers excused themselves. "Governor," executive-protection commander Jeff Ferreira said a minute later, "we have a special gift for you."

That's when they carried out a genuine, full-sized purple surfboard. It had the Maryland flag in purple rather than the familiar red, white, black, and gold. And emblazoned on the front was a slightly abbreviated version of my quote from election night:

> *Deep Blue State in this Blue Year with this Blue Wave . . . it turns out I can surf.*
> —Governor Larry Hogan

They'd all been at the hotel on election night and had heard what I'd said. One of the troopers, Rich Nevy, who'd been with us since the transition and had walked the streets with me during the riots, had a friend who owned a custom surfboard shop on the Eastern Shore. The troopers all pitched in and got this beautiful custom purple surfboard designed and built for me.

It really meant a lot to me that they were so thoughtful and made such an effort. They were proud to be part of the team, and that was their way of showing it. It was my favorite Christmas gift ever.

When I was a kid, I was never that talented a surfer, though I did learn a few moves back in my amusement park days in Ocean City. What I did remember from then was that when I carried the surfboard, the girls thought I was cool. Now, I had an idea where I wanted to bring my new board, and it wasn't to the beach.

January 16, 2019, was blustery and cold in Annapolis, just a couple of degrees above freezing. Not normal surfing weather. The morning was foggy and overcast. The day's events began inside the toasty senate chamber with a private swearing-in. Mary Ellen Barbera, the chief judge of the Maryland Court of Appeals, led Boyd and me through our oaths of office. We each swore to execute our duties "diligently and faithfully, without partiality or prejudice." Now, there was a standard worth living up to! But the real fun was on the snowy grounds beside the State House, where more than a thousand people were waiting in the cold for us. My now six-year-old granddaughter, Daniella, got things off to a rousing start just as the sun peeked out from the clouds.

Encouraged by her father, my son-in-law Louis, Daniella climbed onto a step stool behind the podium and led everyone in the Pledge of Allegiance. Boyd took the oath of office again, in front of everyone this time, for another four years as Maryland's lieutenant governor. Then, it was my turn. I placed my right hand on the same Bible that was used in 1955 to swear in Theodore McKeldin, my two-term Republican role model. "I will support the Constitution of the United States," I vowed, and "will be faithful and bear true allegiance to the State of Maryland and support the Constitution and Laws thereof." It was an old-fashioned way to express it, but I hoped that others would take a moment and reflect on the true meaning of those words. I know I did.

The inauguration of a governor, even one entering his second term, is a highly structured ceremony. This one had the usual military officers standing at attention and the traditional nineteen-gun salute. Four jets from the Maryland National Guard flew in formation overhead. It was all quite moving and exquisitely done. But I had a message I hoped to deliver on this special day. From beginning to end, I wanted to use my second inauguration to highlight how we'd changed Maryland for the better and, even more importantly, to issue a soaring call for a different kind of politics across America, a striking contrast to everything we had been seeing and hearing in Washington. I was pleased we had such a bipartisan turnout. The guests included former governor Bob Ehrlich and former lieutenant governor Michael Steele, both Republicans, as well as Senate President Mike Miller, House Speaker Michael Busch, and former Governor Parris Glendening, all Democrats.

I was especially honored that former Florida governor Jeb Bush, another center-right Republican who had voiced his own frustrations about the increasing harshness of American politics, agreed to introduce me. Jeb, after all, had been one of the earliest victims of 2016's politics of ridicule and division. In his remarks, the former Florida governor described me as "the antithesis of what's happening in Washington, DC, these days," adding that I was "at the top of the list of leaders that I admire."

That wasn't scripted. I had no idea what he was going to say. But Jeb had clearly been paying attention to Maryland.

"Washington's not just our nation's capital," he noted. "It's also the capital of gridlock and dysfunction, and with a divided Congress it doesn't look like things are going to get much better anytime soon. But life outside of DC isn't always that way. Outside DC, good and interesting ideas and strong leadership still hold the power to repair and reinvigorate our institutions . . . Larry embodies the kind of strong, independent leadership America needs now."

Jeb was certainly doing his part to encourage the nascent Hogan-for-president rumbles. Now it was up to me—not to climb immediately into polemic mode but to deliver my big-tent message as powerfully as I could.

I wanted to use this special moment to denounce the divisiveness that seemed to have a stranglehold on so much of American politics, especially the version being practiced in Washington. Though I never uttered the name

Donald Trump, and neither did Jeb, I don't think anyone could have missed the stark differences between my tone and that of the president.

"Four years ago," I said, "I committed to usher in a new era of bipartisan cooperation and prosperity in Maryland, one filled with hope and optimism. I pledged to govern with civility and moderation, to avoid attempts to drive us to the extremes of either political party, and to uphold the virtues that are the basis of Maryland's history as 'a state of middle temperament,'" a phrase that dates back to 1634, when Father Andrew White cast his gaze on what was to become the state of Maryland, a region he said exhibited "a middle temperament between [New England and Virginia], and enjoys the advantages, and escapes the evils, of each."

"I believe it's because we kept that promise to put problem-solving ahead of partisanship and compromise ahead of conflict that I'm standing here again today just as humbled and eager and awed as I was at the start of my first term," I said.

I invoked the names of three American leaders I had long admired, men from the not-too-distant past who'd proven that concern for the common good could rise above the rancor of the moment. We'd lost all three of them since I became governor. One was Jeb's late father, President George H. W. Bush, whose memorial service I had attended just a month earlier at Washington National Cathedral. "Throughout his remarkable life, he showed us the true meaning of honor, integrity, courage, and humility," I said. Another was the late senator John McCain, whose funeral I had attended under the beautiful dome of the United States Naval Academy chapel, now clearly visible from where I was standing on the State House lawn. "Senator McCain wasn't someone who would yield easily," I said. "But he never hesitated to reach across the aisle to get things done, and he always put his country before his party or himself." It wasn't entirely by accident that the senator's longtime friend and speechwriter, Mark Salter, had contributed some nice lines to my inaugural address. Finally, I quoted my own father's eloquent words from the House Judiciary Committee during Watergate when he became the first Republican in Congress to call for the impeachment of Richard Nixon. "'Party loyalty and personal affection and precedents of the past must fall before the arbiter of men's actions: the law itself,' Lawrence Hogan Sr. said that day. 'No man, not even the president of the United States, is above the law.'"

People stood and applauded at that.

"I learned a lot about integrity and public service from my dad," I said. "I miss him a lot, especially today."

My kind of politics isn't a solo act, I explained. It requires contributions all around. That's why I issued a special invitation to "my partners" in the Legislature, with whom I had alternately battled and cooperated over the past four years: "Join in reaffirming our pledge to continue on this bold new path," I said to them. "Rather than engaging in mere rhetoric, let's continue to deliver real results for the people who sent us here."

Clearly, the times were ripe.

"Let's keep putting the people's priorities before partisan interests," I said. "Let's continue to tackle our common problems by accepting our shared responsibility to solve them. Let's repudiate the debilitating politics practiced elsewhere, including just down the road in Washington. Where insults substitute for debate, recriminations for negotiation, and gridlock for compromise. Where the heat, finger-pointing, and rancor suffocates the light and the only result is divisiveness and dysfunction. Where getting something done for the people no longer seems to be a priority. There is plenty of blame to go around."

Ah, yes: the people. Remember them? They're the ones we're all supposed to be serving here. I addressed the people directly.

"You should be able to have confidence in the character and competence of the people you elect to office regardless of their party affiliation," I said. "You should be able to trust that we'll do our best for you to solve our problems. Those of us blessed by your trust should give you a government that doesn't act as if it is something apart from you but one that is of the people, by the people, and for the people. A government that appreciates that no one of us has all the answers or all the power. A government that tolerates contrary views among a diverse citizenry without making them into enemies or doubting their patriotism. A government that can discuss and debate with as much civility as passion and with a view to persuade, not intimidate, to encourage, not demonize or defeat. That is exactly what we have succeeded in providing to the people of Maryland."

––––––––––––––––––

Message delivered, it was finally time to let loose.

For the 2019 Inaugural Gala that night, we sold out the MGM National Harbor in Prince George's County. More than 3,000 people attended, enjoying a sizzling dance band, open bar, chicken and hamburger sliders, and oysters and shrimp. Other than the fact that I and many of the male guests wore tuxedos and the women were in fancy dresses and gowns, the evening was about as far as you could get from the stuffy inaugural balls that are such quadrennial fixtures in Washington.

"Surfin' USA," the Beach Boys classic, came blasting through the hotel's Vegas-level sound system. Flanked by a smiling Yumi and Boyd and his wife, Monica, and all their kids and all our kids and grandkids—this beautiful, multicultural portrait of modern Maryland—my bald head and I marched onto the stage in sunglasses, carrying the shiny purple surfboard the troopers had given to me. The crowd went wild.

I gave the shortest speech any politician has ever given at an event like this. "I still remember when we had our first event five years ago," I said to the crowd. "I think we had, like, seven people. Man, we've come a long way. Now we're selling out the MGM Grand just like Cher and Bruno Mars."

This was not a night for political speeches. It was a night for celebration—and one big thank-you. "I want to thank the people of Maryland for putting their trust in us and giving us a chance to continue to focus on changing Maryland for the better and setting an example for the rest of the nation," I said. "We're all about working hard. But tonight, you deserve to have a party!"

My speech quickly over, another perfect song came up as my "walk-off" music, a song that nicely captured my feelings about the extremes of either party. "Clowns to the left of me," the lyrics said. "Jokers to the right. Here I am, stuck in the middle with you."

And that was right where I wanted to be.

I climbed down one side of the stage onto the teeming floor in front of us. Yumi climbed down the other. Boyd and Monica and our various children beat their own paths into the roaring crowd. We spanned out to greet as many people as we possibly could, while the troopers struggled mightily to keep up with all of us.

At that point, the band was back onstage. The lights came up in the ballroom. The whole place was all lit in purple now.

And the band, through that incredible MGM sound system, did one of the finest versions I've ever heard of Prince's "Purple Rain."

Over the next several hours, I swear I hugged every person, shook every hand, and took a selfie with nearly every human being in that room.

It was a wonderful Maryland crowd. There were lots of Republicans in the room, supporters and lawmakers and friends—and lots of Democrats, too: Prince George's County Executive Angela Alsobrooks, Senate President Mike Miller, and Baltimore City Council president Jack Young, who would go on later to be the city's mayor. "The governor invited me," Young told a reporter who asked what the heck he was doing there with me. "I don't care what party he is. If the governor invites you, you go. I can work across the aisle."

It was the culmination of a lifetime of struggle and achievement. But it was also something more important. It was a celebration of a divided people, coming together as one. Election night had been amazing. But this was much, much bigger. People were dancing and celebrating and having a wonderful time. I was thanking people all night long for believing in me.

I may have been the guy on the purple surfboard, but there were literally thousands of people who helped me ride that giant wave.

CHAPTER 33

BEING DRAFTED

I n the days and weeks that followed, the drumbeat grew louder and more insistent. On cable news. In private phone calls. In conversations with fellow Republicans, donors, and members of the media. Even with a couple of Trump Administration cabinet secretaries.

You really should consider challenging Donald Trump for president.

America needs you.

There is nobody else.

The future of the Republican Party depends on it.

That's what people were saying, anyway.

Candidly, all that national attention, supplemented by heartfelt personal appeals, can become intoxicating, especially in politics. Fortunately, I remained fairly well grounded in reality during all of this.

The media, I understood. They were itching for a tussle in 2020. They wanted a Republican primary race to cover. After three years of being smeared as "fake news" and "enemies of the people," the reporters and commentators were fed up. They were also enamored by the idea of a popular Republican governor, a *real* Republican, with a proven record of electoral success, going toe to toe with Donald Trump inside the GOP.

But cabinet secretaries? Encouraging me to consider running against their boss, the president? That one surprised me. But their words, whispered during a visit to the White House, were unequivocal: "Thank you," one cabinet secretary said. "A lot of us appreciate the things you are saying. You have no idea how important it is to the party and to the country that you are saying them."

The analysts and columnists combed through the words in my inaugural address, looking for clues to my intentions. They quoted the flattery from Jeb Bush, calling me the antithesis of Donald Trump.

"He's a savvy pol," Never Trump commentator Bill Kristol said of me. "He wanted people to see that he had some interest in the national scene."

"The question for pundits and politicians is not why Maryland Gov. Larry Hogan may be considering a primary run against President Trump in 2020, but rather, why there aren't many more who are doing the same," anti-Trump conservative Jennifer Rubin wrote in the *Washington Post.*

In magazine profiles and on TV, the reporters kept retelling the Watergate story about my dad, reprising the time a Maryland Republican named Larry Hogan stood up to a president from his own party. Now, they wondered, would I live up to that legacy? When word spread that I had booked a trip to Iowa in March—well, that created even more chatter. If I wasn't thinking seriously about running for president, why else would I go to Iowa, the site of the first Republican caucuses of the 2020 presidential campaign? Several commentators pointed out that I was in line to be the next chairman of the National Governors Association, starting in July. That in itself would be a valuable platform for launching a presidential race, they said. Given my landslide re-election in deep-blue Maryland and my still-soaring poll numbers, all these people kept telling me I should take my act onto a larger stage.

The White House was clearly paying close attention—and not in a happy way. The president's political team was closely monitoring events in Maryland, the commentators said. According to *Politico,* Trump aides "regarded the inauguration speech as an unmistakable act of aggression," noting that "Trump 2016 primary rival Jeb Bush was a featured speaker at the ceremony and that Mark Salter, a longtime Republican speechwriter and a fierce Trump critic, helped craft Hogan's address."

I didn't encourage any of this speculation. But I also did nothing to silence it, as the "Run-Larry-Run" engine gained steam. I knew that making provocative moves like visiting Iowa would raise my profile and allow me a seat at the national table to discuss the future of the nation and my party.

There certainly seemed to be an opportunity. The "Never Trumpers" inside the Republican Party were still licking their wounds from 2016. Their roster of potential candidates was getting longer, but no real standouts had emerged yet. The list of maybes included Nebraska senator Ben Sasse, former Arizona senator Jeff Flake, former Tennessee senator Bob Corker, and former United Nations ambassador Nikki Haley—all of whom were good people but none of whom had declared any intention to run. And notice how most of them had *former* in front of their names. On February 14, former Massachusetts governor Bill Weld, who'd run for vice president as a Libertarian in 2016, announced he was exploring a Republican run this time. Former Ohio governor John Kasich, who'd run against Trump four years earlier, was said to be thinking of jumping in again.

But the vast majority of high-profile Republicans, including the ones who'd been dropping all those negative anonymous quotes, had no intention of running this race. They'd stayed publicly silent for the past three years. They weren't about to open their mouths, much less step into the ring, at this point.

I will admit I wasn't opposed to the idea of bringing common sense and civility back to Washington. I had learned so much about pulling people together and achieving practical results in Maryland. And I truly believe those lessons could be applied anywhere.

As all this talk hung in the air, I was getting far more national media invitations than I'd ever gotten before. In fact, nearly all the network and cable news shows were constantly calling. I don't think they were suddenly interested in our latest Maryland initiative. I turned down most of them, but I did say yes to a few, just enough to let people know what I stood for and what I believed our party and our country needed most.

Too often, I said February 20 on *CBS This Morning*, Donald Trump was "his own worst enemy," acting "irrationally" and behaving in ways "that aren't great for the Republican Party and for the country or for him and his agenda."

I pointed to an order Trump had just issued, claiming that illegal immigration was such an emergency that he should be allowed to pay for his pet-project border wall with money Congress had refused to allocate. "I don't think using emergency powers was the right thing to do here," I said. "I do believe there are people in Congress and other leaders in the Republican Party who have not stood up when they disagree or when they think the president is doing something wrong," I said. "I've not been afraid to do that."

Asked how I was reacting to all the people who'd been pressing me to run, I smiled and said the same thing I'd been saying since the run-for-president talk began: "I guess the best way to put it is I haven't thrown them out of my office."

———————————

On February 24, I was back at the White House with my fellow governors. If I had good reason to expect a cold shoulder two years earlier, I was really expecting it now. That time it was just that I had failed to endorse candidate Trump for president or vote for him. Now the media was awash in stories saying I might actually run against President Trump—for his own party's nomination. How was bad-cop Jared going to respond to this new development?

These National Governors Association visits to the White House are the same every year. Sunday-night dinner with the president, vice president, and key members of the cabinet. Back-to-back meetings all day Monday. I had been through the drill twice with Obama. This was my third time with Trump.

Vice President Mike Pence ran the charm offensive this time.

I consider Mike a friend. We served together for two years on the Republican Governors Association executive committee before he became vice president. When I was first running for governor, it was Pence who had seconded Chris Christie's plan to support me. I had not forgotten that. A week after the presidential election, Pence had come back as the vice president–elect to speak at the RGA, and he had told me almost exactly the same thing Christie had about Trump: "He's totally different than what you see onstage. Behind closed doors, one-on-one, you'd really like him."

I still wasn't persuaded.

"I know you have had to cut your own path in Maryland," he told me at the White House that day. "And that's great, but I promise we're gonna work together."

"I look forward to it, Mr. Vice President," I said. "Congratulations. It will be great having a governor as vice president. I'm proud of you."

A lot had happened—with Pence and with me—and I knew he was in a different position and had been under enormous pressure. I was pleasantly surprised at the 2019 Governors' Dinner when Yumi and I were assigned to sit with Mike and Karen Pence.

"Mr. Vice President," I said. "I'm really honored that I actually got to sit at your table. I was thinking they were probably going to put me in the kitchen."

He laughed hard at that line.

"Yeah," he joked, "I'm a little surprised too. But, no, seriously, you know Karen and I love you and Yumi."

The next morning the president spoke to the governors before he had to leave for Vietnam to meet with North Korean dictator Kim Jong-un. I was sitting at a small round table near the podium. Ivanka was assigned to sit next to me this time. I was glad Jared wasn't there too. *Man, they're really working me here.*

Just then, the president marched over from the podium. I have to say I could feel some tension from him this time. He didn't ask how I was doing or praise my poll numbers. He leaned over and gave Ivanka a goodbye hug before his flight to Vietnam.

Then, he shook my hand and put his left hand on my shoulder and said, "Governor, it's great to see you. Take care of my daughter, will you?" Which I thought seemed a little awkward, but it was a lot better than what I was expecting from him.

There are plenty of people—every elected Democrat, the commentators on every cable channel except Fox, and a few disenchanted Republicans like John Kasich—who spend all day every day bashing the president. They just hate Trump and want him destroyed at all costs. And then there are others—including the vast majority of Republican officeholders at every level—who won't ever publicly disagree, refusing to utter a single negative syllable about him no matter what crazy thing the president says or does. They are afraid of being attacked on Twitter. They don't want to upset the base. They're petrified of being primaried.

I've never been in either of those categories.

I never attack the president personally. Never call him a name. I'd really prefer not to talk about him at all. I stay focused on my job as governor. But when something rises to the level that I really disagree with, something that's just so offensive or that directly hurts the people of Maryland, I stand up and say something. That's my responsibility. He's still the president. I was respectful of President Obama. I'm respectful of President Trump. But unlike a lot of Republicans, I won't just stay silent, swear allegiance, and blindly toe the line. I have never been someone who would just sit down and shut up.

When I showed up March 4 in Iowa, the national media attention grew. Never mind that I had come to Des Moines for a meeting of the National Governors Association. I was, after all, vice chairman, preparing to assume the leadership of the nation's governors in a few months. I explained that I was there mainly to support the group's chairman, Montana governor Steve Bullock, an assertion that absolutely no one believed. A Democrat from a Republican state who was preparing to launch his own run for president, Bullock is a friend who has also governed from the middle. In Iowa, he was pushing better jobs for all Americans. And maybe, just maybe, Bullock picked Iowa for this meeting to get some national attention, too.

"I'm not here to do any campaigning," I insisted, though I did concede: "It is safe to say there are a lot of people in the party and outside the party who are approaching me."

I tried to keep things light. During my short walking tour of Des Moines, I said I was pleased that the temperature had doubled—"from one to two degrees." I fully understood how hard it would be to challenge a sitting president in his own party, and I said that was why I was in no particular hurry to make up my mind. "It currently makes no sense with a president that has the kind of approval rating that he does in his own party," I said. "Having said that, things can change, and we don't know what it might look like a few months from now."

CHAPTER 34

KEG PARTY

As the presidential talk still raged, I was invited to be the keynote speaker at a black-tie event in Washington on the night before Saint Patrick's Day, the annual fundraising dinner of the Society of the Friendly Sons of Saint Patrick. The Friendly Sons dinner, which raises money for charity, is packed every year with a who's who of Washington, including many well-known figures from business, politics, and the media. The speakers are welcome to have a message, but tradition demands they deliver it in a teasing, sentimental, just-this-side-of-insulting way.

I'm about as Irish as you can get without actually being born in an Old Sod county. And the Friendly Sons dinner seemed like an excellent venue for my message of across-the-aisle unity. Who knew? I might even get to poke some fun at all the talk about me as a potential Trump challenger. I'm not sure if my invitation was a tip of the Paddy cap to bipartisanship or just a clever ploy to put more Maryland behinds into the Capital Hilton seats. But the Friendly Sons' legendary jocularity was certainly out in force that evening, as were the heavy pours of Jameson.

When my time came to speak, I gave a shout-out to my own Irish heritage and my Irish-immigrant ancestors, "truly the only thing that Martin O'Malley and I have in common." I told the Watergate story about my dad and recalled how, as a seventh grader at Saint Ambrose Catholic School in Cheverly, I'd been "sworn" into Congress at my dad's side, ready to cast a second vote for the fifth district of Maryland. "Steny Hoyer made sure that I never did actually get the chance to cast any votes in Congress," I said. "Thank you, Steny, for saving me from all that divisiveness and dysfunction."

I celebrated the still-fierce rivalry among Washington-area Catholic boys' schools with a personal plug for my own beloved DeMatha: Go, Stags!— which, come to think of it, could also be a slogan for the Friendly Sons. I explained that "family circumstances" had forced me to transfer out after sophomore year, but school officials had recently offered me an honorary DeMatha diploma. "I asked them if we could push the event off until after the election," I explained. "I was afraid the *Washington Post* would run a headline that said, 'High School Dropout Hogan Acquires Counterfeit Diploma.'"

I told about my harrowing brush with lymphoma and my blessings from the pope. And I delivered a special tribute to fellow Irish Marylander (and my long-ago babysitter) Mike Miller, who'd served as president of the state senate longer than anyone else in history. "The Friendly Sons of Washington held its first banquet exactly ninety years ago tonight," I told the well-dressed crowd. "Herbert Hoover was president of the United States, William Howard Taft was chief justice of the Supreme Court, and Mike Miller was president of the Maryland Senate."

It was that kind of night at the Friendly Sons. The room was just as I expected it to be.

Then, I got to the topic all the swells were waiting for: the 2020 election for president, the future of the Republic, and my rumored role in both of them. This wasn't a room for Trump-bashing, and I didn't engage in any—certainly not explicitly.

There was, I noted, "a little bit of buzz in the national media and some speculation about 2020. I did just get back from Iowa, but I want to assure everyone that the trip had nothing whatsoever to do with presidential politics."

I could hear the groans in the room.

"I just thought that spending forty-eight hours in Des Moines in sub-zero temperatures would be a fun thing to do."

George Will, the intellectual conservative columnist and commentator, had recently written a column encouraging me to challenge Trump for president. "I appreciated the nice things he had to say," I conceded. "But he opened the piece by saying that I 'resembled a beer keg with an attitude.' First of all, I'm not sure George Will is actually an expert on beer kegs. I'll admit, at first, I was a little sensitive about that comparison because I've been trying hard to lose a few pounds. I've been on a low-carb diet, cutting out beer and potatoes, which probably means I'm no longer one hundred percent Irish."

But I had decided to own the whole beer-keg thing, I said. "Tonight, I want the Friendly Sons to be the first ones to know that I do intend to form a new political party. We're going to call it the Keg Party. I have quite a bit of experience organizing keg parties. The movement could help bring people like Chris Matthews and Brett Baier together under one tent." Both TV anchors were sitting at the head table with me, as was the next man I mentioned. "Heck, I think this is something even Brett Kavanaugh could get behind."

I didn't have to remind this crowd that the newest Supreme Court justice had bragged in his confirmation hearing: "I liked beer. I still like beer." Various members of the Friendly Sons had publicly defended Kavanaugh, publicly denounced him, or at least gotten nine days of columns out of the allegations against him.

I left plenty of time for the important message that was woven through my stabs at humor. Given the laughs and applause my talk generated, I would have to call this a very receptive audience, despite the DC zip code. "Like many of you," I said, "I'm completely fed up with the debilitating politics here in Washington, where insults substitute for debate, recrimination for negotiation, and gridlock for compromise, where getting something done for the people no longer seems to be a priority."

I wasn't here to point fingers, I said. "There is plenty of blame to go around. People on both sides of the aisle refuse to give up even a little to get a lot done." But something has to change. Lately, I said, we'd been making a lot of progress in Maryland, where "we've put problem-solving ahead of partisanship—and compromise ahead of conflict—and reached across the aisle to achieve bipartisan, common-sense solutions that work for the people."

It's really not that complicated, I explained. "The biggest crisis facing our nation isn't a wall between Mexico and the United States. It's the wall that has divided us right here in this country."

I paraphrased my hero Ronald Reagan but with a Trump-era emphasis, tailored just for today. "We need to tear down *this* wall," I said.

One dinner speech does not a movement make. I understood that. But if I could get a thunderous standing ovation in a crowd like this one in Washington, right in the belly of the beast, there was nowhere I couldn't deliver the same message. Even before the applause died down, I was already asking myself where I could take that message next.

My trip to New Hampshire was viewed as a much more serious move than my Iowa visit. I was invited to Saint Anselm College in Manchester on April 23 for *Politics & Eggs*, a time-honored proving ground for presidential candidates and would-be candidates in the nation's first primary state. But even before I went, my visit seemed to be causing concern around the White House.

David Bossie, a senior Trump operative who also represented Maryland on the Republican National Committee, was hustling around the state, trying to embarrass me politically. His tactic: pressuring Republican state senators, delegates, and others to come out early for the president's re-election—before I'd even made up my mind about running—thereby depriving me of political oxygen and making me look weak at home. "The White House has kept careful watch on Hogan's moves for months as a result of his criticisms and heightened national profile," a *Politico* story read.

Creating dissention in our limited Republican caucus in the middle of a legislative session was an idiotic idea. Our numbers were already decimated by the anti-Trump voter anger in the last election.

I called Bossie before I left for New Hampshire. "What the hell is wrong with you?" I said. "They asked me to speak at a breakfast. What are you guys so panicked about?"

He tried to assure me the timing was just a coincidence and gave me some bullshit about how the Trump campaign was doing this in all the states. "Look, Dave," I said, "what you're doing doesn't hurt me. It gets me more attention. It makes Trump look weak. But none of that matters. You just can't divide the state party in the middle of the legislative session and make legislators choose between their unpopular president, who is at twenty-six percent approval in Maryland, and their governor, who is at seventy-eight."

I wasn't done yet.

"I was just at the White House," I told Bossie. "The vice president was very nice. Ivanka was incredibly sweet. Now they're sending your ass in here like a bull in a china shop to try to bully legislators to scare me off. You should know that's not going to work, and it's likely to backfire."

He immediately backed off, agreeing to delay his scheme for the time being.

Politics & Eggs was a neat experience. I had heard about it for years. But my own speech was the first one I had ever attended.

My remarks were well received and broadcast live on C-SPAN, which I presume meant I had at least dozens of viewers nationwide. But the real action was outside the breakfast, where a giant scrum of national media people waited for me. They asked about the report from Special Counsel Robert Mueller, which had just been released. The president made "an attempt to obstruct justice" in the FBI investigation of Russian interference in the 2016 election, I said straight out. The report "did not completely exonerate the president."

Of course, the questions quickly turned to my possible candidacy for president. I had been to Iowa. We had trips to other states planned. "I'm not just wandering around the states hitchhiking," I joked. "I'm just going to continue to listen to people and just feel it out."

I had no interest in launching "a suicide mission" if I didn't think I had a prayer to win, I said. But a short, energetic campaign might be right up my alley. "I'm pretty good at retail politics," I said.

Several of the reporters wanted to know where all the other Republican Trump critics were and how come so few Republican officeholders had dared to raise even the gentlest complaints or criticisms. "There are no profiles in courage here," I said. "They're afraid of being primaried. They're afraid of being tweeted about. Very few of us are willing to say what we really think."

For a while, I'd been expecting to get one of Trump's insulting nicknames. I figured it was coming any day now. The president had no problem insult-tweeting potential rivals like Kasich, Flake, and Weld. I assumed he would go with "Fat Larry," an obvious choice as I had admittedly put on some weight since my cancer battle. Or maybe "Cancer Boy." That would be a good one. But it didn't happen. Trump treated me differently from almost anyone else except for maybe Chris Christie in 2016. During this entire period, he kept his thumbs completely off the Twitter keys when it came to me. I can't explain it. Maybe Trump really did respect my high approval ratings. Maybe he just figured it was better to let sleeping dogs lie. But even when I was openly critical of him, he had never once taken a single shot at me.

Not yet, anyway.

CHAPTER 35

BEST HOPE

So, was I or wasn't I running for president?

The talk kept building through the spring of 2019. Me being touted as a different kind of Republican. Someone who could guide the country past the divisions of the present. Someone who could work with both sides and build coalitions. Someone who could begin to solve the nation's problems instead of just fighting over them. Someone who could help to bring America back together after four volatile years of Donald Trump without swerving the country recklessly to the left, as most of the Democratic hopefuls would.

Our blue-state landslide had ignited this conversation. My second inauguration had defined it. And the media ran with it for six solid months.

I was the businessman-turned-governor crowned by the *Washington Post* as the "un-Trump Republican," running a government that Jeb Bush called "the antithesis of what's happening in Washington." A popular Republican officeholder with a record of achievement, who could attract votes from all sides and wasn't afraid to stand up to the current president. As the 2020 election grew nearer, there certainly weren't too many other people in that category.

All the hoopla felt a little strange to me. As far as I was concerned, I was just being me, doing exactly what I said I would do. For four years, I had tried my best to stay out of national politics. My plan was to keep a low profile and to stay focused on Maryland. But suddenly, there was this rising swirl of national interest—*Run, Larry, run!*—providing a much larger stage for my ideas and the things that I believed in.

At some point, though, I really did have to decide.

What's the rush? some of my senior political advisors asked me—smart people, all of them. The filing deadline for the February 11, 2020, New Hampshire primary, they pointed out, wasn't until the third Friday in November 2019. But waiting that long didn't feel right to me. I didn't want to drag the decision out. I was not going to be one of those perpetual political teases, thinking about running, hinting about running—then pulling the plug only after everyone around me was totally exhausted. That wasn't me. Either I was in it or I wasn't. I've always been the guy who tells it like it is. And I hate playing those political games.

In making my decision, I applied the same test I had used when I was first thinking about running for governor. If I was going to do this, I certainly didn't need a guarantee of victory. But there would have to be at least some possible path to success. Running for president is a deadly serious undertaking. I wasn't interested in launching a kamikaze mission. I wanted to know if we had an actual strategy for potential victory and a reasonable prospect of making a real difference.

Some national Republican leaders and consultants were telling me that Trump would eventually cross some red line. He would do something beyond the breaking point for the party faithful that would finally make him vulnerable to a primary challenge. But realistically I knew that waiting for Donald Trump to implode was not a viable strategy to build a campaign on.

As I studied the political landscape around me, frankly, I just didn't see it.

Donald Trump was clearly vulnerable in a general election. In fact, he was getting more so every day. He hadn't followed Reagan's big-tent doctrine to expand the party. He had alienated group after group of swing voters along with women, young people, and almost anyone who wasn't a white male. His approval ratings were dreadful. Never once had half of the country approved of the job he was doing. The country was more bitterly divided than ever.

But inside the Republican nominating process, he still looked unbelievably strong. The numbers varied from state to state. But among base Republican primary voters, he was polling consistently in the 80 percent range. They were a small slice of the nation, but the people who loved him seemed to love him unshakably. What Trump had said about his most ardent followers—in Iowa, January 2016—still seemed to be true: *"I could stand in the middle of Fifth Avenue and shoot somebody, and I wouldn't lose any voters, OK? It's, like, incredible."*

Yes, "incredible" is exactly how I would describe it.

The idea of advancing my message, talking about things I cared passionately about, did appeal to me. Across America, there was clearly an audience for my politics and my message. I think a majority of the American people felt just like I did. But that audience was not necessarily among Republican base primary voters. They still seemed to be all-in for Trump.

Even the Mueller report hadn't shaken that. Thousands of negative stories in the media hadn't either. Neither had the attacks from Democrats or his own former cabinet and senior staff members, which were piling up by the week.

Even the growing threat of impeachment was having no impact.

For now, at least, there seemed to be no immediate path forward for any credible primary challenge to the president.

On Saturday, June 1, I decided to put an end to the presidential talk. "I truly appreciate all of the encouragement I received from people around the nation urging me to consider making a run for president in 2020," I said that day. "However, I will not be a candidate."

Instead of running, I explained, I would complete my second term as governor and keep changing Maryland for the better. And we would keep setting an example for the nation, showing how common-sense, bipartisan leadership really can work to solve the serious problems of the day.

Starting in July, I would also assume leadership of America's governors as chairman of the National Governors Association. It would be an excellent opportunity to showcase how Republican and Democratic leaders across the country can and do work together in a bipartisan way. Something the politicians in Washington seem completely incapable of.

I also launched a national nonprofit advocacy group, An America United (www.AnAmericaUnited.org), for people fed up with politics as usual. The focus is fixing the broken politics and bringing people together to achieve bipartisan, common-sense solutions to the serious problems facing the nation.

"I believe there's going to be a future in the Republican Party beyond Donald Trump," I told the *Washington Post*. "It's either going to be next year or four years later. But at some point, we're going to be looking for what the future is going to be like."

I was asked what the future holds for me politically. "I'm not so concerned about my future *in* the Republican Party," I said. "I'm really much more concerned about a future *for* the Republican Party."

And that was supposed to be that. Now I could get back to being 100 percent focused on solving problems in my state.

But here's the thing about politics in America these days, especially since Donald Trump did a hostile takeover of the national Republican Party and captured the White House. Crazy and unpredictable things keep happening at lightning speed. It could be something head-scratching. It could be something outrageous. It could be something embarrassing or divisive. The one thing it won't be is nothing at all.

After the Mueller Report was issued, it seemed as if the president's potential impeachment problems were behind him. But in September 2019, news leaked of a federal whistleblower's report about a call between President Trump and Ukrainian president Volodymyr Zelensky. In that call, it was alleged, Trump had pressured Zelensky to open a criminal investigation against former vice president Joe Biden and Biden's son Hunter. To turn up the heat on Zelensky, the White House allegedly blocked $400 million in military aid that Congress had already appropriated for Ukraine. Biden, at the time, was the likeliest 2020 Democratic rival for Trump, and Ukraine was fending off military threats from Putin's Russia.

Within days, the White House released a summary of the call, which largely confirmed the allegations. But the summary predictably became a political Rorschach test where—yet again—each side saw in it what each side wanted to see, and all rallied to their respective talking points, projected at the highest possible volume. Democrats wanted a formal impeachment inquiry and wanted witnesses called. Republicans argued the call summary fully exonerated the president. Many of the Democrats, it seemed to me, were as reflexively anti-Trump as the Republicans were unwaveringly pro-Trump.

So where did I stand? The national media was airing 1974 Watergate hearing clips of my father and demanding to know my thoughts. The first to ask me straight up was Margaret Hoover, host of the PBS program *Firing Line*. "I think we do need an inquiry," I told her on October 10. "We have to get to the bottom of it. I'm not ready to say I support impeachment and the removal of the president, but I don't see any other way to get the facts."

Like my father, I wanted to be guided by the evidence, and the evidence suggested there was something that needed looking into. That didn't mean I thought that Pelosi and the House Democrats would give the president a fair hearing based on the evidence and the facts. "I'm concerned about—can we have a fair and objective one, and I'm not sure we can in this Democratic Congress," I told Hoover in the interview.

In speaking out, I wasn't entirely alone among the nation's Republican governors. Phil Scott of Vermont and Charlie Baker of Massachusetts both backed an impeachment probe. In the US Senate, Utah's Mitt Romney was speaking out as well. But this was still a lonely place for a Republican officeholder to be. The vast majority of Republican politicians were drinking the Kool-Aid and refusing to even look into the facts or, more often, were just too afraid for political reasons to speak out. And once the impeachment process got rolling and witness after witness was called to Capitol Hill, the predictable occurred: The parties immediately split into their separate warring camps. It quickly became clear that the impeachment process would be the exact opposite of the fair and balanced one that my father had insisted upon when Richard Nixon's future hung in the balance. This time around, the whole thing was unshakably tribal and partisan. Inconvenient facts were the last thing most people in Washington cared about. America's leaders were, as usual, trapped in divisive politics.

As a new year and a new decade were dawning, the president was impeached by the House of Representatives in a party-line vote, and Washington was its usual frenzied, angry, dysfunctional self. Gridlock. Finger-pointing. Spinning and sniping across the partisan divide. The only thing Democrats and Republicans seemed able to agree on was how wrong the other side was. The articles of impeachment charged Donald Trump with "abuse of power" and "obstruction of Congress"—serious allegations that did deserve a sober and factual airing in Congress. A man, after all, is innocent until proven guilty. "Let the facts be our guide," as my father said.

But that was simply never going to happen in today's national political environment, especially in a presidential election year. Democratic House Speaker Nancy Pelosi and Republican Senate Leader Mitch McConnell were locked in another of their drawn-out back-and-forths, even before the Trump impeachment trial could begin. Was there any doubt how that drama was going to end in the Republican-led Senate? No more doubt than there'd been in the Democratic-led House. Each party pushed its own narrative. In the House and in the Senate, where you sat seemed to determine where you stood. And all the while, Washington was getting hardly any of the people's business done.

When Richard Nixon faced impeachment, my dad was fighting for a fair and objective hearing for both sides. But forty-six years later, Congress had failed to do its job. Neither the House nor the Senate even came close to meeting the high standard set by my father.

As it happened, both the Senate's impeachment vote and my sixth State of the State address were set for February 5. The juxtaposition couldn't have been any starker. At noon, as anticipation built for the Senate impeachment vote in Washington hours later, I walked into our historic State House in Annapolis. Instead of looking for enemies in the packed chamber, I sought out allies and friends. "As we come together once again for this time-honored tradition," I began, "it is my distinct privilege to be the first Maryland governor to begin a State of the State address by saying, 'Madam Speaker.'" Just a few months earlier, Adrienne Jones became the first African American and the first woman elected to lead Maryland's House of Delegates. She's a Baltimore County Democrat with strong beliefs and a genuine desire to serve. There's plenty we don't agree on, but I'd rather seek common ground than trade insults across the aisle. It was a warm moment with a standing ovation for the new speaker at her first State of the State address.

In the speech, I appealed to the Legislature's Democratic majority to help me reduce violent crime, provide record funding for our schools, pass non-partisan redistricting, and provide the largest tax cut in two decades to help our retirees. Politically, these were all heavy lifts, but I struck an optimistic tone. "As I look back at all that we have been through and all the progress that we have made together here in Maryland over these last five years," I said, "my experiences do not burden me with dread. They fill me with hope. I believe that in spite of all that divides us in America today, there is far more that unites us."

Meanwhile, the US Senate was lurching toward the largely party-line vote everyone expected, acquitting the president on both impeachment counts. No new evidence had been taken. No witnesses had been heard. In the end, the only senator who broke party ranks on either side was Republican Mitt Romney, who voted to convict the president of abusing the power of his office. Mitt is an honorable man who I believe did what he felt was right. Like my dad so many decades earlier, he was attacked for voting his conscience.

Things weren't all *kumbaya* back in Annapolis. I was still a Republican governor in an overwhelmingly Democratic state. We had philosophical dif-ferences, lots of them. The other party controlled a supermajority of the Leg-islature and could easily override any of my vetoes. And I'll admit, sometimes I found the Democrats in the Legislature frustratingly locked in. I wished I didn't have to negotiate and maneuver quite so strenuously to get things done. Honestly, some days I wanted to pull my hair out—before I remembered I didn't have much left to grab hold of. But I felt like we'd found that middle ground where we could all stand together. I could cite many examples, but here's one: The Capital Beltway, the interstate highway that surrounds Wash-ington and runs through Virginia and Maryland, has suffered for decades with the second-worst traffic congestion in the nation. In early 2020, while Washington was still locked in gridlock over impeachment, we succeeded in approving a major traffic-relief program for the region. The *Washington Post* called it the most important infrastructure initiative since the 1970s.

Our regional accord will ease backups for hundreds of thousands of commuters every day and build a new and expanded American Legion Memorial Bridge across the Potomac River connecting Maryland and Virginia. It's the largest public-private transportation partnership in the nation, and we negotiated it with the Democrats in Maryland and with Virginia's Democratic governor, Ralph Northam.

As it turns out, this was just the kind of leadership nearly everyone was desperately crying out for, regardless of party, race, age, or gender. The latest proof of this was in an independent poll of Marylanders by Gonzales Research. Donald Trump's job approval rating was a dismal 37 percent. His disapproval was 61 percent. By contrast, our numbers were stunning. Five years in, in this overwhelmingly Democratic state, 75 percent of Maryland voters approved of the job I was doing. Only 17 percent disapproved. Clearly, people all across the political spectrum preferred the way we had chosen to govern as "the antithesis of Washington." In these times of bitter tribalism and warring camps, we were somehow managing to earn the approval of 70 percent or more of every single demographic group.

Seventy percent of African Americans.

Seventy-three percent of Democrats.

Seventy-five percent of women.

Seventy-seven percent of Republicans.

Seventy-eight percent of independents.

Pollster Patrick Gonzales was quoted as saying: "In this age of extreme political polarization, it is astonishing that men and women approve of Hogan in identical numbers, as do voters under fifty and those fifty and older. Further, in our thirty-five years of polling the voters of Maryland, we have never found a pol who was supported by 73 percent of Democrats, 77 percent of Republicans, and 78 percent of independents. These numbers indicate a versatile, Protean-like appeal we have not witnessed in a politician before . . . anywhere."

We were on a roll. We'd worked hard. We'd stuck to our values. And we were genuinely getting amazing things accomplished. I also felt like I was getting pretty good at this job of governing. I was really feeling comfortable and confident in my role. I don't want to say I'd grown complacent or anything like that. The way I approached it, being governor was still 24-7-365. I certainly wasn't phoning it in. I knew I'd be giving it all I had until the day I handed the office over to my successor in January of 2023.

But after all I had been through, I did not expect that my greatest challenge by far as governor was still in front of me.

Silent.

Invisible.

Deadly.

Growing exponentially by the day.

PART VI

SAVING LIVES

CHAPTER 36

GROWING THREAT

I had no idea what coronavirus was.

Unless you count political science, my only scientific background consisted of taking Meteorology 101 as a science requirement with all the football and basketball players back at FSU. I have a couple of honorary doctorates from Mount St. Mary's University in Emmitsburg, Maryland, and Hanyang University in Seoul, South Korea. They give those to governors sometimes. But that doesn't make me a real doctor. Not even close.

Actually, I did know a little about pandemics. Over the past five years, our emergency management team had briefed me on our pandemic plans. From time to time, they ran tabletop exercises on how the state might respond to the swine flu or SARS or other scary-sounding epidemics. *If something like that were to happen, would we be prepared?* We certainly wanted to be. But it was always more of an academic exercise. There had been flare-ups around the world since I'd come into office. But thankfully, none of those deadly diseases had ever swept toward the shores of Maryland. And no one I had spoken to had ever predicted anything like the novel coronavirus that jumped from an animal to a human in Wuhan, China, in late 2019—until suddenly, it happened.

Starting small but spreading quickly.

Delivering disease, death, and economic destruction wherever it went, which soon enough would encompass the entire world.

By the time this virus got a grip on us, everyone's life would be changed, including my own. I would be thrust into a whole new arena as a leader. I would face enormous scrutiny and the toughest demands of my public life. I would take responsibility for the lives of the six million people in my state. As chair of the National Governors Association, I would have to go toe-to-toe with the president of the United States and fight every day to help people nationwide.

There were a lot of things I wasn't certain about as I went into this global pandemic, but there was one thing I knew for sure: whatever the coming challenges might demand, I absolutely could not fail.

The first case was revealed to the world on January 11 by China's state-controlled media—a sixty-one-year-old man who had been a regular customer of one of Wuhan's famous wet markets, where bats and other animals are freshly slaughtered for sale. We now know that this announcement came at least two months after the coronavirus had actually begun to spread. There was nothing in the earliest reports, predictably downplayed by the communist Chinese government, that made me think this was going to become a global crisis. But I was concerned enough by the Chinese announcement that I told our emergency management folks and our health department people and my senior leadership team in Annapolis, "Better keep an eye on this, and let's start coming up with some plans."

The virus wasn't wasting any time. The first cases outside China were confirmed by the World Health Organization on January 20—in Japan, South Korea, and Thailand. The next day, the first US case was announced in Washington State: a man in his thirties who had just returned from a trip to Wuhan. "While originally thought to be spreading from animal to person, there are growing indications that limited person-to-person spread is happening," said a statement from the US Centers for Disease Control and Prevention.

And that was true, except for the word "limited."

To me, the news all sounded ominous. If this thing showed up in Seattle, couldn't it also travel to Maryland? Those emergency management tabletop exercises were suddenly seeming like a smart idea.

Our team jumped in, gathering quite a bit of information in those early days. My senior advisor Ron Gunzburger and Matt McDaniel, a young lawyer who'd recently joined our staff, began tracking the daily reports on the disease and sketching out preliminary plans. Fran Phillips, our deputy secretary of health, brought her terrific expertise into the room. Matt Clark, my chief of staff, began reaching out to top infectious disease and public-health experts across Maryland. Our state is home to Johns Hopkins University, the University of Maryland Medical System, and the National Institutes of Health. Our medical and science talent is among the best in the world. We were learning as we went, but our efforts were up and running before most people were paying much attention, including America's president.

On January 25, a Saturday, we got our first scare in Maryland. Three travelers who'd been in China landed at Baltimore Washington International Airport with sniffles, coughs, and lung distress, symptoms that mirrored the new virus. State health officials responded promptly, testing all three travelers and ordering them to isolate themselves at home. Though the tests came back negative, we were already making decisions in the governor's office about how we should react when the first positive cases arrived.

"It won't be long," I assured our team.

On Wednesday, January 29, at a meeting of the Maryland Board of Public Works, I made my first public comments about the approaching public-health threat, even before we had a single case in Maryland. I didn't want to panic anyone, but I did want people to be alerted about what seemed to be heading our way. As always, I wanted to err on the side of transparency. "At my direction," I calmly explained, "the state is taking every precaution to prepare and mobilize whatever resources are necessary to address the coronavirus. Our state government team is in close communication with federal officials and will continue to remain so on an ongoing basis. Maryland is fortunate to have some of the top health research facilities in the world, and I am confident in our state's ability to respond to any potential cases of the virus. I expect that we will be a leader in developing treatments, and perhaps even a vaccine."

———

For whatever reason, President Trump's first public utterance on the coronavirus sounded more like denial. He was in Davos, Switzerland, on January 22, after the first American case was revealed.

"Are there worries about a pandemic at this point?" asked CNBC anchor Joe Kernen.

"We have it totally under control," Trump responded unhesitatingly. "It's one person coming in from China, and we have it under control. It's going to be just fine."

And off the president went for the next eight weeks. The rest of January and February were peppered with cheerful or sarcastic comments and tweets, downplaying the outbreak's severity and the need for Americans to do much of anything.

In a January 24 Twitter post, Trump lavished praise on the Chinese government. "China has been working very hard to contain the Coronavirus," he tweeted. "The United States greatly appreciates their efforts and transparency. It will all work out well. In particular, on behalf of the American People, I want to thank President Xi!"

Four days later, the president retweeted a headline from the fledgling pro-Trump One America News network, the first of many offering false hope of a cure: "Johnson & Johnson to create coronavirus vaccine." Where that came from, I have no idea. The folks at J&J may have been just as surprised.

"We have it very well under control," the president said at a January 30 campaign rally in Michigan. "We have very little problem in this country at this moment—five. And those people are all recuperating successfully."

Despite the upbeat prognosis, the president was receiving the same dire warnings as we were in Maryland. In fact, we would all learn later, he was getting barraged with them. From alarmed intelligence officials who were hearing urgent reports from China. From State Department epidemiologists. From others. In a January 18 phone call from Health and Human Services Secretary Alex Azar, who was trying to pass along warnings, all the president reportedly wanted to talk about was his opposition to banning flavored vaping cartridges. Officials at the National Center for Medical Intelligence, a small but vital outpost the Defense Intelligence Agency, were gaming out how America might quarantine a city the size of Chicago. No one had ever done that before. White House trade advisor Peter Navarro sent up a major flare in his January 29 memo, warning that the Wuhan coronavirus could become a "full-blown pandemic," risking half a million American lives and trillions of dollars in economic productivity.

On January 30, nearly 9,800 people were reported to have been infected around the world, with 213 dead. The next day, the Trump Administration restricted travel from China.

It was a positive step. It almost certainly saved lives. And Trump took some criticism from Democrats who questioned the move's effectiveness and accused him of unfairly singling out the Chinese. It wasn't a total clampdown. For one thing, the ban didn't apply to Americans returning home, potentially bringing back the virus. But in hindsight, the Chinese travel ban was absolutely the right thing to do. Unfortunately, it harkened no change in White House messaging.

On February 2, Trump phoned into Sean Hannity's show on Fox News. "Coronavirus," Hannity said. "How concerned are you?"

"Well," Trump answered, "we pretty much shut it down coming in from China. We have a tremendous relationship with China, which is a very positive thing." Too bad the virus was already spreading rapidly around the world. There were 14,557 reported cases by then, many of them in Europe now, especially in Italy—and a lot of missed opportunities in Washington.

So many nationwide actions could have been taken in those early days but weren't. No public warnings were issued from the White House. No fifty-state strategy was drawn up. No personal-protective equipment or life-saving ventilators were dispatched to American hospitals from the national stockpile. At the same time, the federal government was making poor decisions about coronavirus testing. That might have been the biggest mistake of all. While other countries, South Korea most impressively, were racing ahead with well-coordinated testing regimes, the Trump Administration rejected international testing protocols and tried to go it alone. Without clear leadership in Washington, the test being used by the federal Centers for Disease Control was fraught with inaccuracies, and the nation's private labs were kept at arm's length. The resulting disorganization would delay mass testing for almost two months and leave the nation largely in the dark as the epidemic spread.

Instead of listening to his own public-health experts, the president was talking and tweeting like a man more concerned about boosting the stock market or his own re-election plans. Thank goodness we had governors who were willing to step up and be counted.

America's governors descended on Washington in early February for the annual winter meeting of the National Governors Association. As chairman, I had worked closely with the staff for months, assembling the agenda. We had a full weekend planned. At the end of the third day, Sunday, February 9, right before the governors had to change into tuxedos or gowns for dinner at the White House, I squeezed in a private, governors-only briefing at our hotel, the Marriott Marquis. We brought in five of the federal government's top experts to address us about the growing threat.

We had Dr. Anthony Fauci, the longtime director of the National Institute of Allergy and Infectious Diseases. Dr. Fauci was highly admired in the public-health field, although his awesome knowledge and straight-talking style hadn't yet made him a national rock star. We had CDC head Dr. Robert Redfield. We also had Ken Cuccinelli, the acting deputy secretary of Homeland Security, as well as Jay Butler, the CDC's deputy director for infectious diseases, and Robert Kadlec, assistant secretary for preparedness and response at the Department of Health and Human Services. It was an all-star panel of top professionals who really knew their stuff, the farthest thing imaginable from one of those dull, plenary sessions that government conferences are famous for. We were hit with a series of detailed, factual presentations and some frank back-and-forth, detailing the knowns and unknowns of this scary virus. We got the unfiltered truth, as well as it was known at that point.

"This could be catastrophic . . . The death toll could be significant . . . Much more contagious than SARS . . . Testing will be crucial . . . You have to follow the science—that's where the answers lie." It was jarring, the huge contrast between the experts' warnings and the president's public dismissals. Weren't these the people the White House was consulting about the virus? What made the briefing even more chilling was its clear, factual tone. It was simply a case of the nation's greatest experts telling us: "This is what you might be faced with" and "This is what you have to do." All of it was a harrowing warning of an imminent national threat.

Cuccinelli told the governors that when we got back home from Washington, we needed to consult with our legal teams to find out what public health emergency powers we had. Could we order the quarantine of individuals? Of communities? What if people didn't comply? Cuccinelli, who had been the attorney general of Virginia, explained that governors have a wide range of authority in a public-health crisis.

It was a sobering warning. We all took it seriously, at least most of us did. It was enough to convince almost all the governors that this epidemic was going to be worse than most people realized.

That eye-opening briefing in early February gave the governors a giant leg up before the epidemic was officially declared a global pandemic. With the president largely unengaged in this crucial early period, the governors were ready to step up and lead in the early months of what was quickly becoming a terrible plague.

———

A couple of other things happened that weekend in Washington. They didn't seem so significant at the time, but they ended up planting seeds that would bloom quite dramatically later on.

On Friday night, the Republican Governors Association sponsored a dinner with President Trump. Backstage beforehand, I said hello to the president. We took a photo together. He was perfectly cordial. Then the president came out and gave one of his unscripted rally speeches that seemed to go on at least an hour too long. He touched on all kinds of disconnected topics. I don't remember him mentioning the virus, but he did talk about Asia. How much he respected President Xi of China. How crafty he'd been negotiating a better trade deal with the Chinese. How much he liked playing golf with his buddy "Shinzo," Prime Minister Abe of Japan. How well he got along with North Korean dictator Kim Jong-un. Then, the jarring part, how he really didn't like dealing with President Moon from South Korea. The South Koreans were "terrible people," Trump said, adding that he didn't know why the United States had been protecting them all these years. "They don't pay us," Trump complained.

Yumi was sitting there as the president hurled insults at her birthplace. I could tell she was hurt and upset. I know she wanted to walk out. But she sat there politely and silently.

The next night, on Saturday, Lee Soo-hyuck, the South Korean ambassador to the United States, hosted a reception at his official residence on Glenbrook Road for all the governors and their spouses. Yumi had worked with the ambassador to plan the event. During the reception, President Moon Jae-in delivered a video message, welcoming the governors and thanking them for Korea's very special relationship with the United States. Speaking in Korean with English subtitles, he said how proud he was of Yumi as the first Korean American first lady in America. Then he referred to me as the *han kuk sahi,* or son-in-law, of the Korean people. It meant a lot to us to hear him say that, though it would take a couple of months before we would learn just how much his warmth would truly mean to the people of my state.

CHAPTER 37

IT'S HERE

As soon the governors' conference ended, President Trump hit the campaign trail. I returned to Annapolis and summoned my team the very next day. I told them about the briefing from the infectious-disease experts and warned everyone: "This thing is going to be a serious crisis."

By then, the *Diamond Princess* cruise ship, quarantined off the coast of Japan, had 174 confirmed coronavirus cases. No one knew whether to hold the passengers offshore or let the ship pull into port, and no one informed us that there were a dozen Marylanders aboard.

We were following all the reports from Europe and Asia. Italy and Iran were big concerns. Germany was struggling too. Ron Gunzburger and Matt McDaniel carefully charted the spread of the disease. They kept a special eye on California and Washington State, where the early American case count was ticking up. Matt Clark and Fran Phillips mapped out potential responses, asking whether lockdown measures that seemed to be working in authoritarian China were even thinkable in a free society like Maryland. Ron and Matt

McDaniel also prepared a memo on the legal powers of a Maryland governor in a health emergency, along with some early steps I might take. We made a list of special Maryland vulnerabilities. The cruise-ship terminal in Baltimore. Our nursing homes, schools, universities, and prisons. And we began seriously asking ourselves: Despite Maryland's renowned health-care system and the state's world-class medical facilities, would we have the hospital capacity to handle a major outbreak of COVID-19, as the respiratory disease caused by the virus was now officially being called? I had genuine concerns that we might not.

From the evidence I was seeing, we easily could run short of everything and everyone we needed. Too few ICU beds and ventilators and lifesaving personal protective gear. Too few N95 masks, surgical gowns, and coronavirus testing supplies. Too few doctors, nurses, and respiratory techs—and what would we do if those frontline workers started getting sick? There were so many issues to consider.

But as we were busy working our way through them, February was fast becoming one of the biggest wastes of a month in the history of Washington. At his February 10 campaign rally in New Hampshire, President Trump was all over the map. Impeachment. The economy. Grievances with the "fake news" media. He lingered on the spreading coronavirus just long enough to dismiss it as a threat.

"Miraculously," he predicted, the virus could disappear. "A lot of people think that . . . as the heat comes in, typically that will go away in April." Referring to the United States, he added: "We're in great shape, though. We have twelve cases, eleven cases, and many of them are in good shape now."

While the president was downplaying the threat, governors around the country were showing leadership and racing to prepare. California's Gavin Newsom and Washington's Jay Inslee (two Democrats) and Ohio's Mike DeWine and Massachusetts's Charlie Baker (two Republicans) stayed especially focused. The president, by contrast, was anything but. A MAGA rally in Phoenix on February 19. Firing the acting director of national intelligence because the president didn't appreciate a briefing he gave Congress on Russian interference in the upcoming 2020 election. A rally in Colorado Springs. A rally in Las Vegas. Flying off for a two-day state visit to India with lavish banquets and gigantic gatherings—and additional dismissals of the corona-virus threat.

"The Coronavirus is very much under control in the USA," the president tweeted on February 24. By then, the confirmed US case count was at fifty-one.

Two days later, Trump took a great step by appointing Vice President Mike Pence to head the federal government's coronavirus task force. I have always liked and respected Mike Pence. As a former governor of Indiana, he had an instinctive understanding of the importance of governors and what it means to run a state. But even that sensible appointment didn't mean the president was coming to grips with the threat. "It may get bigger," he told reporters at the White House. "It may get a little bigger. It may not get bigger at all. We'll see what happens. But regardless of what happens, we are totally prepared . . . When you have fifteen people and the fifteen people within a couple of days is going to be down to close to zero, that's a pretty good job we've done."

Unfortunately, the case count was going in the opposite direction, and so was the growing list of those the president was ready to blame: Demo-crats, CNN, MSNBC, Chuck Schumer, the Obama Administration. "One day—it's like a miracle—it will disappear," he said on February 27. Two days after that, he promised that a vaccine would be ready "very quickly." At a rally in South Carolina, he compared the Democrats' criticism of his coronavirus response to their impeachment efforts, saying, "This is their new hoax."

February ended with 85,403 confirmed coronavirus cases around the world and no national plan in place in the United States.

———————

On March 1, a Sunday, around 2 PM, I got a call from New York's Dem-ocratic governor, Andrew Cuomo. His state, like Maryland, hadn't gotten a case yet. But like me, he knew the virus was coming, and he was getting focused on how to respond. "What would you think of trying to get the gov-ernors together for a call about this?" he asked me.

"Great minds think alike," I told him. "We are actually working on that right now. It's important to have all the governors talking to each other." I was looking to schedule a call for early in the week, I said.

Later that day, I was visiting with the family of an old friend who had died—not from COVID-19—when one of my troopers pulled me aside and said: "The vice president's office is trying to get ahold of you. He wants you to come to the White House tomorrow and be in the Situation Room. They want to do a video conference with all the governors." I confirmed I'd attend and round up the other governors. That night, Governor Cuomo announced New York had just confirmed its first case of COVID-19: a thirty-nine-year-old female health-care worker who lived in Manhattan.

I went to the Situation Room on Monday, sat next to Vice President Pence with the top leaders of the White House Coronavirus Task Force. We did the video call with the governors. I was the only governor in the room. Dr. Fauci was there. He was joined by Dr. Deborah Birx, who had just been named as coordinator of the White House task force. It was obvious that Mike Pence was taking the pandemic seriously. Without President Trump in the room, Pence was all business. Sober. Methodical. "Here are the facts as we know them," he said. "Let's hear from the professionals."

I attended one more of these meetings in the Situation Room a week later, before doing the rest of them with some of my team via videoconference from the Maryland State House. These twice-weekly White House conferences with the governors would remain informative and productive. Not surprisingly, they were somewhat less so on those occasions when the president himself participated. While I appreciated the opportunity to speak frankly and directly to him, I'm not sure everyone felt as comfortable speaking their minds when the president was presiding.

It was only a matter of time before the virus would reach Maryland. I was constantly trading texts and phone calls with governors around the country, from states where the virus had been detected and states where it hadn't yet. "What are you guys doing? . . . How bad do you think this is going to be?" There was no doubt now: the governors would be leading the frontline response, and as chair of the National Governors Association, I would be leading the governors.

My team and I had been running hard for the past two months, and nothing was letting up. Luckily, I had one short break on the calendar. Weeks earlier, I had agreed to fly down to Florida on Thursday, March 5, for a children's charity weekend at the Baltimore Orioles spring-training facility in Sarasota. I would throw out the first pitch and attend a bunch of spring-training events. All that week, I kept thinking I probably needed to cancel. I was getting constant updates from our team. The health department was testing one or two symptomatic people a day, though so far everyone had come back negative.

"Don't you think we need to cancel the Florida trip?" I kept asking the staff. "The last thing I want is to be in Florida when we get our first case in Maryland." We'd made a commitment to the Orioles, the staffers kept reminding me, adding that it was easy enough to fly home from Florida should that become necessary. So we decided to go ahead with the trip. "Just keep me informed up to the minute," I said. "I don't want to be finding out about our first cases after I am already in Florida."

That Thursday morning, I spoke on Capitol Hill to a bipartisan group of senators and congressmen hosted by No Labels, a terrific group trying to combat partisan dysfunction in politics. Then, I made a speech at a Republican Governors Association event before rushing to meet Yumi at Reagan National Airport for our 1:50 PM American Airlines flight to Tampa. As we waited in the departure lounge, we ran into Karen Pence, who was catching a flight to fill in for the vice president at a campaign rally. She and Yumi chatted while I got updates from the office about our coronavirus preparations. Still no cases. Checking. Double-checking. Then checking again.

Relieved that no Marylanders had tested positive yet, we boarded the flight—then promptly sat on a runway for more than an hour, as I continued texting back and forth with the office. Finally, at 3:05 PM, the pilot said we were cleared for takeoff.

Ten minutes into the flight, I loosened my tie and ordered a drink. For a moment, I almost started to relax. Even with a full schedule, a thirty-six-hour trip to Florida was something Yumi and I could really use. She was smiling in the seat beside me. That's when I looked up to see my assistant Collin Cummings leaning over me.

"Sir," he said, "we just got notified of our first three positive cases of coronavirus, all in Montgomery County."

Really?!?

"Find out when the first return flight is," I said to Collin. "I want to get back as quickly as we possibly can."

Collin and our executive protection detail began furiously texting and phoning with our team in Annapolis, checking flight schedules and doing their best to answer my many questions. They gathered early details about the three patients. Apparently, they had all been on a Nile River cruise in Egypt before returning to Maryland. And here was the immediate logistical challenge for us: Our American flight, now an hour late, wasn't scheduled to land in Tampa until 5:10. The last and only nonstop back to BWI that evening was a Southwest flight, scheduled to depart from a completely different part of the airport at 5:10.

I said to Collin: "We cannot miss that plane. They cannot take off without us. If you have to, have Matt Clark contact Gary Kelly [Southwest's chairman and CEO]. We need that plane to wait for us."

Collin was on it.

I asked Yumi to stay behind in Florida and fill in for me at the Orioles events, just as she had at the Korean ambassador's residence in Washington the night the Baltimore riots exploded. These emergency U-turns were starting to feel like a pattern.

We landed in Tampa, where we were met by our advance detail team and local police officers. "Good luck, honey," Yumi called out as the police, Collin, and I bolted into the crowded terminal. Down one concourse. Onto a tram. Through another concourse. Onto another tram. Then onto the waiting Southwest flight. We took the only open seats, back in the very last row of the plane.

If anything, the return trip was even more eventful than the journey down. I had just begun reviewing details of the new cases and editing some remarks for the press conference when the plane's Wi-Fi went down. Corporal Thomas Scott, the leader of my detail, was trying to communicate with the Maryland State Police and the Maryland Transportation Authority police at BWI airport. No luck. Collin and I were trying to connect with my chief of staff, health secretary, communications director, and others to get critical information on the public-health emergency and to discuss the announcement I would need to make as soon as we landed and got to Annapolis.

The flight attendants were apologetic about the Wi-Fi. "Isn't there some other way for us to communicate with the ground?" I asked. "Isn't there a way that the pilot can make calls from the cockpit?"

"We can patch through calls but only in a health emergency," one of the flight attendants said.

"This *is* a health emergency!" I assured her.

I asked her to keep it confidential but whispered the reason why. The Maryland-based crew could not have been any more accommodating after that.

The MTA police and Maryland state troopers met us on the tarmac at BWI. In a caravan of half a dozen SUVs with a motorcycle escort, we raced back to Annapolis in record time, just shy of twenty minutes. I appreciated the speed, though, with all the sirens, I couldn't hear everything everyone was trying to tell me on the conference call as we raced back.

I jogged into the State House a little after eight o'clock and climbed the marble staircase to the second floor. I stopped quickly in my office and signed the state of emergency order that my legal counsel, Mike Pedone, had prepared, the first of many emergency orders he would draft for us. The media were already assembled and waiting in the Governor's Reception Room, the same spot where I had announced my cancer diagnosis almost five years earlier. But this time, I wasn't the only person whose health was at risk.

If I'd learned anything from the public part of my own cancer battle, it was this: If you are transparent and let people know what's happening, give them the straight facts, they will stand beside you through thick and thin.

Clearly, I would need that support again.

I announced that three positive coronavirus tests had been confirmed at the Public Health Laboratory in Baltimore. A husband and wife in their seventies and a woman in her fifties, just back in Maryland from an Egyptian cruise. The patients were now in isolation at home, as state health department investigators tracked down others who might have come into contact with them.

"While this news is serious," I said, "I want to again remind everyone that this is exactly what our state has been actively and aggressively preparing for."

Right then and there, I declared a state of emergency and fully activated the state emergency operations center, just as we had when the riots erupted in Baltimore.

The riots, my cancer—all the lessons from my past challenges would be guiding me through this one.

CHAPTER 38

GLOBAL PANDEMIC

The days and weeks that followed were a blizzard of executive orders, press conferences, phone calls with the other governors and federal infectious-disease experts, briefings with our Maryland coronavirus response team, consultations with local elected officials and legislative leaders, endless strategy sessions with my senior staff, and constant reminders that I should sanitize my hands—*again*. Running a state and leading the nation's governors during a deadly pandemic is not a job for the faint of heart. Frankly, it was physically and emotionally exhausting.

On March 11, the World Health Organization officially declared COVID-19 a global pandemic.

"This is going to be the most important challenge of our lives," I said to the leaders of Maryland's twenty-four counties in a March 13 conference call, as five more positive tests were confirmed. "But this will also be the most important thing we ever do."

Not a single person disagreed. As diverse a group as they were—Republicans, Democrats, urban, rural, and suburban—every one of these local leaders could feel the weight of the moment. We were all in this together, even if none of us knew exactly what *this* was. There was just so much to be done.

The day before, I had announced that all public schools would close for two weeks beginning March 16 and outlined a series of other extraordinary steps: calling up the Maryland National Guard, prohibiting large gatherings, and delegating all my non-coronavirus state duties to Lieutenant Governor Boyd Rutherford so I could focus exclusively on the crisis.

On March 14, I expanded emergency care for the children of critical personnel, as we got our twenty-sixth case. The next day, with community transmission obviously growing, I issued an order closing the state's casinos, racetracks, and betting facilities, as the Legislature raced toward an early adjournment, wrapping up everything from the budget to education reform.

I heard some scary numbers during my morning senior staff meeting on March 16. New modeling from Johns Hopkins University projected that if we imposed no social distancing orders, Maryland would have 360,000 coronavirus cases by June 1. And with the virus's current 3.4 percent mortality rate, that would come out to 12,200 deaths over the next three months. Clearly, more actions were needed to flatten the infection curve. So later that day I ordered that all the bars and restaurants cease sit-down service and that gyms and movie theaters close. Because we were so clear in explaining the reasons for these drastic actions, we got overwhelming public support.

On March 17, the quietest Saint Patrick's Day ever, I postponed the April 28 primary election to June 2. We couldn't have hundreds of people lining up at polling places in the middle of a deadly pandemic. That same day, the Preakness was postponed until September at the earliest. On March 18, we recorded our first coronavirus death, a Prince George's County man in his sixties who had underlying medical issues. Terrible news, but you couldn't exactly call it a surprise.

That day, I told the senior staff: "I know you're working as fast as you can, but I need you all to work faster." And here was the inspiring part: they didn't roll their eyes at me. They did whatever was needed and more. They opened the hospital surge beds faster than anyone thought possible. They procured more supplies and equipment. They organized programs to feed kids around the state, and on and on. It didn't matter the task. Everyone stepped up and gave it their all.

"I don't want to scare people," I explained, "but I don't want to BS them either." By March 19, we had 119 positives, including a five-year-old girl from Howard County. That day, I ordered new restrictions on public transit and at BWI airport.

The virus was sweeping across the state and the nation. I wasn't the only governor taking bold, unprecedented steps, but I was among the most aggressive and the earliest. While I heard a few muffled complaints that I might be overreacting, I was certain I wasn't. And sadly, the virus kept proving me right.

And so it went, shutting down big parts of the economy and major aspects of everyday life because we had to. The actions we were forced to take were beyond painful, and I was acutely aware of the severe economic impact they would have on people's lives. But it was the only way to reduce the spread of this deadly disease, protect our health-care system from being totally overloaded, and save the lives of thousands of people. On March 23, I ordered the closing of all nonessential businesses and offered unprecedented financial assistance to those businesses and their employees. We turned the Baltimore Convention Center and a neighboring hotel into field hospitals. On March 25, I announced the schools would remain closed for at least another four weeks. On March 28, we shut down all state park beaches. And on March 30, I issued an executive order directing Marylanders to stay home. That order wrapped in many of my previous orders, which had effectively closed down the state even before the stay-at-home order was issued. But I needed people to get the message and take it more seriously.

I would end up signing more than three dozen executive orders, not one of which I could have ever imagined signing before any of this.

At the White House, mid-March brought a change in tone. On March 16, President Trump acknowledged for the first time that COVID-19 was much more serious than he had previously let on, urging older Americans and those with chronic health conditions to stay at home. Without enforced social distancing around the nation, the president warned, 2.2 million Americans could die. He also conceded that the economy may well be careening toward recession. The way the stock market had been tumbling lent strong credence to that. It could be a while, the president added, until things returned to normal. "If we do a really good job, people are talking about July, August, something like that," he said to the same reporters he'd been assuring for months that there was nothing to worry about at all.

Trump's change in tone was certainly welcome. Unfortunately, it didn't last very long. By the very next day, he was again downplaying the dangers of the public-health emergency and praising his own performance. He attacked New York's Andrew Cuomo and "failing Michigan governor" Gretchen Whitmer and insisted he had taken the threat seriously from the start. In the weeks and months to come, these zigzagging, confusing messages would remain the one constant in the White House pandemic response.

Nothing was more important than testing to get the spread under control, as the cases really began to skyrocket. If we didn't know who had the virus, how could we possibly target our response? One of the biggest frustrations—not just for me but for most of the governors—was trying to get our hands on coronavirus test kits and the chemical reagents that were needed to put those tests to work.

On the topic of testing, the president, as usual, was all over the place. "Anybody that wants a test can get a test," Trump had asserted unequivocally on March 6, which was blatantly false. By then, exactly 2,252 tests had been performed in the entire United States, according to the COVID Tracking Project. All across the country, my fellow governors were desperately pleading for help on testing. But Trump kept insisting the administration had it under control: "1.4 million tests on board next week and five million within a month," he promised March 13. "I doubt we'll need anywhere near that."

Not surprisingly, people kept asking: *So where are the tests?*

Soon enough, Trump shifted from boasting to blame. "We inherited a very obsolete system" from the Obama Administration, he claimed, conveniently ignoring the fact that his own CDC had designed the troubled US testing system and that his own Food and Drug Administration had waited a full month before allowing US hospital labs to develop their own. On March 25, the president was back to bragging again. "We now are doing more testing than anybody by far," including South Korea, whose widespread testing program was being praised around the world. Trump's comparison held up only in raw numbers. *Per capita,* we'd tested far fewer people to date than the Koreans had. During the daily White House briefing on March 31, Trump jumped in to answer a question directed at Dr. Fauci, asserting again that coronavirus testing was no issue at all. "I haven't heard about testing for weeks," the president insisted.

Really?

I felt a duty to set the record straight. That's "just not true," I shot back the next day on NPR's *Morning Edition*, adding that, when it came to testing, the states are all "flying blind." I knew Trump hated being contradicted, but I was speaking up for all the governors.

On April 6, the president made another sudden surprising declaration on testing, saying testing wasn't the federal government's responsibility after all. It was the states' job. "States can do their own testing," Trump said when he was pressed yet again about the continuing testing delays. "We're the federal government. We're not supposed to stand on street corners doing testing."

This was hopeless, waiting around for the president to get federal testing up to speed. After being assured for weeks that mass testing was coming and the Trump Administration had everything under control, the governors had to recognize that we were entirely on our own. It was sink or swim. By that point, I knew: I would have to do something dramatic or we would never have enough tests in Maryland.

At the daily White House briefing on April 6, Trump described a two-hour phone call that Vice President Pence had just completed with the governors. "They are very happy, every one of them," Trump declared.

It was a "great conversation," the president added. "Were there any negatives?" he turned to Pence and asked.

"No, sir," the vice president assured him. I'd led the call on behalf of the governors. I can tell you that wasn't the way I would describe it.

The only grumbles Trump had been hearing lately, he said, were coming from "partisan Democrats and maybe a couple of RINOs," the insulting acronym for Republicans In Name Only. "One RINO, in particular," Trump added.

I don't think there was much doubt which governor the president had in mind. Did I have to show him my Republican *bona fides* all the way back to my dad's 1966 campaign? This was the same Donald Trump who in 1999 told Larry King he was "very liberal" on some issues and who in 2004 told Wolf Blitzer that he identifies "more as a Democrat."

Trump didn't attack me directly. Not yet. Only in this passive-aggressive way. But I could feel the friction from him on some of our governors' calls. White House aides would often complain later to my staff, saying I should have shown more appreciation and not raised issues like the lack of testing and personal protective equipment.

I kept talking with Vice President Pence, cabinet secretaries, and members of the president's coronavirus task force. By and large, they seemed to be on the ball, attentive, and helpful. Jared Kushner even called me for the first time. It was the day his father-in-law put him in charge of rounding up ventilators. Jared and I had spoken only a couple of times at the White House in what I recalled as brief, chilly exchanges. But he was open and friendly now and sincerely asked for my help.

"We only have 9,300 ventilators in the entire national stockpile," he said, "and Cuomo says he needs 40,000 in New York." Could I survey my fellow governors and get an honest count of who really needed how many? I agreed to do whatever I could to help. It seemed a little weird to me that Jared Kushner, who wasn't a medical expert, would be put in charge of something so vital. But honestly, I was impressed with his critical thinking, how fast he was on top of the issue, and the directness of his conversation with me.

At the same time, I was growing increasingly worried about an issue even closer to home. The outbreak around New York City was getting most of the national attention, along with New Orleans and Detroit. But I was seeing evidence that the Washington, DC, region, which includes Maryland and Virginia, could well be an impending hot spot. Of the region's 3,411 known cases by the end of March, almost half were in my state. My senior staff showed me projections of the growing number of cases the region could expect over the next few weeks. Those numbers, pretty much on the mark, helped me make the case.

"Don't forget about the Baltimore/Washington corridor," I started saying to anyone who would listen. "Our numbers are going to be growing as some of these other places are leveling off." And this was no mere parochial concern. If the virus took off in our region, that was bound to have a major impact on the very people who were leading the fight for the rest of the United States, 400,000 federal workers who were critical to the nation's response. Maryland alone was home to the National Institutes of Health, the Food and Drug Administration, Walter Reed National Military Medical Center, and the Army's Fort Detrick vaccine testing and infectious-disease center, not to mention the National Security Agency, the US Cyber Command, and—well, the list went on and on.

I called President Trump directly to raise this concern. I didn't get a call back. I phoned Vice President Pence, who usually returned my calls promptly. This time he did not. But I spent the first weekend of April on the phone with all the other people who needed to hear about this: Dr. Anthony Fauci, NIH chief Dr. Francis Collins, Assistant Health Secretary Admiral Brett Giroir, Defense Secretary Mark Esper, and Army Secretary Ryan McCarthy.

"I know you guys are focused on the big picture," I said to Dr. Fauci, "but I'm paying attention to something important that's happening right here in your own backyard."

I laid out my capital region concern.

"I think you're exactly right, Governor," Fauci said to me in his famous gravelly voice. "Right now, as we speak, I'm pulling into the parking lot at the White House. I'm going to raise the issue with the whole task force."

I went through the numbers on my call with Dr. Collins at the NIH. He did not sound surprised. "Governor," he said, "we look at similar numbers every morning at seven o'clock. I think you're right to be concerned."

I told him we had made a request to the president on March 15 to conduct joint testing at NIH, and now that was even more urgent, given the rising numbers and the threat to the federal workforce. Dr. Collins stopped me there. Not to argue but to plead.

"Actually, Governor," he said, "I'm glad you called because I was going to ask *you* for help."

At NIH headquarters, he explained, his people had the capacity to perform only seventy-two tests a day. "I don't even have enough tests for my immune-compromised patients or for my staff," he said. "I was hoping you could help me." He wondered if I might prevail upon Johns Hopkins, whose Suburban Hospital was across the street from the NIH, to do some testing for him.

I could only shake my head at that. The National Institutes of Health was actually asking *me* to help *them!*

As governors, we were happy to do the hard work, make the tough decisions, and take the political heat. But an undertaking as large as a major national testing program—that required Washington's help. We expected something more than constant heckling from the man who was supposed to be our leader. In an especially fiery session at the White House briefing room on April 18, Trump defended his handling of the crisis and boasted that America's testing capacity was "fully sufficient to begin opening up the country totally."

The next morning, I was back on CNN correcting the president's misstatements. "To say that the governors have plenty of testing and they should just get to work on testing—somehow we aren't doing our job—is just absolutely false," I told Jake Tapper.

None of the states had the tests they needed, I said. "Every governor in America has been pushing and fighting and clawing to get more tests, not only from the federal government but from every private lab in America and from all across the world, and we continue to do so." That was certainly true in Maryland, where we'd increased our testing by 5,000 percent in a month. "But it's nowhere near where it needs to be," I said.

Talking about testing was important. The governors deserved a forceful voice on their side. But at the same time I was talking about testing, I also knew we had to do something about it.

Not enough tests in Maryland? I had said to myself and my team back in March. *We'd better do whatever it takes to get the testing we need!*

Luckily, I had a special ally on my side.

Yumi Hogan, Maryland's Korean-born first lady.

We'd all been hearing what high marks the South Koreans deserved for their coronavirus testing. They'd been among the hardest hit by the virus. But they'd gotten on top of their outbreak with a swift program of social distancing combined with a commitment to test, test, and test some more.

Yumi was almost a celebrity in her home country. I remembered the cheering people waiting on the sidewalk outside our hotel in Seoul. *"First Lady! First Lady!"* She was certainly admired by President Moon. And hadn't he recently called me a Korean son-in-law? Maybe there was some way the Koreans would be willing to help.

On Saturday, March 28, I asked Yumi to join me on a call with Ambassador Lee. We spoke about the special relationship between Maryland and Korea, and Yumi made a personal plea in Korean, asking for the nation's help.

That request set in motion what we called Operation Enduring Friendship, twenty-two days of vetting, testing, and negotiating an unprecedented set of protocols. Our scientists and doctors spoke to their scientists and doctors. Eight Maryland government agencies got involved, as did their counterparts in Korea. It took dozens and dozens of phone calls, night after night—sometimes it seemed like all night—working through language barriers and a thirteen-hour time difference.

President Moon's team helped to cut through miles of bureaucratic red tape and connect us directly with executives at the molecular diagnostics company LabGenomics, one of the world's leading medical testing firms. We explained what we were trying to achieve in Maryland and how desperate our need was. The LabGenomics people seemed to understand.

We aimed high, ordering kits for 500,000 coronavirus tests, airlifted to us as quickly as possible in Maryland.

We had to draft international procurement contracts. We needed clearance from multiple US agencies, including the FDA, the USDA, and Customs and Border Protection. We didn't tip off the media. We certainly didn't tip off the White House.

Even as the plane took off from Seoul, I couldn't risk anyone stepping in and botching our lifesaving mission.

CHAPTER 39

SECRET MISSION

In cloth face masks, Yumi and I stood on the tarmac at a far-off corner of Baltimore Washington International Airport on Saturday, April 18, as a Korean Air Boeing 777 stopped in front of us at 10:50 AM. The very special chartered passenger jet, which had been flying for fourteen hours, had a crew of five and no passengers aboard. It was the first Korean Air flight ever to land at BWI.

The vicious pandemic had already infected 12,761 Marylanders, taking the lives of 463 of them, and the numbers were still climbing. So what cargo could possibly be any more precious than a half million LabGenomics coronavirus tests?

As the pilot turned off the engines, I looked at Yumi. Smiling through my mask, I said: "Congratulations, honey. You helped save a lot of lives."

The crew members all came down together, walked over, and stopped six feet from Yumi, me, and a representative of the Korean embassy. In a sign of the times, the social distancing rules seem to be the same worldwide. Yumi bowed, and the other six bowed in return. Following the lead of the Koreans, I bowed too.

We said *Gamsahabnida,* thank you in Korean.

I presented ceremonial Maryland governor's coins to each of them. Then a masked and gloved team from the Maryland National Guard went immediately to work, unloading kits for the 500,000 coronavirus tests, which were packed in chilled and pressurized shipping containers.

I can't remember when I'd ever seen anything more beautiful than that.

There was one lone US Customs officer standing off to the side, watching but not interfering with anything, along with several dozen of our armed Maryland National Guardsmen, just in case.

The test kits cost $9 million, which was a lot of money for the state to pay, though the price didn't sound so high when compared to the $2.8 billion in revenues we'd already lost by having to shut down such a large part of our economy, albeit temporarily. It was quite a bargain, actually. No one knew how many lives those 500,000 tests might save, but it would be a lot.

I knew many people would be surprised to learn about this side of Yumi. Marylanders already knew and loved her as their gracious and caring first lady. But they didn't know about her international diplomacy skills or her tenacity. Without her involvement, this deal would not have happened.

I had enlisted my Korean-born wife and my special "son-in-law of Korea" relationship. With help from the relentless Roy McGrath, who directed my team's emergency procurement efforts during the crisis, I had navigated some hugely complex terrain to make this deal happen. And half a million Korean-made tests were now in Maryland, by far the largest supply in any state in America.

I could finally exhale.

A caravan of Maryland National Guard trucks escorted by the Maryland State Police drove the tests from the airport to a refrigerated, secure warehouse at an undisclosed location. From there, in a careful and orderly fashion, the huge supply of tests would be deployed to help defeat this horrible epidemic in our state.

———————————

As I returned from the airport, the street in front of the governor's mansion wasn't as tranquil as it normally was on a COVID-era Saturday afternoon.

There were a few dozen cars and trucks snaking around, protesting "Lock-down Larry" and our state's coronavirus precautions. Independent polling data showed our actions had the support of 84 percent of Marylanders. They understood. These steps were saving lives.

People have a right to protest, and I certainly understood their frustrations. I was frustrated too. The whole focus of my administration had been on expanding our economy, helping small businesses grow, and putting people to work. As a lifelong small businessman, I was well aware of how many people were being hurt economically. That broke my heart. But I also knew that to save lives, we had to reopen in a smart and careful way.

———————

On Monday, two days after the Korean jetliner landed at BWI, Yumi and I walked out onto the steps in front of the mansion to address the state and national press corps. Yumi was wearing a pink coat, silk scarf, and blue face mask. She had a pin on her coat with US and South Korean flags. I put on a suit for one of the first times since the pandemic began, and I too was wearing a face mask.

I explained all the details of Operation Enduring Friendship, the confidential mission, the secret flight, and the half million tests. "The administration made it clear over and over again they want the states to take the lead, and we have to go out and do it ourselves. That's exactly what we did," I said.

———————

The successful mission got tons of attention in the national media. Congratulations poured in from everywhere—from Marylanders and from people across the country. Individual American states don't normally do this sort of thing. It was also big news in Korea.

One reaction gave me a special smile. It was from Andrew Cuomo, the Democratic governor of New York and vice chair of the National Governors Association. He had learned about our operation while watching the evening news with his daughters, he said. One of them said to him: "Wow! That was really smart," while another asked, "Why didn't you think of that, Dad? Why didn't you think of buying test kits from South Korea?"

"I was really feeling *de minimus* as a governor," Cuomo self-deprecatingly told a room full of reporters. "Larry Hogan is a better governor than I am."

I knew he was joking, but I told him later that I appreciated his political endorsement!

Truly, the story was larger than politics. It cut across every line. *The governor who'd grown tired of waiting went out and found his own tests.* Everyone seemed to appreciate it. Well, *almost* everyone.

After the press conference on Monday, I thought we might even get a congratulatory word from the president. Donald Trump had always had a taste for bold gestures—but, apparently, only for bold gestures he could claim. The president spent much of that afternoon's White House briefing criticizing me and dismissing what we had done.

"No, I don't think he needed to go to South Korea," Trump grumbled. "I think he needed to get a little knowledge . . . The governor of Maryland could've called Mike Pence and saved a lot of money . . . The governor from Maryland didn't really understand" about testing. "He didn't understand too much about what was going on."

It seemed the president was confusing test kits with testing labs but, *whatever.* It was a great day for Maryland.

Mike Pence called me a few days later. We had a friendly and productive conversation on a whole range of topics related to Maryland and the National Governors Association. At the end of the call, I jokingly said: "By the way, the president said that instead of working with South Korea, I should have just called you to get tests. If I had known it was that easy, I could have saved a heck of a lot of effort!"

CHAPTER 40

WAY FORWARD

We had a right to be proud of all we had accomplished in Maryland. I felt good about my role leading the nation's governors and, when needed, being a factual and calming counterbalance to the president. I had worked across the aisle again, just the way I always have. Though the pandemic danger wasn't entirely behind us, we could finally start looking ahead. A vaccine would come—*soon,* we hoped—quite possibly one developed in Maryland. Until then, all the governors, myself included, needed to use a combination of containment and mitigation, along with robust testing and contact tracing. But until the coronavirus was fully eradicated, I also needed to do everything in my power to get my state back on its feet.

It was like when I went through chemotherapy. They pumped my body full of just enough poison to kill the cancer without killing *me.* Then, slowly, methodically, guided by science and medical expertise, the doctors built up my strength again and pulled me back from the edge. I am walking proof of the value of that gradual, safe, and effective approach.

The healing formula this time was a highly detailed, thirty-page action plan called "Maryland Strong: Roadmap to Recovery." It was based on facts and data, not politics or wishful thinking. The plan was drafted by Ron Gunzburger and Matt McDaniel, based on recommendations from the National Governors Association, Johns Hopkins, the American Enterprise Institute, and the president's own coronavirus task force. Our plan was closely vetted by some of the nation's top public-health experts, including former FDA commissioner Dr. Scott Gottlieb and Dr. Tom Inglesby from the Johns Hopkins Bloomberg School of Public Health. We couldn't just flip a switch and recklessly return to normal. We had to be smart about it. The plan accounted for personal protective equipment, surge capacity, testing, and contact tracing, all the factors that would keep us moving forward. It was the most detailed recovery plan anywhere in the nation.

Our economic recovery would move forward in three stages. The first phase lifted the statewide stay-at-home order while still urging people (especially the elderly and those with underlying conditions) to remain voluntarily "safer-at-home." Phase one also reopened some small shops and businesses, outdoor recreation and religious gatherings, and similar low-risk activities. Phase two raised the limits on public gatherings, allowed nonessential employees to return to work, and reopened restaurants, bars, and other businesses, as long as they followed masking and distancing rules. When we reached phase three, higher-risk activities would be allowed again—eating in crowded restaurants, visiting hospitals and nursing homes, and attending larger religious services and other big events.

No one was more eager than I was to bring life back to normal. I love being with the crowds on opening day at Camden Yards. I missed the hugs and handshakes and all the everyday human interactions I rarely thought twice about until we couldn't do them anymore. In early May, the COVID numbers were finally beginning to plateau in Maryland. We were ready to gradually move forward as long as we carefully gauged our progress and responded accordingly. "Until a vaccine is developed," I told the people of Maryland, "the way we go about our daily lives and the way we work is going to be significantly different." To pretend otherwise just wouldn't be honest.

From my long-shot 2014 victory in the governor's race to the riots that shook Baltimore. From my late-stage cancer battle to a global pandemic. You can't say I haven't been tested. Thankfully, I've learned some valuable life lessons along the way. One thing I've learned is that what most people want from their leaders is an optimistic, can-do, results-oriented approach. People just want the problems solved. They are sick and tired of divisiveness and paralysis. They believe that civility and pragmatism are more effective. They don't think compromise is a dirty word. And they do think straight talk is more valuable than empty rhetoric. These are things that my Republican party is going to have to focus on if it expects to have a future and win national elections again.

Regardless of who wins this election in November of 2020, a large majority of Americans are thoroughly convinced that our political system is fundamentally broken, that we as a people are tragically divided, and that Washington is completely dysfunctional. People are frustrated that they can't trust politicians of either party, that nobody appears focused on solving the problems, and that nothing ever seems to get done.

As soon as the smoke has cleared in November, the talk will immediately turn to the race in 2024. Sadly, unless we begin to change the self-destructive course that both parties are on, this mess will likely just repeat itself. After the pandemic crisis subsides, Washington could simply return to the same toxic politics that had been infecting America long before COVID-19. That is not what America needs.

How did it get so bad? There is more than enough blame to go around. People on both sides of the aisle have been unable to find that middle ground where we can all stand together. Don't they understand how little we will ever achieve apart? Sometimes, it seems, neither side really wants to make progress. Each side just wants to win arguments. That's not governing. That's political theater, and most Americans are sick and tired of all the drama.

Look, I'm willing to stand up and fight for the things that I really believe in. But not for status quo politics as usual and not to perpetuate polarization and paralysis. I come from the get-to-work and get-things-done school of politics, and I'll work with anyone who is willing to do the people's business. Come to think of it, that should be a prerequisite for anyone who wants to be involved in public service.

In spite of our differences and the serious national challenges ahead, I still believe that what unites us is far greater than that which divides us. Those who believe our political system is too broken and can't be fixed should look to us in Maryland. We have already shown a better path forward. And if we can accomplish that here, then there is no place in the nation where these very same principles cannot succeed. They are the best hope America has.

ACKNOWLEDGMENTS

Forget everything you've ever heard about quiet inspiration and lonely nights at the keyboard. Writing a book, like running for office or governing a state, is never a solo endeavor. As I have now discovered firsthand, book writing is always a team sport. Especially for someone like me who already has a seven-day-a-week job (plus a part-time gig as chairman of the National Governors Association). So I am lucky to have had such generous and talented teammates on the literary field with me.

In *New York Times* bestselling author Ellis Henican, I found the ideal collaborator, a natural-born storyteller brimming with humor and curiosity. Ellis knew how to pull the good stuff out of me and make it sing, even the good stuff I didn't know I had. And he brought along an unmatchable backfield. Researcher Roberta Teer can find out anything about anyone. Transcriber Janis Spidel now officially knows every secret I have. Peter McGuigan and Kelly Karczewski of Foundry Literary + Media are top-notch agents who have guided us shrewdly through the strange world of publishing and delivered us into the deft hands of BenBella Books, our publisher, and Recorded Books, our audio partner. BenBella publisher Glenn Yeffeth, deputy publisher Adrienne Lang, editor-in-chief Leah Wilson, senior editor Alexa Stevenson, developmental editor Brian Nichol, copyeditor Elizabeth Degenhard, art director Sarah Avinger, production director Monica Lowry, marketing director Jennifer

Canzoneri, and vendor content manager Alicia Kania are total pros who have brought our book beautifully to life. Troy Juliar, Recorded Books' chief content officer, and VP Laura Gachko made my transition to professional voice actor a blast, not a burden. And who knows? Maybe now I have at least one career prospect for my post-governor years!

Without my own dedicated crew, I'd probably still be on page 1. Andrew Brightwell, who's been with me since before Change Maryland and is now helping with the launch of AnAmericaUnited.org, was our air-traffic controller, at the center of everything book-related.

Ron Gunzburger, my longtime political and gubernatorial advisor who goes all the way back to my "giving Steny Hoyer nightmares" days, spent many nights and weekends editing and questioning assumptions.

The two amazing young women who've been my right and left brain for six years, Kara Bowman and Amanda Allen, helped jog my memory and correct some details. I think of them like daughters, but both say that most of the time they were more like my mom. My political director David Weinman, a great new addition to our team, helped with valuable planning and input on the book.

My communications director, Mike Ricci, a veteran of Speakers John Boehner and Paul Ryan, gave excellent input. My former comms director, Amelia Chasse Alcivar, who worked in John McCain's campaign and is now the director of communications for the Republican Governors Association, gave incredibly thoughtful advice.

Our media guru, Russ Schriefer, never loses sight of the deeper meaning in the messages he helps to convey. No wonder George W. Bush, Mitt Romney, Chris Christie, and so many other presidential candidates have turned to him.

To write it, you have to live it. That's one of the key lessons I learned here. So there wouldn't have been much to write about if it weren't for the many people who helped me get to where I am. I'm deeply grateful to every last one of them.

Nobody reads books about people who lose elections. So big thanks to all the miracle workers in our campaign family. Tom Kelso was the hardest working campaign chairman anywhere in politics. Steve Crim managed a winning 2014 campaign hardly anyone thought was winnable, and our re-election campaign managers were equally on it in 2018. Jim Barnett, who'd done Scott Brown's Senate race in Massachusetts, and Doug Mayer, who'd honed his talent working for Chris Christie and Nikki Haley, proved that passion and utter doggedness are almost impossible to beat. Allison Meyers, an RNC veteran who served as our finance director, helped raise an incredible amount of money to support our efforts. Gary Mangum, Elaine Pevenstein, Jim Brady, Ed Dunn, Sam Malhotra, and so many others—I am especially thankful to those who've been with us from the start. I am eternally grateful for our entire dedicated campaign team and the thousands of volunteers and contributors who showed faith in me when the experts said our cause was hopeless. Look at all you have helped to achieve!

Major thanks to my running mate and wingman, Lieutenant Governor Boyd Rutherford, who has been with me every step of the way and has been a true partner. Same to my chief of staff, Matt Clark, and my former chief, Craig Williams, two amazing men who both excelled in a very demanding job. And the same to my chief legislative officer Keiffer Mitchell, a Democrat who has been with me since the first day I took office and who walked with me every day through the streets of West Baltimore during the riots.

I am so grateful to our entire staff and cabinet, who are incredibly dedicated and talented. To all those serving in our administration who are working hard every single day to change Maryland for the better, I am constantly amazed by what you have accomplished.

A special thanks to my oncologists, Aaron Rapoport and Arun Bhandari, and all the other dedicated doctors, nurses, and medical staff who helped save my life. When I say, "I wouldn't be here without you"—I mean it. I literally would not be here without you.

A special nod to my fellow cancer survivors, many of whom went through even tougher battles than my own. You taught me so much about grace and staying positive when things get tough.

My sincere appreciation to Pope Francis, Tim McGraw, and the thousands who stood by me with prayers, support, and encouragement. Surviving cancer, it turns out, is also a team sport.

Many thanks to my brother Tim, Victor White, Jake Ermer, Kevin Setzer, and all the guys at my real-estate business for stepping up and allowing me to take an extended leave of absence that's gone a little longer than any of us expected it to. You have done a great job of making me look *dispensable.*

Thanks to my fellow governors, Republicans and Democrats alike, who unanimously elected me to lead them as chairman of the National Governors Association. Despite the bitter politics that have divided Washington, it's the governors all across America who are setting an example of working together to get things done. I'm proud to serve with all of you.

A special thanks to Chris Christie, who believed in me when almost nobody else on the national political scene thought I had a chance to win, and for being such a true friend from the first day we met. A very rare thing in politics.

Thank you to the more than six million people of Maryland, who put their faith in me in 2014 and haven't stopped yet: You have believed in me, allowed me this incredible opportunity to serve, and given me the most important work of my life. There has not been a single day, good or bad, when I was not grateful for the privilege.

Finally, words can't express how much it has meant to have the love that has surrounded me since the day I was born. It is the foundation of this book and of everything else I have ever accomplished. That love came first from the family I was born into—my dad, my mom, my sister, and, later, my four younger brothers—who together helped make me who and what I am.

Then, when I got to choose a family of my own, I found a family who, thankfully, also chose me. It has been wonderful to share this journey with Yumi and our extraordinary daughters, Kim, Jaymi, and Julie, who have enriched me, completed me, and given me so much to live up to. Now our own family has grown with three sons-in-law and four grandchildren. I am truly blessed.

I'm so deeply grateful to all of the many people who have been such an important part of my journey. Looking back, I'm amazed at the experiences we've been able to have together and the accomplishments that you have made possible. I'm not entirely certain exactly what the future holds. But there is one thing you know you can count on. I'm going to keep giving it everything I've got, each and every single day that I am given.

A special note: 100 percent of the proceeds of this book will be donated to An America United (www.AnAmericaUnited.org), the national citizens organization I founded to advance bold, common-sense, bipartisan solutions to the serious problems facing America.

ABOUT THE AUTHOR

Larry Hogan is the 62nd governor of Maryland and chairman of the National Governors Association. Recently reelected in a landslide, he is only the second Republican governor in Maryland history to win a second term. Known for his practical solutions, his stark transparency, and his ability to work across party lines, he is also a survivor of late-stage non-Hodgkin's lymphoma. His wife, Yumi Hogan, is the first Korean-American first lady in America. The Hogans live in the historic state capital of Annapolis.

INDEX